W9-AEW-159

UNIVERSITIES AND LIFELONG LEARNING SERIES

A new imperative:
regions and higher education in difficult times

MANCHESTER
1824

Manchester University Press

UNIVERSITIES AND LIFELONG LEARNING SERIES

Series editor:
Professor Michael Osborne (University of Glasgow)

Universities and lifelong learning analyses the external engagement activities of universities and third-level institutions and is concerned with the range of activity that lies beyond the traditional mission of teaching and research. This is an area that until now has seldom been explored in depth and has rarely if ever been treated in a holistic manner.

Lifelong learning, the arts and community cultural engagement
in the contemporary university: International perspectives
Edited by Darlene Clover and Kathy Sanford

Knowledge, democracy and action:
Community–university research partnerships in global perspectives
Edited by Budd Hall, Edward Jackson, Rajesh Tandon, Jean-Marc Fontan and Nirmala Lall

A new imperative

Regions and higher education
in difficult times

Chris Duke, Michael Osborne and Bruce Wilson

Manchester University Press

Manchester and New York

distributed exclusively in the USA by Palgrave Macmillan

Published by Manchester University Press
Oxford Road, Manchester M13 9NR, UK
and Room 400, 175 Fifth Avenue, New York, NY 10010, USA
www.manchesteruniversitypress.co.uk

Distributed exclusively in the USA by
Palgrave Macmillan, 175 Fifth Avenue, New York,
NY 10010, USA

Distributed exclusively in Canada by
UBC Press, University of British Columbia, 2029 West Mall,
Vancouver, BC, Canada V6T 1Z2

British Library Cataloguing-in-Publication Data
A catalogue record for this book is available from the British Library

Library of Congress Cataloging-in-Publication Data applied for

ISBN 978 0 7190 8830 8 *hardback*
First published 2013

Typeset in Minion with Aptiva display by
Koinonia, Manchester
Printed and bound in Great Britain by
CPI Antony Rowe Ltd, Chippenham, Wiltshire

Contents

Tables

Abbreviations

AUCEA	Australian University Community Engagement Alliance
CDG	Consultative Development Group
CEDEFOP	European Centre for the Development of Vocational Training
COAG	Council of Australian Governments
CSO	civil society organisation
CSR	corporate social responsibility
EC	European Commission
EMS	Environmental management system
ERDF	European Regional Development Fund
EU	European Union
EUA	European Universities Association
GDP	Gross Domestic Product
GFC	global financial crisis
GM	Genetically Modified
GNP	Gross National Product
GSJ	Green skills and jobs
GUNI	Global University Network for Innovation
HE	higher education
HEFCE	Higher Education Funding Council England
HEI	higher education institution
HRD	human resource development
ICT	information and communications technology
IGO	Intergovernmental organisation
IMHE	Institutional Management in Higher Education (OECD)
INGO	international non-governmental organisation
ISO	International Standards Organisation
IT	information technology
LR	Learning Region
MoA	Memorandum of Agreement
MoU	Memorandum of Understanding
NIU	Northern Illinois University
NGO	non-governmental organisation
OECD	Organisation for Economic Cooperation and Development

OKC	Office of Knowledge Capital (Melbourne)
PASCAL	International Observatory on Place Management, Social Capital and Learning
PFI	private finance initiative
PURE	PASCAL Universities and Regional Engagement
QUANGO	Quasi-non-governmental organisation
R&D	research and development
RCG	Regional Coordinating Group (for a PURE region)
RDA	Regional Development Agency
RDA	Regional Development Australia
RIR	Regional Innovation and Renewal
RMIT	Royal Melbourne Institute of Technology University
RVR (1 and 2)	Regional Visit Review (1st and 2nd)
SMEs	small and medium enterprises
S&P	Standard and Poor rating agency
SRRR	sustaining rural and remote regions
TAFE	technical and further education
TEC	Tertiary Education Commission
THE	*Times Higher Education*
three Ms	Massification, Marketisation, Managerialism
TS	Tertiary system
U21	Universitas 21
UCL	University College London
UK	United Kingdom
UNCSD	United Nations Conference on Sustainable Development (Rio + 20)
UNEP	United Nations Environment Programme
UNESCO	United Nations Educational Social and Cultural Organisation
US(A)	United States (of America)
VU	Victoria University (Melbourne)

Participating regions

Buskerud County, Norway
Darling Downs and South West Queensland, Australia
Devon and Cornwall, England
Essex, England
Flanders, Belgium
Gaborone, Botswana
Glasgow, Scotland
Helsinki, Finland
Jämtland, Sweden
Kent, England
Lesotho (as a small whole-country region)
Melbourne, Australia
Northern Illinois, United States of America
Puglia, Italy
South Transdanubia, Hungary
Thames Gateway (south-east London), England
Värmland, Sweden

Introduction:
regions and universities
in the post-2008 world

Something extraordinary is underway around the world, the outgoing President of Tufts University and of the Talloires Network, a 'global coalition of engaged universities', tells us in a 2011 international volume: 'institutions of higher education are directly tackling community problems ... the engaged university is replacing the ivory tower' (Lawrence Bacow in Watson *et al.* 2011, outside cover and p. xx). Why, how and how far is this occurring? Community service is fully a century and a half old in the American university. Is the 'extraordinary something' a rediscovery, as the 'ivory tower' suffers the slow death of a thousand cuts? Yes in part; it is also something different, in a very different world.

It is a world characterised as global–local. As the 2008 global financial crisis (GFC) persists and extends, the idea of the learning region attracts wider attention as a policy proposition. It is central to this study. Its appeal has waxed and waned over the years, finding more favour in some parts of the world than others, depending on countries' political arrangements and traditions. As national- and international-level government systems remain bemused in ever-more disturbing and unpredictable times, the logic of devolution to more local levels gains in appeal. Can and do regions learn? Can and do they involve higher education(HE) in their learning and development? The need may appear self-evident; achieving it is another matter.

Research or knowledge-making is the more glamorous second arm of the familiar twin tasks of industrial-age universities, alongside teaching. The production of knowledge may be 'pure' 'blue-skies', 'curiosity-driven', the preserve of Dr Strangelove and the boffins, a world of mystery and mystique remote from working people and their diverse cultural communities. On the other hand, in recent decades the idea of (civic) engagement revives community service, the 'third leg of mission', accompanied by newer words and arrangements – partner(ship), commitment to region, locality or place, sustainability. Vulgar notions of relevance and utility enter through the philosopher's side entrance.

Mid-twentieth-century research commissioned by powerful government and industry agents aroused concern that the industrial–military–government complex would corrupt integrity and disinterested scholarship. Realism ensured that such contracts did not cease; an arm's-length relationship might be secured if academic knowledge production went with semi-arm's-length diffusion of research findings

1

in the form of 'knowledge transfer'. Essentially similar arguments, couched as liberal education, have sought to nurture thinking citizens while remaining safely apolitical. This formulation has in turn been challenged. Knowledge transfer on academics' terms seems almost arrogant. It keeps academic control of the agenda, passing on as if by grace and favour those findings which the academy has discovered in its own time and way and chooses to share.

More relevant to the daily work and even survival of many universities is teaching: in modern managerial and economic language; the production of 'human capital', or human resource development. A neo-liberal competition-driven world demands knowledge that can be turned to profit through application as 'innovation'; and education, now often 'training' or vocational education and training for skills development and renewal. Much of the vocational and professional development work of universities is for non-profit roles in public life and civil society; but these trends arouse widely shared deep concerns about 'the death of the public university' and the desertion of disinterested inquiry and education for the public good. So does the call to show the impact, meaning in effect the utility, of research.

Fundamental and universal change in the world of higher education from the late twentieth century is described as 'massified', 'marketised' and spoiled by 'managerialism'. Ever more demands are made of universities. There is much literature and intense public debate about the peril or demise of the public university. This is a quite different take on the 'something extraordinary' that is going on. Both propositions can be true. With increasing scale national higher education systems can homogenise and diversify simultaneously, the latter most probably including some form of steeper status hierarchy.

So far this Introduction has referred to universities; whether all universities or only those without the high standing and prestige bestowed by advanced age and high research output is a hotly contested matter. The consideration should be widened to include all higher education institutions and tertiary systems – the post-school colleges that carry different names. Partnership on a university's terms, using university discourse to speak with others whose language, traditions and *raison d'etre* are different, will surely be university-centric and unequal. If postmodernism threatened the rationality basis of academic scientific knowledge, Mode Two engagement questions its apparently natural monopoly, proposing a vigorous and constructive new identity for the modern university. For this to be fruitful the language and terms of engagement must be considered *de novo*.

Coming from another direction, from work on the nature of knowledge itself, more scholars now see value in the modern complex and fast-changing world in the *co-production* of knowledge between universities (the old knowledge industry) and other parts or stakeholders in what is commonly called the 'knowledge economy' or 'society' (see in particular Gibbons *et al.* 1994). Different kinds of skill and other resources, access and expertise held by different agencies or stakeholders are brought together. This allows a research agenda to be defined, designed and executed together, and the results co-owned and applied, perhaps in continuing partnership, by different collaborating partners. It may also allow the

2

curriculum, the full learning experience of students, to be developed and provided in partnership, with the educational institution in the lead but co-owned by other parts of modern learning society.

That perilous other world, the 'real world out there' beyond the university of which higher education is inescapably part, lurches from crisis to crisis. Leadership lacks confidence and is prone to narrow-focus, quick-fix, short-sighted policy-making. Often insensitive to the unintended later consequences of acts taken under political pressure, it leaves these as problems for others to resolve and pay for. Instant global communication, overwhelming information overload, intrusive media and incomprehensible 'butterfly-wing' connectivity added to old-fashioned power politics make for a toxic brew. In this global world local action and local solutions become more attractive and more compellingly effective. Here things can be handled with better judgement based in better understanding of diverse realities – 'context is everything'.

The concept of the learning region is central to this way of problem-solving. Like 'lifelong learning' the term is used variously and carelessly. Chapter 3 explores the meaning and importance of the learning region. Not all universities warm to such local–regional engagement. The unwise pride of global forces and nations undermines it; but even the most prestigious and 'global' university has a local footprint and ever-watchful neighbours.

The 'something extraordinary' is certainly there; yet most university planning and activity appears to run on in an internally referenced parallel universe. Both parties must learn to listen, to give as well as to take: the academy and the multiple community cohabitants of regional space who might be its partners. Each must learn more of the other's world in order to co-create sustainable healthy development. It is a long step beyond being merely decent neighbours.

This book arises from the work of PASCAL, an international non-governmental network Observatory. Its name exploits echoes of philosophical depth as well as technical modernity of language, taking the concepts of Place, Social Capital and Learning together with the vital connecting conjunctions of And, to define its mission. PASCAL seeks also to connect scholarship with the practice of governance in its widest sense. It explores these matters without assuming the right of the university to dictate terms in some spirit of academic 'noblesse oblige'. The book is not a recipe or toolkit. Instead it uncovers and analyses problems behind the difficulties confronting those in communities, local regions and universities who try to 'engage' – to work together in sustained collaborative partnership to the benefit of all concerned. PASCAL Chair Jarl Bengtsson's ten-point outline sketches the storyline thus:

1 university engagement has a long history, for example in extramural programmes;
2 it has not however generally affected mainstream university activity;
3 missions 1 and 2, teaching and research, remain dominant;
4 'The third mission' is however of growing importance as university leaders come to see its importance: as investment to the benefit of society at large,

and for improving universities' often poor public image;

5 it is in this context that outside partnerships have become of greater interest;

6 there are big differences between public and privately funded universities; the challenge is particularly urgent for the public ones;

7 this means that there is a serious gap: universities have disciplines whereas cities and regions have problems; these two different kinds of knowledge and approaches to work do not communicate well with each other;

8 cities and regions are struggling with critical problems concerning the economy and unemployment, green issues and social cohesion;

9 there are barriers and obstacles to bridging this gap such as failure to share information, lack of a clear legal and administrative finance, lack of funds, and the absence of joined up administrative and academic work in universities;

10 there are various examples of these different problems being overcome in the PURE studies (see below) but the gap often remains wide and sustained effort is needed to bridge it.

Readers keen to understand the PASCAL Universities and Regional Engagement – PURE – project may wish first to go to Chapter 5, which explains the PURE project and the PASCAL context. Before that the four chapters comprising Part I examine the central themes and the large issues which preoccupy us: first the 'global problematique' and the changing structure of society and its management; then the two key partners in engagement: the local region and the university. At the heart of our story is PASCAL's experience of working with multiple regions and their universities on their experience with engagement. It is a microcosm of the larger story of the unrequited love which engagement often is. Part II examines in turn several central strands mainly of policy but also of process that are illuminated by the PURE project. The book offers an opportunity for deeper reflection on the issues which arise, a process which is assisted by wider analysis and reflection in the concluding Part III.

Finally, by way of introduction, an apologia. The language that surrounds engagement is fraught, as is much of today's discourse about public life in general. We thought of including a set of clarifying definitions and explanations of such key terms as 'third mission', 'lifelong learning', 'community', and 'engagement' itself. This threatened to become a full tome of essays on keywords. Instead we ask the reader to bear with us, and to settle as we do for discussion of such terms as they become significant within the text.

PART I

Towards Mode Two knowledge production

1

Complexity and diversity
– the 'global problematique'

Crisis – what crisis?[1]

Why 'a new imperative'? Is it an exaggeration to use this expression about engagement – a subject that many inside and outside the world of the academy still consider marginal, an interruption to the main business of universities?

We live at a time when many of our assumptions about the economy, politics and social identity are being deeply challenged. In 2007–08, diverse regions volunteered to undertake action research to understand and strengthen the contribution of their higher education institutions (HEIs) to regional development. By the time the study was launched late in 2008, what came to be called the global financial crisis had already broken, dramatically in the case of the United States, where it is referred to as the Great Crash of 2008, and Europe, including the UK. Major financial institutions were collapsing. Some were in effect nationalised by a conservative US Administration. There was deep worry that the global economy was about to collapse, heralding the onset of a new Great Depression. As a result the project ran in a period when even small sums of money for anything not short term and essential became unavailable. The context in which the work was planned changed, perhaps, so it appeared three years later, permanently and irreversibly.

One April morning in 2011, two and a half years after the GFC had swept the world, the business page of a leading British broadsheet newspaper carried two adjacent stories. The International Monetary Fund was quoted as denying talks over the crisis 'of Greece's crippling national debt' while the Eurozone shuddered over the 'crisis to the euro'. Alongside this, the record pay-off of UK mortgage and other household debts was described as an ominous development, with a cumulative household debt reduction over three years of £57b (*The Independent*, 5 April 2011, p. 34).[2]

Here is a gross disjunction: reckless borrowing brought global financial capital and several European national fiscal systems to their knees. Yet households would further threaten financial stability by obediently reducing borrowing, being more economical and living more within their means. Can one thing be true at national and global levels while the opposite applies to local- and individual-level behaviour? Is there a contest, a life-and-death worldwide struggle, between national and individual competitive acquisitiveness and a more traditionally embedded culture of harmony, balance and sustainability expressed at more local community levels? What is the connection between the national, the global and the local? Here is an underlying theme.

This example well illustrates the state of confusion into which economic wisdom has fallen. Three months later the French broadsheet *Le Monde* headed its Editorial 'Ces gamins qui nous gouvernent'. In reviewing the feebleness of Europe's finance ministers in Brussels and of the US President struggling with his republican majority adversaries in seeking a way out of the crisis threatening both continents, the leader concluded that the ministers were keeping themselves busy with a cold while cancer threatened (*Le Monde*, 13 July 2011, p. 1). In an entirely different, ophthalmological, context I find a headline from an Australian ABC National news headline a decade earlier, that seems long-sighted and well fitted for wider use: 'There is a growing expectation of short-sightedness round the world.'

Quick-fix short-sightedness in times of crisis is a curse of democracies in the modern mass media age, obsessed as many are with hostile tabloid newspapers, opinion polls and impending elections. Another problem is the persistence of discredited economics as a still-dominant perspective. Along with connecting global and local, myopically limited thinking generated by conventional neo-liberal economics and the imbalance between economic and other perspectives and realities are recurring issues. How far can regional administrations redress these problems? How and how far if at all can higher education, itself feeling under pressure, assist?

Response – what response?

The sense that governments lack the will and ability – leadership is a favoured word – to take decisions necessary for the longer term undermines faith in elected governments, feeding apathy and cynicism. Intergeneration conflict is evident: immediate voting age cohorts versus the needs of future generations including today's young. The near-paralysis of the US federal political system in 2011 provided a stark and serious example ('US budget stalemate threatens to turn debt crisis into catastrophe', *The Guardian (Financial)*, 15 July 2011, p. 26). On the other hand, in the wake of the GFC and angry opinion about continuing very high banker salaries and bonuses, wealthy citizens in several countries, including France and the US, have called for higher taxes on people like themselves. Some governments are beginning to respond (see for example Buffett 2011).

There is ample evidence that a tipping point has been reached across several dimensions of shared human experience; our rate of adaptation is too slow. It appears evident that technological fixes alone will not suffice. Bigger efforts at smarter technological innovation, and larger budgets for new kinds of infra-structure and smart technology, provide only part of the answer. A formidable difficulty is that adaptation has to be society-wide and deep; cultural rather than just political-technical. Can existing traditions and wellsprings of knowledge and intelligence be tapped? If reactivated will they provide solutions by drawing on socio-cultural capital – even old 'folk' wisdom – to rediscover more serviceable *mores*? More comfortably perhaps, we ask whether the humanities and the social science can and should add a more useful and effective voice to the contributions of the university coming from sciences and technology, thus guiding and informing how public policy is made and executed.

The global financial crisis put to an end a long period of largely unquestioned and uninterrupted growth in wealth in the West. It was soon acknowledged that it was at least initially a crisis of the North and the West, more precisely a North Atlantic crisis. It has however affected personal incomes and spending power, even hope for survival, in poor as well as rich countries. It comes on the heels of further rising inequalities within and between nations. Until recently it was widely asserted and possibly accepted that prosperity would continue to increase: trickle-down theory lived on. Prosperity was however predicated on continuing growth, and that assumption has scarcely shifted. There will be no different tomorrow. Even so, there is a new mood abroad about soaring inequalities and new doubt about rising GNP and GDP as ends in themselves.

The GFC, however, came on the back of earlier ongoing and chronic 'crises': global warming; climatic disasters, including increasingly violent and unpredicted weather events; rising concern over world food supply; and inadequate reserves of essential natural resources, especially water and oil. For a brief spell there appeared the prospect that a new version of Keynesian economics would arise: countries would build their way out of stagnation and rising unemployment by innovating and investing in green technology innovation which demanded green skills and new green jobs. Quickly enough preoccupation with rising national indebtedness was fuelled by a few influential rating agencies. This led to battening down, and a reasserted small-state neo-liberal agenda. Three years after the GFC began, the dominant narrative was about a return to growth and the reduction of debts by countries which in earlier times had carried higher levels of debt without question.[3] A more vociferous street-wise alternative discourse was rising, however, during 2011.

Before the now widespread awareness of serious global eco-crisis, the rise of new world regions seemed certain and inexorable. The rate of economic growth and the cumulative speed of economic travel between old and new nations and regions make for another of the great historic declines. Like the Roman and other empires and colonial systems, old and more recent, including unpleasant and ultimately failed twentieth century political experiments like Stalinism, fascism and apartheid racism, we see the relative decline of the West including even the mighty US empire and economy. East Asia, Latin America and others close the gaps and overtake.[4] Uncomfortable as it is to those falling back, such change may be easier to manage than a shift to very low growth, and more probably contraction in energy consumption and living standards, such as global warming implies.[5] No world leader has yet made a speech on these matters to compare with British Prime Minister Harold Macmillan's end-of-Empire 'winds of change' address half a century ago. Al Gore came nearest, but not while holding high office.

A seldom questioned response to the complex crisis confronting peoples and governments is to go on doing rather more of the same – a critic would say being in a hole and digging deeper. Those who stand to lose most obstruct the development of the more fundamental, alternative, 'green' solutions that may prove to be essential. This flows from a failure of 'connectivity' – the absence of joined-up thinking and action. It also derives from obvious immediate discomfort, and from expected and likely political and social consequences.

Above all, there are divided perceptions of the hitherto little questioned assumption about continuing growth and rising prosperity. This has prevailed, effectively from the time of the Renaissance in the West, and continues to be held by mainstream political parties of almost every persuasion, if only because suggesting otherwise would be judged suicidally unpopular. These assumptions are however being challenged academically and by other 'public intellectuals', also by small Green parties and ever more confident popular street and tweet movements.[6] Political leaders trail behind their followers. Any sign of economic recovery is greeted as the end of incipient crisis. No ambitious politician wishes to admit the inevitably looming crisis of rising world population and competitive aspiration for finite natural resources, even without global warming, implying an end to growth.

Deeper roots of the GFC malaise

This is a time of chronic multifaceted complexity and difficult long-term trends affecting many sectors. An almost universal response, especially in the 'old North', still rejects ideas of a planned society and European, especially Scandinavian-style, 'big government' socialism: rather, allow a 'liberal economy' based on free trade, more open competition and 'the wisdom of the market' to produce a high and rising quality of life. This has implied creating more 'human capital' – an ever-better skilled and innovative workforce with higher education bent to more direct economic service. Yet this free-market model has come under damning criticism as the consequences of unfettered financial 'vulture' capitalism are realised.

There is then an instinct in times of crisis to tighten up, manage short term and control more closely – and an opposite, countervailing but weaker emphasis on sustainability. Thus the GFC is seen from one point of view as a great lost green opportunity to invest our way out of economic difficulties like high unemployment.

A different response might be towards decentralisation: localisation of initiative and responsibility to sub-national regions. Looking to the increasingly global 'market' in economic terms does not however mean automatically leaving things to more local regions, where governance is still required in political and administrative senses. Smaller regions are still less likely to be able to contend with the wealth and power of huge global corporations which can out-play whole nation states. Given national governments' propensity to defer and deflect hard problems for electoral purposes, it is important how far resources are also devolved when regional devolution is adopted. It is not uncommon, as in Britain and France, to see difficult problems and unpopular, costly responsibilities passed down to local regions without the centrally controlled budgets being transferred to match them. In its work with PURE regions the international non-governmental organisation PASCAL found some regions hamstrung by central government reluctance to trust, delegate and empower. Any wish to work with local universities as development partners was hampered by central regulation and control. We find examples of this in Part II below.

This is not the place to try to explain much less solve the problematique of a world out of balance. There are many scientific and social scientific studies. Some are apocalyptic, especially where global warming is concerned. More now also look at rising inequalities and latent political unrest; see the ever-growing literature, both non-fiction and fiction, on the broadly ecological (in particular Princen 2010; also Camilleri and Falk 2009; Gardiner 2006). The GFC is part of a process whereby economic and ultimately other forms of power and leadership are moving away from North America and Europe to 'the South', notably Asia and Latin America. Most of the dominant international intellectual energy, and the international governmental and non-governmental leadership, still comes from the North and controls the discourse, but this is fast changing. The crisis is also about a long-term shift in global power, and rethinking the assumptions and structures on which it has been based.

Modern-optimist belief in inevitable sustained growth assumes ever-rising production and consumption, growth being the engine of past and present success. There is an almost anthropomorphic belief in the decisions – the acts of wisdom – of *the market*. Its most obvious manifestation is belief in a small, minimally interfering state and low taxation, with innovation driven by markets and the profit motive. The market is accorded an intelligence and will that are superior to human planning and intelligence,[7] but not however seen as blessed with long vision.

Even ahead of productive employment, the first duty of the contemporary citizen is to consume. Choice is a duty, an enshrined civic virtue. It is incumbent on each person to exercise choice which, it is thought, will neutralise the monopolistic tendencies and perverse consequences of global capitalism. Any failure of the free market is the failure of each freely choosing individual citizen, much as poverty is also personal failure. The wider assumptions surrounding this 'paradigm' are seldom recognised and questioned in the West. A different approach comes from PASCAL's regional office in Africa however, where Catherine Hoppers speaks of an African way and of the Commons. The dilemma or tragedy of the Commons arises from the clash between individuals' short-term interests and the long-term interests of the group, and a resulting unrestricted demand for finite resources. She notes the continuing existence in Asia of common village land. She calls for the university to become a kind of cultural Commons as a place to realise citizenship in the production of knowledge.

A further twist to the bankruptcy of conventional economics in a world of 'unreal wealth' and fluid global finance markets was manifest as the 2011 'Euro crisis' rolled on. Nations can be condemned within a narrow and seldom questioned economic paradigm, by one or other of just three recognised rating agencies: Standard and

Poor's, Moody's and Fitches Ratings. These are inside the phenomenon and part of the problem.[8] The excessively rapid and unstable behaviour of global finance markets (again anthropomorphically) 'attacking' and picking off one economy and nation after another that is weak as rated by the agencies, fosters the instant migration of trillions of dollars of 'funny money'.

To the lay observer there is little connection between these phenomena and economic capability, much less social capital. The phenomena rob ordinary people, and even ordinary national governments, of any sense of power and self-determination. They appear plausibly to legitimate the asset-stripping of the weak by the strong on a global scale. Meanwhile the influence of media and their opinion-forming businesses conspire to inhibit or prevent open and open-minded reflection that would lead to sound judgement and different paths of action. Absence of transparency undermines public trust. Citizens tend to withdraw into private worlds. Political apathy and cynicism become more common, good governance yet harder to achieve, although the social media provide an increasingly powerful and relatively safe means to remain active and connected.

A deeper problem accompanies belief in the wisdom and supremacy of market forces. We may call this anthropocentrism, meaning that only our species has rights. Everything else derives its meaning and right to exist from serving human purpose and human need (Garlick and Matthews 2009). By implication, unbounded competitive acquisition is fine, so long as it serves ever-higher consumption and continues to fuel a now-global economic machine. Curiously, what we see, partly in the name of consumer-citizen choice, is reduction of diversity and the loss of species and whole ecosystems on a scale unprecedented for many millennia.[9]

This is exacerbated by the continuing if slowing rise in world population, and the increasing economic success of now more populous world regions. Their rising aspirations require more energy, more and better food and other commodities. They aspire to surpass the living standards, and in the process the natural resource consumption, of the West. This again shows a looming crisis and not merely a technically complicated and technically fixable problem. A critical end-point of literally unimaginable changes approaches. We have either to plan a way out or to confront yet larger challenges and deeper crisis later.

This would require superbly good governance, demanding the rapid and collaborative evolution of applied intelligence that can draw on and draw together different academic disciplines, administrative departments, and different kinds of wisdom, knowledge and skills. Absence of long sight, long-cycle planning and investment is the predictable consequence of the short-cycle political leadership produced by the only kind of democracy that we know how to make work. Public opinion is fuelled by instant news. Journalism is 'embedded', intrusive and compromised in all kinds of ways and places. There is too anxious a political eye on too frequent changes in electoral fortunes as profiled through opinion polls, with the next election never far from sight. These combined elements make for almost endemic failure to take a long view and to act on complex difficulties. The electoral cycle fuels the kind of contradictory behaviour exemplified above about debt: governments lead ever deeper into more national debt to the future by deferring payment on services taken out today, leaving problems and costs to a future generation.[10] This political dimension of the syndrome taken with the other dimensions sketched above does suggest a crisis, not merely a complex problem needing to be solved.[11]

Global and local

Seen as inexorable, 'globalism' takes many forms. It is a catch-all term clutching many complex phenomena. The global feels remote from local action, from active citizenship and self-determination, although organisations and interests are becoming ever more agile in making the connections. Social networking offers real power and a part-illusionary sense of connectedness. It can depoliticise and disempower. It can also empower an Obama campaign or an Arab Spring.

Going local is a natural, many maintain a healthy, response to the predicament of awesome, remote and incomprehensible globalism. Localisation implies recognition of diversity. People and places differ: different resources, needs, problems and possible solutions. The more one localises, the more different contextual realities become apparent; and the closer people can come to being able to understand and take part in the sane management of their affairs. Those charged with the governance of local regions however encounter formidable difficulties to do with limited authority, stature and resources as well as capabilities. They face complex global problems, and often uncertain and untrusting national governments. There is clear logic for all universities and other higher education institutions in part also to 'go local', partly grounding their mission and *raison d'être* in their different and unique regional circumstances. This can only happen if universities, and especially their leadership, can act with determination. This means resisting the homogenising global forces of competition and consumption. These are big questions in the quest for ways to govern and manage more effectively than one-size-fits-all central planning and execution allow.

We have approached the subject mainly from European and Anglo-Saxon experience; the issues are however now essentially global. They appear to apply also to the aftermath of the Soviet system, and to other systems and traditions including China, and other parts of Asia and the South. The swelling literature on innovation as the key to competitiveness, often at a city or region level, is also mainly Western; but this too is becoming more diverse.

Regions and regions

This chapter has used the term 'region' in two different senses. The two well-established uses, and the difference, are obvious. The larger sense in particular can however be infused with emotion. We need to be clear and sensitive in using the term.

The smaller sub-national regions are the central subject of this study, as considered in Chapter 3. They may coincide with the States in federal systems like Australia, Canada, Germany and the United States; or with administrative regions and localities in unitary systems, as in the regions and departments in France, and the English counties, municipalities or regional development authority areas. Some regions have old names, long histories and a deep sense of identity. At the other extreme, the European Commission has caused the creation of new regions with and usually within its Member States, which are designated and targeted for European development funds.

The regional development work of the Organisation for Economic Cooperation and Development (OECD) recognises regional and local administrative authority areas as defined by OECD member governments. PASCAL as a flexible non-governmental organisation (NGO) also includes regions defined locally, for example by patterns of HEI catchment and provision, as well as official sub-national and sub-State administrative regions. Even allowing for this, the local region is in fact commonly a complex, plural and contested reality. Its meaning shifts according to interest and perspective. There may be several different and equally correct answers to the question 'what is the region?' It is better to ask what sense and use of the term works best for which identity and development purpose; and whether, when and why identity is an important aspect of being a region for its residents, its economy and its well-being.

The other kind of region, geographically large continental-scale, tends to have broad historical and possibly cultural affiliation as well as obvious geographical connection. Yet there is huge diversity in every case other than Australasia. Even there, New Zealand, a quite distant oceanic appendage to what is otherwise Australia, may object to an imposed identity, identifying rather with Oceania. Across the Pacific, the United States is to North America as Australia is to Australasia, and so too Canada to New Zealand.

Europe is historically distinct and still globally powerful. Historically however its eastern limits have fluctuated and are debated: Russia reaches to the Pacific, and southwards into the distinct region of Central Asia. Despite relative diminution as a global power, European influences penetrate to Central Asia. There is also renewed European interest in the Mediterranean basin, where the 'Arab Spring' fuels new regional consciousness.

Asia contains over half the world's population, with huge diversity across all conceivable criteria. It has large sub-continental regions. Each has meaning and stands comparison with other world regions – East Asia, the South Asian sub-continent, South-East Asia. More distinct, though far from homogeneous, is South or Latin America, economically flourishing, more self-confident, steadily 'invading' North America. Africa, pejoratively and with xenophobia called the Dark Continent, is (re)gaining its own voice and articulating an 'African way'. It too is 'invading northwards' (see also Watson et al., 2011. Chapter 8; Duke 2012a). Geopolitically the changing power reality is reflected in the international political construct of BRICS – Brazil, Russia, India, China, South Africa – counterbalancing the older Northern 'rich man's club' of the OECD. Tectonic grinding occurs as political power, based in economic success, moves between these large regions, contributing to the sense of global problematique.

What can regions and HEIs do?

What can local regions do to lead and manage better in these circumstances? Deliberations and sometimes decisions occur increasingly at global and international levels – in the agencies of the UN family of organisations, among groups of nations such as G20, in policy discussions of the OECD and acts of the European Union and Commission. Some global forces, especially in the world of global markets, mobile finances and 24/7 trading, appear beyond the reach even of international and national government systems, let alone more local administrations.

Most decisions and rules determining what local regions can and cannot do emanate from national political and government systems. Some are centralised, and jealous of power. Most perversely from this regional perspective, there is a temptation and a tendency, at a time when politicians at least pay lip service to participation, choice, decentralisation and so to more local control, to devolve responsibilities for key services to regions, but not to make available centrally controlled funds to do the work. Thus a local region, for all that it is closer to the needs of diverse local communities, may end up attracting the opprobrium of service failure, without means of redress.

A corresponding and linked question arises as when we turn from the region (Chapter 3) to the higher education provided in each locality, and to the leadership of HEIs (Chapter 4). What can each institution do, using often unique expertise as an intellectual powerhouse for the 'knowledge society'? Can it work in partnership with the local region, applying expert knowledge in ways that tackle complex puzzles, problems and imminent crises, making knowledge serviceable and useful?

As we will see in Chapter 4, these institutions are also in part victims of the global problematique. Many are pulled or tempted away from their local communities and regions into global contests. Many are under increasing pressure. Resources are reduced, the need for more, and ever more diverse, services rises. Accountability becomes more demanding. How realistic is it, looking at both parties in the 'engagement transaction' between regional administration and university, to expect them to respond to the new imperative, when each can barely cope with what they are already expected to do? Is it, as advocates argue, a 'win–win' situation? Or are the odds stacked too heavily against an effective contribution? These are questions to be explored in what follows, drawing on case studies of attempted partnership in different regions, mainly within the PASCAL project known as PURE and also from other studies of engagement.

Conclusion

Open and fearless examination of reality, of truth and its meaning for ethics, morals and *mores* in the widest sense, and hence culture and behaviour, has often been seen as a preserve of universities and public intellectuals, perhaps too of the seers and visionaries of organised religion. Religions alas seldom seem to come up with new and different, promising answers. What the more fundamentalist within all faiths prescribe is often unattractive, drawn from *a priori* dogma rather than from any communicable evidence base. As to politics, only the greatest and least trammelled statesperson sounds plausible; often it is only after demitting office that wisdom outshines pragmatism. Can we look to universities today to chart paths through such a problematique? This is the question to be tested through experience below.

This chapter has scanned large issues, ecological financial and economic. Social, civic and political dimensions have scarcely been mentioned. They too are important, and equally subject to change. Together they show that we have reached a critical turning or tipping point. Science and technology applied to human interests and affairs have overwhelming power for good or ill. The question is whether we have the will and the means to use the resulting knowledge and intelligence better to govern ourselves and to manage our affairs, our environment, our social and ecological heritage.

This is the bewilderingly turbulent setting in which PURE made one particular contribution to understanding and enhancing the contribution of higher education to regional development from 2008 and on into 2011. These localised studies were more or less directly impacted by the global context: how to handle the great complexity of governing and managing ourselves in modern societies; and how to ensure that the resources of HE (capital and running costs, time and human endeavour, big systems for the creation and transmission of knowledge) are put to best use.

At the heart of this are questions of culture, values and ethics. If these are neglected remedies will be shallow-rooted and fail. Culture and values cannot be changed by local regions, or by universities, alone. Parameters and policy directions are set nationally and globally. A new paradigm based on sustainability and reduced resource consumption is needed. So is a new economics which abandons growth as its mantra. Regional administrations cannot achieve these things alone. Regional governance that draws on and draws together the commitment and resources of local stakeholders, including higher education, may make the attempt more realistically.

Notes

1 Compare Larry Elliott, economics editor of *The Guardian*: 'Three years on, it's as if the crisis never happened' (*The Guardian*, 30 May 2011, p. 22).
2 Amusingly the Prime Minister's closing conference speech to the British 2011 Conservative Party Conference had to be amended at the last moment to remove the challenge to everyone to pay off credit card debts, 'a move that some calculated would shrink GDP by 15 per cent at a stroke' (Wintour 2011, p. 1). The incident illustrates the paradoxes and contradictions bemusing policy-makers.
3 For a cogent analysis of crisis and opportunity from a Keynesian perspective see Stiglitz (2010). Ho-Joon Chang, another critic of the current myopic economics, calls for a reform of the entire financial system (*The Guardian*, 9 August 2011, p. 26). Tony Judt (2010a) makes an 'impassioned plea for a new politics to heal a society stricken by rampant materialism and gross equality' in *The Guardian*'s Review section (*The*

Guardian, 20 March 2010, pp. 2–4). In another example of an increasing chorus of challenges to what is seen as *status quo* inertia in the face of a dangerously changed world, Harvie and Milburn colourfully call for civic mobilisation to 'regain control of our lives' and beat what they call the zombie of neo-liberalism 'marching on as it decomposes' (*The Guardian*, 5 November 2011, p. 37).

4 The recognition is now publicly dawning that economic predominance is rapidly flowing from the US to China.

5 Anticipating what follows in Part II, among PURE regions, the only place where the idea of managing contraction was seriously referred to was Puglia in the Italian south, where non-governmental energies are very evident. The question is becoming commoner in a context of seeking to measure not just GDP and economic growth but quality of life, with a 'happiness index'. Letters in the UK media discussing a year of 'flatline economy' suggest ways to live sustainably and more equitably without growth, to tax higher incomes and invest the proceeds in disadvantaged regions, and to invest and to manage any further 'quantitative easing' via a Green Quantitative Easing fund (*The Guardian*, 27 July 2011). In similar vein George Monbiot defines 'the monetarisation and marketisation of nature' and its 'reduction to a tradeable asset' as the definitive neo-liberal triumph (Monbiot 2011). See also Chapter 7 in this book.

6 A sample of headlines at this time reads: 'What is to be done' (a call for a new politics); 'Three years on, it's as if the crisis never happened'; 'The end of economic growth'; and 'A man for our times', meaning Socrates, condemned to death for telling follow-countrymen things they did not want to hear. See also Stiglitz (2010).

7 Or alternatively portrayed as an all-destroying cartoon monster. During 2011 awareness grew how far sophisticated algorithms built into complex software allow the financial markets to run virtually without human interference and control, and the possibly disastrous consequences of these automatic processes.

8 As the Euro crisis intensified in the latter part of 2011 around the Greek and Italian economies and the security of the banks, the behaviour of these agencies in downgrading institutions and economies began to attract more serious critical scrutiny. Thus, on the occasion of its downgrade of the US debt, the *Financial Times* condemned S&P's action as showing stunning and irresponsible ignorance. The three agencies are described here as a 'legally sanctioned oligopoly that regulated without oversight or consequence' Bill Miller, 'S&P's downgrade of US debt is wrong and dangerous', *Financial Times*, 9 August 2011, p. 24).

9 And often, closer to home for the urban and city dweller, loss of diversity in shops and markets as marketing and selling are scaled up and globalised.

10 There is special irony in applying this to the formation of the next generation itself. HE services are consumed now but paid for like hire purchase or a home loan, decades later, with rising student fees and loans in the UK and elsewhere. There is also the deeper hypocrisy that this form of public sector expenditure is thus masked to honour the dogma of 'small government'.

11 The tone of public debate in many countries appeared to shift in 2011 towards greater bemusement as to where leadership should lead, with rising popular discontent even in stable and conservative countries like the USA and Israel. There is then the danger as leadership in democratic systems wavers that more ruthless and arbitrary populist-authoritarian forces will instead prevail. On the other hand recent experience of devolved government, for example in Spain (Catalunya/Catalonia and the UK (Scotland), if disturbing to central administrations, is also heartening.

2

Governance and the changing 'three sectors'

Several crises and probably sustained transformations are taking place in an ever more closely connected and global world. 'Globalisation' itself is a universally acknowledged big change. Global warming implies long-term drastic climate change. Now clearly demonstrated, it remains disputed by diverse interests because of its serious implications. The fiscal and economic changes known as the global financial crisis started with the Great Crash of 2008. The GFC persists without sign of easy relief several years later.

Less obvious and dramatic, another change that affects how regional engagement and development may work is occurring in many societies. This is the blurring, interpenetration and rising ambiguity affecting what we habitually call the three sectors comprising the structure of society. As these become fuzzy, questions arise about who is partnering with whom, about the nature of governance. The meanings of capital, and even capitalism, have also become problematic.[1]

This chapter examines the three main elements commonly distinguished in modern society: the public or first sector; the private or second sector, meaning industry and commerce; and the voluntary, non-governmental or not-for-profit third sector, now often referred to as civil society. It considers the changing identities and stereotypes of each, their interconnectedness and their relationships. Where is higher education located, and how is engagement seen within such a categorisation?

The third sector has been of rising importance in recent years, in a context of more global complexity, including the GFC and the ecological crisis discussed in the first chapter. As the old categories change and their boundaries blur, what does this mean for diversity, one aspect of the difficult moral, psychological and operational tangle with which modern governance has to contend? What can the different parties do in partnership to manage new challenges and complexity? This includes the universities and other higher education institutions, which are also anomalous in this increasingly inaccurate tripartite division. Can they together, as good stewards and effective governors, resist the common urge to control by simplifying and standardising?

The challenge for the local region is considered directly in the next chapter. This includes managing a common instinct to cope by dividing up and compartmentalising. Regional administrations need to connect up their own internal (horizontal) elements; manage the matching functions of central government (external vertical links); and work with a multitude of external horizontal private, third sector and mixed-model interests and agencies, including the universities. Being effectively engaged partners, good stewards and governors means managing complexity. It requires avoiding mass standardising and homogenising, and not working in separate compartments.

The 'three sectors' and the new fuzziness

What are the three sectors today? How do old and new ways of distributing and managing power connect with regional administration? Is engagement of regions with their universities made easier or harder? We need to acknowledge stereotypes as well as the identity of each sector, and how these are changing. We may then be clearer as to where higher education is located and how it can engage. It too is caught up in contemporary churn and has its own crises of identity and stereotype.

Stereotypes matter. Their strength and their determination of the behaviour of those internalising them is illustrated graphically by Wilkinson and Pickett (2010, pp. 113–115). Strongly held, they may create formidable or insurmountable obstacles to collaboration. It is almost impossible to enter long-term relations with those for whom there is no trust and respect. At the least negative, stereotypes will cause suspicion and undermine confidence between partners across the sectors, making multilateral partnership impossible. Authoritarian, uncomprehending and venal government, incompetent and corrupt local administrations, inward-looking ivory-tower universities, rapaciously greedy captains of industry, banking and commerce: these are the stuff of popular media as well as serious drama. If real, or perceived as real, they make collaboration difficult indeed.

What is happening to the public sector?

In common speech the public sector means the government, both politicians and civil or public service administrators, at all levels from national to most local. Nowadays it increasingly includes also an international level. Some functions are universally accepted as nationally fitting, such as defence, currency and homeland security; how these are conducted may vary and be contested. Others to do with the economic, social, cultural and moral spheres are contested at almost every level. Tasks and duties taken for granted a few decades ago are now contested or have been moved. An obvious example is state versus private ownership – nationalisation and privatisation.

The very fact of government with powers to regulate, tax, spend and provide is seen, as by the American Tea Party, almost as an unnecessary evil. The capacity for harm rather than for good of the twentieth century state was shown by Nazism and Stalinism in Europe, Maoism in China, Apartheid in South Africa and Macarthyism in the US. The British Welfare State has been greatly rolled back in recent decades and the trend continues. Continental Europe, still seen as the seat of near-communist socialism by many Americans, is moving or has moved country by country to a more free-market model. The situation is however volatile. The tendency for the gap between rich and poor somewhat to narrow has been reversed in more recent decades with the near-universal adoption of neo-liberalism. No sooner had left-leaning governments been voted out of office in most European countries than the pendulum began to swing back, for example in Denmark and France. In early 2012 the euro crisis was however reinforcing change to the right, as in Greece and Spain. Despite the end of the Cold War and the great global divide that followed World War Two, other ideologies have flourished, some explicitly faith-based.

The most central single ideological proposition currently still dominating political thought and public policy derives from economics, rather than from older theories of the state. It concerns the wisdom of the free market, personified and credited with having a will and intelligence of its own. Taking the mantra of economic neo-liberalism, it is characterised as a triumph of Hayek over Keynes. It values economic freedom based in low taxation, open markets and minimal regulation. It takes for granted that capital accumulation driven by competition and the ambition to succeed and become wealthy is best, not just for the wealthy and very rich but for the whole society. Despite the GFC it still means minimally hampered private sector wealth-generation, wealth-creation through enterprising innovation, and a small non-interfering state. The idea of the hidden hand of the market is very old. So is the long-disproved yet persistent belief that growing wealth will 'trickle down' and be shared by all, obviating the need for state intervention to reduce poverty and inequality.[2] Competition, consumer choice and, above all, continuing economic growth are the anchor points of what is now neo-liberalism.

The implications for governance and the public sector are profound. If government is a necessary evil, almost anything that it does is stigmatised. Public or civil servants are treated as non-producers, drones who limit enterprise and productivity, wealth and by implication happiness. In many parts of the OECD world, not only on the US republican right, and especially where the GFC has bitten deepest, progress and even survival is held to mean cutting back the public sector. The primary level of government, the nation state, is normally reliant on quite frequent general elections. It remains the strongest level but is also the most exposed to anti-government feeling. Above it, internationalism is weakened by a xenophobic tendency to revert to one's own and look after oneself.[3] Xenophobia takes different forms. It is exacerbated by South to North invasion on a global scale, including west to east migration within China, and 'south to north' migration of political and economic refugees often in desperate and tragic form. It is illustrated by the instincts of people in many European countries to withdraw from the European Union or the currently besieged Eurozone. Globally mobile financial capital and large corporations further limit the power to govern, internationally, nationally and in local regions.

Faced by these political pressures and hostilities, and the newer imperative to reduce expenditure and manage national debt at almost any price, national governments will squeeze regional and local government of resources, and yet charge them with additional duties in areas from which national government withdraws. Effective and agreed devolution needs high trust and good faith. The UK offers an outstanding case study for such issues, but similar examples can be found elsewhere. In implementing the idea of the Big Society the government in Westminster passes responsibility to local levels in the name of citizen power and local devolution; but has simultaneously reduced the funds transferred from national to local levels to do the work (see, for example, the interview with Merrick Cockell, the new leader of the Local Government Association headed 'Balancing act'). This concludes that the letting go and taking risks essential to localism have not happened (*SocietyGuardian* in *The Guardian*, 27 July 2011, p. 5).[4] NGOs commonly rely on modest public funding accessed locally to support their infrastructure and by contract for activities. These are curtailed or terminated in the quest to drive down national indebtedness, with little recognition of damage and new resulting costs.

The private sector

The global financial crisis was created in the finance industry within the private sector. The cost of the immediate policy response fell mainly on the public sector. Until recently *private sector* was equated with industry, or with industry and commerce. Banking and the financial sector – 'the city' – barely featured. The old opprobrium attaching to the 'greed of corporate capitalism', meaning ruthless captains of industry, largely transferred to banks, bankers and their bonuses, which appear to hold governments and economies to ransom. Within the neo-liberal paradigm industry now enjoys a more positive image as the productive sector, relied on to generate rising productivity and continuing growth. Within the industrial part of the private sector, small and medium enterprises (SMEs) have become significant as a major area for innovation and job creation.

Older stereotypes of greed and ruthlessness that coloured academic dealings with industry and government, especially in relation to the military, have weakened, but are refuelled by bad chemical disasters and environmentally catastrophic oil spills. A less dramatic example of locally damaging behaviour by global corporations is the transfer of investment and employment between countries wherever more favourable conditions can be found. This hurts regions losing business and employment, making corporations unreliable partners for long-term development. Globally fluid capital and the opaque world of big corporations attract hostility. When industry campaigns for example against State public health and protection of the environment it feeds the old negative, colliding with the preferred benign image of corporate social responsibility (CSR). In 2011 the interwoven wealth and influence of the Murdoch 'media empire' attracted universal opprobrium when it came before a British House of Commons inquiry.

Business ethics, CSR and the notion of a triple bottom line attempt to change the image and perhaps the conduct of industry. High-profile acts of concern and generosity by wealthy captains of industry, outstandingly Bill Gates of Microsoft, and by wealthy entertainers, may also soften the negative popular image of the sector. As universities have become more 'business-like', entrepreneurial and competitive, their conduct attracts similar scrutiny and their own ethics debate spills out beyond research ethics to the conduct and management of the institutions themselves. Individual scholars of course vary enormously, but they tend to be more socio-liberally inclined than the generality of the population. At the most generous it is seen as a profession of public intellectuals using their autonomy to 'speak truth to power'.

For engagement to work well, belief in the good as well as the utility of collaboration with the 'private sector' as well as regional administration is almost essential. Without the support of scholars' hearts as well as minds, higher education engagement with the public and private sectors may not extend far beyond formal memoranda of agreement; hence the importance of identity and stereotype to engagement.

A main focus of regional engagement is often SMEs. The SME sector often provides a high proportion of local employment, one where the need for local higher education training, support and expertise is most evident. In terms of private sector training and research budgets, government wants to reduce its own expenditure, and looks to industry to spend more on skill training and human resource development. Some of this falls to universities working in partnership, much to the college sector. Universities also want industrial research grants, while worrying about the loss of academic freedom and interference in setting the research agenda that may result.

The Nordic countries in particular offer models of 'tripartite' planning and collaboration between government, employers and trade unions, an approach mirrored internationally by the OECD. Unions might be seen as representing individual and community interests and the third sector to which shortly we come. The loss of traditional bases of large-scale unionism in old industrial areas, including transport and mining with their large labour forces, means that their significance has waned. On the other hand the rise of sometimes unionised professions and white collar employment represents another force in civil society. It has become customary to talk about the productive interweaving of different sectors and strands of complex modern society in one or another variant of a 'triple helix'.

The third sector

Various terms refer to those parts of the social structure that are neither governmental nor profit-oriented. They reflect different traditions and priorities from region to region. Collectively they may be an antidote and almost a substitute for the excesses of big government where this is seen as corrupt, authoritarian, arbitrary, inefficient or out-of-touch; and of the private sector if this is seen as monopolistically exploiting a free market to increase shareholder profits and overpay senior executives. The third sector normally enjoys a more favourable image, other than among those whose institutions and interests are thus threatened. It is however broad and diverse. It can be seen in parts as paternalistic, self-seeking, self-indulgent, inefficient – or on the other hand as dangerously radical. It extends from apolitical 'blue-rinse' middle-class charity, and generous philanthropy and support for good causes, through sharply focused lobbying and direct action on social, health and environmental issues, with or without a specifically political agenda, to out-and-out revolutionary radicalism, as manifest in the Arab Spring of 2011.

The commonest universal term for the third sector is *non-governmental organisations*. In North America the term *not-for-profit* is often preferred. In more politically inclined and international settings the favoured term is *civil society* and so CSOs for civil society organisations. It includes a wealth of other apolitical activities to do with recreation and hobbies, sports and things religious and cultural. NGOs now feature strongly as an international and global force, as well as being very local. The third sector may thus be a partner, counterpoise or alternative to the other sectors, especially the public sector as in the UK Conservatives' 'Big Society' campaign. It depends on an alternative socio-political philosophy from that of 1980s' 'Reaganomics'. Here the autonomous individual is celebrated in Margaret Thatcher's famous if misquoted assertion that 'there is no such thing as society'.

Civil society is where many people sustain their main life and identity, rather than in politics or at the workplace. In some societies it is through communities and neighbourhoods; in others, villages and tribes. David Watson traces civil society from Hegel, located between family–community and the state, as an ethical idea. Here the university is assigned a critical role, avoiding over-identification with the state (Watson 2010 p. 399; see also Watson 2007). We defer consideration of where the university is located, and how it is perceived, to Chapter 4; for the moment, note that higher education may thus be seen as part of the third sector, but is elsewhere treated as a part of the state. Universities are also featured increasingly as businesses, some being for profit, others also private but not as yet mainly for profit. From another perspective higher education is not tidily located in any one sector, but claims special status as a system and institution outside this structure while perhaps connecting to all three. Universities might by seen almost as part of the formal and 'constitutional' structure of society: another 'estate of the realm' like the media and religion, alongside the executive, judiciary and political lawmakers.

These matters of definition and perception materially affect how the third sector is seen, and what different elements are and are not able to do. Trying to unpack them demonstrates how confused and complex the situation has become. The hybrid quasi-NGO or *quango* has long been familiar as an indirect means of making and executing policy 'at arm's length', avoiding direct government control and using essentially voluntary civil society expertise. When the UK government changed after eleven years a new government bravely announced 'a bonfire of the quangos', but modified this as their significance and necessity were recognised. Also now long-lived and still in favour despite numerous examples of costly failure is the private financial initiative or PFI, which melds public and private sector and is replicated in many forms and settings.

More recent and less criticised from any side is a host of social enterprises in what is now called the 'social economy'. Social enterprises based in voluntary and community endeavour take the form of housing associations, cooperatives and joint mutual ventures. They are seen by one university as giving a benevolent identity to non-profit, self-sustaining businesses engaged in good causes, such as recycling computers or running health-related services (*Times Higher Education*, 16 June 2001, p. 1). They marry together features of the private and third sectors, attempting to use skills and attributes of the private sector to achieve public, not-for-profit benefits (Nyssens 2006). Writing in *The Guardian*, Madeleine Bunting sees mutualism and civic participation, new discourse of the then new coalition government, as a way to redesign the battered and unfashionable Welfare State, specifically in the area of social care for the vulnerable by means of local community 'circles' at borough level. She notes that this voluntary sector involvement addressed a reservation that Welfare State founder Beveridge had back in 1948: it was to involve active citizenship, not breed passive recipients (*The Guardian*, 28 June 2010, p. 25).

Such a proliferation of new organisational forms and arrangements for achieving broadly public interest outcomes suggests how unserviceably rigid the employment of traditional three-sector political thought has become. It points to new forms of partnership and engagement which may be open to regional authorities operating on a more local level and in a more differentiated way than is practicable for nation states and national departmental bureaucracies. In such a world, born of the shortcomings of older approaches and the exigencies of twenty-first century crisis, new possibilities for the involvement of higher education in local–regional development also emerge.

Interconnectedness and the new importance of the third sector

Seemingly distinct phenomena are found connecting in a time of increasing complexity and specialisation, the more so with the sense of financial, ecological and political crisis that pervades the early twenty-first century. PASCAL set out to connect the making and managing of *place* with social capital and learning, and to connect and cross-fertilise the academic world with the policy arena. It sees the social policy realm as deeply interwoven with the economic (Duke, Osborne and Wilson 2005). Dealing separately with the economic and taking no account of social welfare, like attempting political liberalism and practising social conservatism, will ultimately fail.

On the other hand, trying to manage ever more complex government usually requires different policy realms to be administered separately. They need specialised units and sub-systems. These have a propensity to become narrow and competitive, rather than to integrate; 'silo' or 'stovepipe' administration results. Joined-up government is essential to handle complexity. It has been attempted in many ways, for instance by matrix forms of organisation, usually with limited success. Massively powerful electronic information-handling systems also have limitations. They frequently result in high-cost overruns, sometimes in complete failure. They can only be as clever and connective as they are designed to be. Human collaboration, shared trust, tacit knowledge and common sense are all also needed.

Returning to the classic three sectors, there is another problem: 'third' is also third in power and status. Yet it has risen dramatically in importance as national prosperity has stalled, the scope of the state has contracted and new social problems have emerged. This 'sector', for all its growth and diversification, lacks the political power and authority of the state, and the economic power of the private sector. It carries some negative stereotypes alluded to above. It is now so diffuse, inter-permeated with and by the private and public sectors, that its contemporary identity is ambiguous. In recent decades it has grown hugely in influence, reach and duties, and so is gaining new identity and stature. It has extended beyond middle-class charity towards the poor, for example in the UK, to become a major player at all levels from the local community to the international. It is now indispensable to regions and local authorities for managing ever more burdensome devolved responsibilities. It is increasingly assumed and asserted that without the resources, efforts and goodwill of the voluntary or civil society sector, essential social welfare services, let alone newer, larger and less obviously tangible development aspirations being articulated as quality of life, or happiness, simply cannot be achieved.

The rising importance and effective governance of the third sector must now be included in any study like this, the more so while political philosophy inclines towards 'big market, small state'. The explosion of social networking from the essentially interpersonal and largely narcissistic, as in the now-filmed story of Facebook, to the intensely political, as in the Arab Spring, adds a new dimension. It can connect and empower individuals, create a potent political vehicle and add to the complexity of governing. Twitter gets blamed for hard-to-contain riots along with illegal 'raves'. To those in government, social networking involves not-always-'civil' civil society; it has become subversive anti-social networking. It can also be seen as the third sector equivalent of e-commerce in the commercial and business world.

The difficult necessity of diversity and the quest for simplicity

Diversity in the management of higher education systems is divisive, frequently extolled, but fiercely resisted as being unavoidably hierarchical. Diversity of mission is thought desirable; yet avoiding upward 'mission drift' seems impossibly hard, such are human ambitions and institutional reward systems. A different yet comparable dynamic causing difficulty occurs where national governments acknowledge the diversity of local and regional needs but cannot resist the urge to control. They see the good sense in the principle of devolving authority and decisions to more local levels of governance which are closer to and understand better the different needs and strengths of different local communities.

Where power has grown locally and upwards from diverse origins into federated national systems, diversity may be historically and culturally embedded. At a higher level of administration this is the subsidiarity principle of the European Union. Elsewhere, even in federal systems where demands on government and the ambitions of national politicians combine, the instinct to centralise and standardise administration can be overwhelming. Diversity becomes an unaffordable luxury in hard and impatient times. Albeit human and easily understood, this fallacy is fatal to the notion of regional governance responding effectively to actual diverse needs, and building on the actual diverse and often rich social–cultural assets of different people and places. It also weakens efforts to collaborate effectively regionally between local academic, private and third sector partners.

Diversity is a vital element in the difficult moral, psychological and functional tangle with which modern governance must contend. Standardisation is more tempting, the more complicated the task. In an audit era (see Chapter 10) common targets, rules and measures handled by big IT systems look sensible. But even the most advanced and sophisticated electronic systems cannot accommodate real-world diversity as they force subjects into artificial categories. They lack the flexibility and responsiveness which effective and sustainable devolved arrangements allow. Social capital comes to be rejected and generalised. Mainly economic targets prevail.

Chapter 1 examined problems that confront societies and their governance with rising complexity, but said little about why diversity matters. Apparently a fundamental characteristic of health and survival in all species, human and other, it is untidy, and difficult to value and manage. As we witness destruction of species and reduction of diversity on a scale not experienced since the demise of dinosaurs however, awareness is dawning that the survival of different ecosystems, species and even human cultures, languages and ways of life really matters. Learning to manage, support and gain from diversity has become a central challenge for civil societies and their governments. The degrees of difference that we find tolerable seem to be limited. An instinct favours xenophobia, hence the controversies surrounding multiculturalism. Recognising and supporting diversity demands political courage on the part of governments and Voltaire-like integrity of universities. It becomes a central test of good governance, illustrating how difficult yet important regional collaboration across the sectors is.

Working together – regions and higher education

It should be evident why it is hard to engage well, drawing on the resources especially of universities and local communities as required for good governance. Being effective partners, stewards and governors means managing complexity, not standardising and compartmentalising. Embracing diversity and collaboration requires learning different 'languages'. It requires understanding different *mores* and moral codes.

What this means for administering a region applies on two axes: horizontally between the departments and divisions within a regional administration such as a province, or a State in a federal system; and vertically, to connect the policies and powers held centrally with those devolved to the region. Only the first is directly amenable to region-level management. Yet it is essential, if the region is to manage well and long term. The second is determined principally by the philosophy and leadership of those in power nationally. Sometimes deep traditions and prejudices within the permanent administration obstruct. For a region looking to the national capital, the implications have mainly to do with representation, lobbying and persuasion. Regions may unite in representation to national government, or seek to carve out more autonomy alone. In terms of the other kind of lateral linkage, cross-sector engagement, local regions have more room to operate with the changing private and third sectors, but may lack the experience, imagination and skills to do this well.

Essentially similar segmentation occurs with universities: specialised areas are divided and sub-divided within academic disciplines, carving up reality to be owned in bits by competing departments and sub-departments. This may create divisive affiliation to specialised international professional associations and career identities, which compete for loyalty with the local employing university. Academic boundaries ignore the untidy problems of the 'real world', its governments and communities.

Efforts have long been made to penetrate these barriers and to work across the boundaries: inter-departmental committees, matrix forms of organisation, cross-disciplinary research groups. More familiar identity and 'membership' structures often persist. The need to connect powerfully challenges higher education systems, institutions and traditions with the need to reconfigure their teaching, research and management to the requirements of modern societies for higher education expertise. Engaging with regions, communities and real-world problems goes against the grain of academic instinct. On the other hand, the university is also part of the community by virtue of its staff and students. The community's culture, hopes, needs and values reside within each HEI insofar as it is in and part of the region. Change can be stimulated from within, given that the community is in the university, as is the university in the community.

Challenges for local regions and for universities

The next two chapters look in turn at the two main 'partners' of this study – local regions and higher education institutions. The second part of the book turns to some empirical findings of PURE and other field studies. We have seen that regional administrations have to connect their own internal (horizontal) elements with the matching functions of central government (external vertical links), and with a multitude of (external, mainly horizontal) private and third sector interests. They need also to work with often cantankerous universities. Can these essential forms of collaboration and interconnection be managed by local regions; or are the problems in the years and circumstances of the GFC simply too daunting?

David Watson points out how widely the term 'stakeholder' is used in these settings, yet how oddly anomalous it is: 'Stakeholder is one of those words which has almost exactly the opposite meaning now, since [sic] when it was originally coined. The stakeholder used to be the person who held the coats – and the prize-money – while the fight was on; the notion was one of scrupulous disinterest.' He proposes that a modern 'stakeholder', as now understood, has to put something on the table and at risk (Watson, 2010, p. 402) – to commit a stake rather than merely watch and 'hold the ring'. The anomaly is most evident when you ask who the prize-fight is supposed to be between. All are now in the ring, engaged in a common struggle. But it can be an ill fit, given the love affair of so many administrations with competition. Fighting rather than collaborating is seen as the driver of progress. The optimistic alternative of well-managed engagement means not a win–lose or a winner-takes-all competition, but a win–win for all parties.[5]

Many feel and some assert that the global forces and tectonic power shifts that this generation witnesses within and behind the GFC are just too much. How can they overcome barriers and enable collaboration with prospective partners: in higher education and in other parts of the increasingly intermingled sectors of private and community civil society? Rather than seeing the crisis as an opportunity to be taken, is it a matter of battening down and waiting for the storm to pass, tightening belts and carrying on as before? In considering this let us turn to the local region.

Notes

1 From 'good' venture capital we have among other terms corporate (ambiguous) and responsible capital confronting crony and vulture, with debate whether and how free-rein capitalism can be consensually constrained.

2 The issue is taken up by Stewart Lansley, who has written on the cost of inequality with three decades of the rising 'super-rich' and the further widening of the income gulf through the GFC period (*The Guardian*, 5 October 2011, p. 32; see also Wilkinson and Pickett 2010).

3 There are many examples of this kind of assertiveness from Iceland and Finland to the Netherlands, Britain and the USA; a variant is the separatist tendency of Italy's Northern League.

4 A sample of headlines in one national UK daily over a few days serves to illustrate: 'A happy ending? – end-of-life care has been transferred wholesale to charities at two health trusts...'; 'Kicking charities while Serco profits isn't a plan with legs'; 'Charities fight for survival as funds slashed'; and, heading five letters to the editor, 'False economy of cutting support to charities' (*The Guardian*, 27 July 2011, 4 August 2011, 2 August 2011, 05 August 2011).

5 An article by the polemical British *Guardian* writer Polly Toynbee on reform of the National Health Service carries the by-line 'Despite the ideological demand for competition, doctors point to evidence that collaboration is what gets the best results' (*The Guardian*, 30 July 2011). Arguing against the anti-collaborative 'world class fixation' of vice-chancellors, policymakers and others, David Watson asks 'If teams work, why do elite winners take all?' (*THE*, 8 December 2011, p. 8)

3

Two key partners – (1) the region

Introduction – partnership between unlike organisations

Engagement between a region and a university is a kind of mixed marriage. It can be difficult to bring and keep together in productive union two very different partners. Academics specialise in teaching, research and academic writing. Regional administrators specialise in making and carrying out policy. Academics colonise the world of ideas. A few study regional development and policy-making, but their identity and professional advancement derive from published writing. Their job is to do research, think and write. That of administrators is to *do* things, often, in today's complex difficult times, to manage crises.[1]

A constant challenge experience in PURE is that regions, especially regional authorities, see universities as relatively opaque and monolithic, accessible only through friendly individuals. This is a problem of and by regions as well as universities, since they lack both the apparatus and any sense of priority in working with universities: neither the systems nor the culture are present. Perception tends to be restricted to one-off transactions rather than sustained collaboration. Regional authorities need to be able to articulate their policy priorities in ways that enable universities to contribute. Regions tend to be blind to the potential role and use of universities. In the case of the southern Queensland region for instance this was very apparent in terms of regional and local strategic planning documents; yet the PURE process of engaging led quickly to keen interest in the many possibilities that working with the regional university offered.

In this chapter we consider the first of these two partners: the region. Local regions have much less formal power and lower status than national governments, whose policies, whims and political accidents circumscribe what they can do. Yet local regions are likely to have the knowledge to do things within their regions better. Universities have tended to enjoy more glamour and mystique. They are an older institutional form than is a modern regional administration. The more prestigious have taken little interest in their region in recent decades; many still do not. In many countries however they now find themselves open to critical scrutiny and obliged to show value for money.

Higher education is a universally acknowledged main seat of learning. We turn to this in the next chapter. Yet learning is also increasingly important in the region, at least in the sense that lifelong learning in 'the learning region' has become an almost automatic policy precept. It is especially salient in the language and policies of the EU. Here and throughout the book we ask what it really means and how it is honoured in practice. We also ask about its place in the problematic twenty-first century world characterised in the chapters above.

Continental regions and local regions

Let us clarify the meaning of the ubiquitous term 'region' before explaining what we mean by the 'learning region'.

We are interested not with the large continental region, the common sense of region in the global and macro-political sense, such as Africa and Latin America. As PASCAL experienced in the course of an international conference held in Gaborone, Botswana, in 2010 Africa, a continental region of many diverse countries, has a rising, at times strongly expressed, sense of identity; not just as a continent historically oppressed by slavery and colonialism, but also in terms of its historic wisdom and cultures – an African way on which to build a distinctive and more optimistic future. The Latin American region has a still stronger sense of distinctive identity, history and destiny, with new purpose and confidence on the global stage.

In the global world of the late twentieth century and today, the identities, and the sense of their present and future, of these large regions are increasingly significant as large-region power relations change. Emotional suffusion may be strong: it was once said that 'East is East and West is West and never the twain shall meet'. They now meet on different terms. Massive world population movements produce more or less destabilising cultural encounter and multiculturalism within nation states. In terms of the large world regions, competition and shifts of economic power between big regions run alongside and partly displace national identities and the kinds of bloody local rivalries that marked European history and energised the 'European project'.[2] In this large-region context the engagement of higher education with (local) regional development takes different forms, depending on the cultures, histories and economies of these world regions.

The creation, extension and contemporary crisis of the EU and the European Community, as an economic, and increasingly an administrative and supranational government region, makes this even more salient. The EU has extended through much of the continent of Europe in its original geographical and cultural sense. The European Community Administration and Parliament, and a large array of EU development programmes, are relevant to academics as well as economists. Unlike the OECD, another intergovernmental organisation (IGO) wielding influence in the work addressed by the book, the EU spends more than a third of its budget on economic and sometimes socially oriented applied research and development (R&D) programmes.

European thought has hitherto dominated most learning region discourse, especially through the organs of the EU, with its Committee for Regions, and of that other advanced industrial nations' rich man's club mainly of the North, the OECD.[3] The higher education and development work of both the OECD (OECD 2007) and PASCAL, comprise mainly European studies[4]. The EU and the OECD differ in that one corresponds to a global-scale region, whereas the OECD is a club of wealthy industrialised nations initially mainly European, but always, and now increasingly, reaching also into other continental regions. The OECD as a European-based IGO active in promoting regional development, including the involvement of higher education, and with a vigorous interest in sub-national regions, provides a vehicle for exchanging experience and extending European understandings of the learning region into other large regions of the world.

Within these big regions and broad identities the most powerful affiliation and identity for most people is national, and often still more local. It is still very local for traditional village communities in wealthy as well as poor countries. It is often also strong at sub-national regional levels, which may or may not align with the national government's administrative divisions. These divisions can be altered quite suddenly by political act without touching deeper underlying place- and community-based affiliations. Often the sense of identity and community or belongingness is based on distinct old historic administrations such as free cities and principalities, residing as much in folk as in living memory.

In many Western countries, there is critical scepticism about the national government. In some places this extends to deep cynicism and alienation at least from national politics, and in other countries to non-violent resistance or outright civil war. What is relevant to this study of engagement is how national politics, policies and citizen-voter attitudes affect regions within the nation. Do they enhance or stunt the capacity for partly autonomous and purposeful regional development? Scepticism in Europe flows into outright hostility as the GFC persists: towards the conduct of Member States faced with this crisis, and towards the 'European project' and the EU itself. Taking refuge in local-region destinies and development is not however simple.

National identity has been strong especially in European minds since the rise of modern nationalism in the nineteenth century. It is less deep-rooted in some non-European parts of the world where expedient colonial administrations were created by colonial fiat rather than as natural nation states, but aggressively asser-tive in others. This does not make devolution to more culturally and geographi-cally meaningful regions easier; a still-new nation state may be preoccupied with fragmentation and loss of minority peoples and territories. Giving development responsibilities to localities may threaten the break-up of the nation. We return to relations between national governments and local-region administration below.

Even in Europe with its diversity of identity, there is an instinct for central control. The UK is an obvious example with weak, now disbanded, regional development agencies, and fear about where Scottish devolution may lead.[5] In Australia, federal–States rivalries remain chronic. However, a modern wave of cultural and political decentralisation is bypassing the nation state. Nations like Spain and even the UK have devolved more authority to sub-national regions. France and Italy wrestle with levels of regional government. Having regions and departments as well as the commune level seems costly multi-tiering; but taking a level out reduces localism, or makes central control harder to manage. Also the EU has created new 'regions', a few of which even cross national boundaries, to support high priority area development.

We see then that *the region* is administratively problematic, but often significant and powerful to many in Spain or Italy, France or the UK. In North America this is obviously the case with the US States and Canadian Provinces. The meaning, strength and character of *region* are diverse and important. No one answer to 'what is the region?' holds true for all circumstances. Nor will any one hypothetical ideal best answer fit them all. Seemingly opposite answers can be equally true and operationally valid. This illustrates that modern governance as well as modern living requires living with paradox and opposites.

The meaning of the local learning region

So far we have examined the global and national contexts within which the sub-national local region exists. What do they identify as their challenges, and how do they marshal the resources to address them? Our central interest is not in the governance and politics of regional devolution as such, but in how this can connect with the resources of higher education to enhance balanced regional development. This brings us to the capacity of a region to do this, and to develop as a learning region.

One definition of the learning city and learning region is 'An administrative region that has developed the capacity to collect, analyse and use data and experience to enhance the quality of its understanding leading to improved practice' (Duke 2010, p. 144).

There are rich and poor, deep and shallower, meanings of the concept, as these passages from the same *Encyclopedia of Education* article explain:

> The learning city is an ideal, rather than a description of any actual place or places. It is an aspiration for the way the city might be better managed and manage itself in a complex world characterized by terms such as global and knowledge economy. The terms learning region and city-region are used also as a way of thinking about the management of a city area or region with an evident identity, boundaries, and some form of government. It reflects a sense that city and regional governance could and should be different, and better than they presently are. Local administrations in many parts of the world have in recent years expressed the intention to be learning cities; a number have announced that this is what they are, will be or are becoming. In the sense that the learning city is a social and political aspiration rather than a well defined and understood condition with agreed characteristic measures, it is best understood as a social construct. ... There is no established definition of what it means. ... It is best understood as heuristic, a metaphor which expresses a set of values and purposes, not an established concept in academic social science. The term is used mainly in policy arenas and among communities of practitioners who are concerned with how things can be done better.
>
> ...there are two distinct levels of meaning to the concept of learning city or city-region. The easier-to-understand term implies an urban or regional authority that makes good provision for many people to learn. It sees learning, essentially in forms supported by high quality and widely accessible education and training as crucial to economic productivity, competitiveness, and so to civic success.

The second, deeper and richer ... meaning concerns the capacity of a city or region itself to learn almost as an individual person or other organism can learn, understand, and adapt its behaviour. There may be a difficulty in a Western democratic and individualistic tradition about accepting the notion of learning outside the individual. The recognition has been strongest and longer established in respect of the learning organisation as an informing principle for the study of organisation behaviour, for consulting to management, and in management education. Subsequently learning has been affixed to many other institutions and phenomena, from schools and universities themselves to other kinds of organisations such as hospitals and banks to events like festivals. In a geographical and political sense it has been applied at levels from the nation to a small locality such as a village. (Duke 2010, pp. 144–145)

In short, the learning region is an ideal. It indicates a direction of travel, with criteria for making and noting progress. There is no simple recipe for action. It is therefore often reduced to a more tangible agenda, such as widening HE and enhancing the relevance of its education and training to meet known labour market needs. What is sacrificed is the longer-term sustainability that a world in crisis and its regions need.

The contraction of meaning from a region capable of reflecting on its own experience and adapting its behaviour accordingly, to a region where there is good and accessible vocational education and training, echoes similar reduction in the scope of the grand concept of lifelong learning: from informal and non-formal as well as formal learning, life-wide as well as lifelong. This ambitious reformulation at the beginning of the 1970s (Faure *et al.*, 1972; OECD 1974) shrank to its more widely used but much narrower interpretation by the end of the century, notably in the programmes of the European Commission (Duke 2012a).

The coming of age of the local learning region

The idea of lifelong learning lay largely dormant for twenty years. It was vigorously revised and interpreted, albeit often narrowly, during the 1990s, in Europe and coincidentally or by emulation also in other parts of the industrialised world as 'knowledge society' discourse became commoner. This study draws on work arising from this new wave from the 1990s.

A scan of reports, and other grey and mainstream literature of that time, illustrates the burgeoning of new interest, mainly in the policy arena and from scholars linking the two worlds of research and practice. This was coming to be called Mode Two knowledge production (Gibbons *et al.* 1994). Different streams of intellectual interest combined around new policy issues. These included competitiveness, innovation and economic success; the identity and place of a generation of new and what came to be called regional universities (Dahlof and Selander 1994; Davies 1997); and the management of higher education systems to include helping local economic and to some extent community and social development. An example of the new salience of the learning region is Chris Benner's 2003 article on learning communities in a learning region, which examines learning networks in Silicon Valley (Benner 2003). It includes numerous book and journal titles in the 1990s referring to the learning region, including Florida (1995), along with work by Castells (1996), Wenger (1998), Amin and Thrift (1994), Steiner (1998) and Garlick (1998). Competitiveness and innovation systems feature strongly. Other relevant much-cited work at this time was by Kanter (1995) and Porter (1990).

One important source of work on policies affecting universities in their regions was the University of Newcastle in North-East England. It was led by Pro- and later Deputy Vice-Chancellor John Goddard with colleagues including David Charles and Paul Benneworth. That University has shown unusual consistency in adhering to regional development and community engagement which continued under new and still current leadership.[6] Newcastle's work was influential in the OECD IMHE's higher education and regional development activity from that time, cascading into different countries of Europe, notably the Nordic region (see Goddard 1997 Centre for Urban and Regional Development Studies {CURDS} 1998; Department for Education and Employment {DfEE} 1998, OECD 1999, OECD 2007). Work in the UK HE policy arena fed into national policy-making settings: the Dearing Inquiry (National Committee of Inquiry into Higher Education 1997), the Higher Education Funding Council, and the Committee of Vice-Chancellors and Principals (Goddard et al. 1994; see also Charles and Benneworth 2001; Charles et al. 2001; Charles 2003).

Charles's work with the Higher Education Funding Council England (HEFCE) was the genesis of the benchmarking of engagement which PASCAL took up through PURE, extending it from HEI to regional benchmarking (see Chapter 10). It is less clear how far these efforts significantly influenced ongoing HE and regional policy in the UK a decade later, other than through the HEFCE's Higher Education Innovation Fund. Nor did regions gain in stature from such efforts, especially with the abolition in 2010–11 of England's Regional Development Agencies (RDAs).

By the beginning of the new century, the idea of regional development for the 'knowledge economy' or society, with emphasis on regional innovation and innovation systems, had well and truly arrived, especially in Europe. It was adopted by and locked into much of the discourse and work of the EU, and of the OECD and its Member States in and beyond Europe. The main focus was on the competitive region and its economy. Rhetorically the learning region had wider scope. It encompassed at least some of the social, equity, healthy, cultural, civic and environmental aspects that PASCAL advocates in the cause of balanced development. And yet for all the flow of rhetoric, case studies, publications and practical learning town, city and region ventures in the first decade of the new millennium, the richer idea of the learning city or region failed to win practical policy adherence (Yarnit 2011).

Notes

1 A university contracting work with a region as research that advances its academic profile encounters this tension in microcosm when the region sees it as consultancy enabling it to perform better.

2 Another emergent example is the idea, and the very name, of the Arab Spring.

3 But see Watson *et al.* 2011, for an example of a case-based study of university engagement where the US and other non-European cases and influences predominate. This unusually attempts to rebalance normal perceptions by means of a South-to-North perspective. The focus however is on higher education rather than local regions and their development, which is the focus here.

4 Five of the fourteen OECD and five of the sevennteen PURE studies were of regions outside Europe. See also Duke 2011, 2012a) for discussion of lifelong learning, engagement and the large regions in a global framework.

5 See for example John Curtice's 'Devolution's slippery slope' – 'Most Scots and Welsh still oppose a full breakaway but the appetite for extra powers looks unsatiated', and David Marquand's 'England's visceral Europhobia may break up the UK' which concludes with the 'possible break-up of the UK, with England staying out [of the EU] and Scotland and Wales going in' (*The Guardian*, 10 October 2011, p. 26; 18 December 2011).

6 The Vice-Chancellor Chris Brink argues trenchantly that the utility as well as the quality of a university's work is fundamental: 'What is it good for? What difference does it make?' (The lesson of hardship: focus on what matters – the people nearest, *THE*, 12 May 2011, p. 17). In the same issue of *THE*, The University of Bradford seeks a Deputy Vice-Chancellor who will advance knowledge transfer as well as learning and teaching, to 'make knowledge work'.

4

Two key partners – (2) higher education

Introduction

Chapter 3 explored two particular issues before considering the region as a partner: the scope and diversity of regions, and the impact of national and global change. Two essential similar questions arise in relation to the other main partner in this study, higher education: what is the scope of HE and how do national and global forces affect the situation?

On this 'other side' – higher education institutions as against public sector governance – there is a swelling literature on the transformation of higher education, universities in particular, to accommodate a fast-rising proportion of the age cohort now standing at over 50 per cent in some places.[1] Explosive growth in size is complicated by global influences and perspectives. There is competition internationally for students, prestige, staff and resources. Global ranking has become influential and much contested almost overnight. There are new and rising pressures to prove utility and value for money, and to diversify income and earn more. There are fears for the survival of the public university dedicated to serving the public good (see for example Readings 1996, and the many HE policy titles that employ the word 'crisis').[2]

Some of these pressures favour engagement and common purpose with the region of location. Others however seriously obstruct it. There is an inclination among those who advocate engagement to underestimate the obstacles and resistance in the hope that enlightened self-interest will prevail. Value for money, relevance and impact have become common discourse. Indicators measure return on investment over the lifetime of the individual learner. Higher education is commonly referred to as an industry, and an export industry. New ideas and language for the HE sector include the concept of 'tertiary', embracing all post-secondary education, training and human resource development (HRD). The talk is increasingly of HE systems and sectors where once it was essentially about individual institutions.

Other changes in recent decades have created new ways of understanding the nature and uses of knowledge, as manifested in the 'knowledge society' which includes and is wider than the more favoured 'knowledge economy'. They prompt questions about how social systems, institutions and governments as well as place-based communities learn, continue learning and apply their learning to managing better. As we have seen in Chapter 3, the concept of a learning region combines lifelong learning with the idea of learning in and as a locality – what PASCAL recognises in relation to place-making. These changes prompt questions about how social systems, institutions and governments as well as place-based communities learn, continue learning and apply their learning to achieving chosen outcomes.

This adds up to massive and rapid cultural change intruding into the 'hidden garden' of the university, its curriculum, research agenda and management. It has far-reaching implications for the nature of teaching and learning in HE institutions. These are unfolding in different ways in different world regions, and with new information and communications technology (ICT)-based distant learning opportunities. Some appear to pull universities away from their natural locality-based character and anchorage into the placeless virtual world of Borderless Higher Education, as the long-established ACU Observatory is called.

How do these issues affect the contribution of higher education to regional development and the nature of local partnership? The focus and interpretation of engagement vary across as well as within the different main world regions. Some privilege individuals' formation and the economic and civic uses to which they put what they learn. Others are more concerned with how higher education supports and gains from the economic and perhaps the wider balanced development of a region.

The scope of higher education and the tertiary idea

Is tertiary education a good way to plan policy and to administer higher education?

In practice, most economic and social policy studies of higher education refer mainly or only to universities. Even when the formal scope is called 'higher education', language tends to revert to university or universities. The OECD favoured and began using the language of tertiary education to include all post-secondary provision some decades ago. This practice has not been widely adopted.

Australia for example had a federal Tertiary Education Commission (TEC) for a while in the 1980s, with three Councils for its tripartite system of universities, advanced education, and technical and further education (TAFE). It then merged the first two higher education sectors and dissolved TEC. HE and TAFE continue to be planned and administered separately, one at federal, the other at State level. On the positive side, this allows different States to try different approaches to TAFE–HE articulation and partnership, as well as diversity within state systems. In Victoria for example two of the dual sector institutions (RMIT and Victoria University) have ratios of 3:1 and 1:3 in their mix of HE and TAFE students.

The UK likewise merged the universities and polytechnic sectors, but also kept the (mainly non-HE) tertiary further education sector apart, more closely managed and differently funded. Views and policies on the older 'binary divide' – the division of HE into ('research-led') universities and vocational universities or institutes – continue to vary between countries and over time. Reform may mean erasing the old binary line in one country, but establishing or restoring it in another. Scotland combined the policy and funding of higher and further education under a single Funding Council while England separated them more decisively. Other countries using different terms face the same conundrum.

The longest record of tertiary planning (without necessarily using that term) is probably in different parts of the USA. The former Master of New College Oxford returns to the theme of the California Master Plan in a recent opinion piece. The Plan envisaged a three-tier system from easy entry community colleges to research universities. The 'articulated and centrally directed three-tier system' achieved what for example the UK binary systems hoped for, with twice the enrolment in the senior two years at University of California Berkeley compared with the first two years, and three quarters of State university graduates starting elsewhere. Despite financial problems internal mobility remains a reality. More generally however there is concern in the USA about the low completion rate of US community colleges (about one third); and recognition that US mass HE has not addressed underlying inequalities. Social stratification is perpetuated – more important than who goes is to which college and for what subjects (*THE*, 15 December 2012, p. 29; 2 March 2011, p. 39; 7 July 2011, p. 59; Mullen 2011).

Such arrangements try to accommodate differences over the character and outcomes required of twenty-first century HE. National administrations have difficulty handling this and other broad ideas within the tradition of departmental responsibilities. These often become policy and programmatic management silos. This bureaucratic dynamic – silos, or what in the old industrial English North-East were called stovepipes – plagues the governance of all complex systems. It is highly relevant to regional partnership. A big 'cake' like education needs managing in slices, given the scale and spread from nursery and kindergarten through schooling to post-doctoral studies and advanced research; yet lifelong learning is held to be seamless.

Many countries have a history of changing the names and remits of ministries and departments to do with education and training, sometimes several times in a decade. The UK's 2011 White Paper is the eleventh new framework for higher education since the 1961 Robbins report. That country has taken branding and separation very far in two senses: by removing higher education entirely from any kind of Ministry of Education umbrella; and by aggressively redefining it as skills, located in a Department of Business, Industry and Skills. From an economic view of regional engagement this might appear to be a good thing. It also constitutes an affront to the traditional more liberal view of the role and mission of the university. Frequent changes of system structure, responsibility and nomenclature are costly. They induce 'innovation weariness' in institutions needing some stability to do well. They also display uncertainty and conflicting intentions for higher and tertiary education.

Any work that looks at the contribution of education to regional development needs to consider the whole tertiary education sector. Research and its commercial exploitation and application belong mainly, though not only, with the more wealthy universities, both traditional and technological. Teaching however makes the most direct contribution, preparing people for adult and working life. For some this means general capacities for living, learning and working throughout life – learning to learn. For others it means more immediately useful and specific work-ready attitudes, knowledge and skills.

How far training and on-the-job learning should be taken towards equating graduation with immediate employability is chronically divisive and contested. For prestigious universities, oriented to research and to teaching only the most capable young people mapped on a global canvas, thinking and administering on broad tertiary principles may be anathema. For a region which needs human resource development and has new skills requirements to diversify, innovate, produce and compete, the college sector[3] may be much more important. Industry, and more particularly the SMEs which are now often the larger part of the productive private sector, frequently criticises the lack of work-readiness of young graduates exiting higher education. The college sector is by its nature and the way it is managed much closer to the needs of local enterprises and the local economy.

Through PURE, PASCAL attempted to promote discussion and policy analysis of 'tertiary' as an ordering principle for engaging the HE section with regions. As a special cross-regional theme it did not attract the interest of other subjects featured in Part II of this book. Yet the subject remains centrally important to the governance, and behind this the identity and functions, of higher education. For now it rests in the policy in-basket – for some perhaps the too-hard basket.

National policies and global forces – mass HE, competition and utility

The second half of the twentieth century saw what came to be called an elite university system expand beyond recognition to become mass higher education. In places it approaches near-universal participation in some form of tertiary education. This came to be seen as a national and personal economic investment equipping countries, individuals and local regions to compete globally in the knowledge economy. Other purposes – equity, social justice and wider access, social inclusion and stability, a culturally richer, healthier and more civically active society – also featured in the rationale for expanding higher education.

The change was led by the world's wealthiest nation, the United States. Virtually no nation and higher education system is exempt; participation multiplied in volume, extending both as a proportion of the age participation rate (APR) and out along the age range through the working age population. The United States' neighbour 'Canada' recognised early that adults were a majority in higher education (Campbell 1984). Newly more prosperous nations, small and medium-sized like Singapore and South Korea, huge like China and India, expanded their provision of higher education at breathtakingly rapid rates.

Older undergraduate students in particular tend to be involved with local institutions, whereas in some nations young people have tended to go away to university to study – in England but less in Scotland and New Zealand for example. Nowadays that tendency has become international where it can be afforded. The traditionally somewhat insular United States provides a good example: a November 2011 annual report by the Institute of International Education shows a year-on-year 5 per cent increase in Americans going abroad to study, and a rising proportion going to unconventional destinations like Egypt, India and China (*THE*, 17 November 2011, p. 10).

Engagement with a region is more likely when large numbers of students are part of the regional economy and its communities. More broadly and taken together, these changes have deep and far-reaching implications for universities' involvement with the local regions. Some aspects of globalisation pull away from local involvement but for many HEIs their destinies and comfort are often significantly entwined with those of their region. With the new generation of virtual or distance universities it may be a different matter. Much of the large private sector of higher education now found in many countries is however likely to be well geared to regional needs, to secure strong enrolment and business success.

Within fifty years higher education has been transformed from a small number of selective institutions to a mass or universal tertiary-HE system. In large countries there are hundreds of university-level institutions as well as branch and virtual campuses and learning centres. Thanks to the Internet, degree-level study can be accessed remotely from other parts of the world. This is altering the meaning of the *higher* in HE, and raises questions about local engagement in what is now a major export industry. It may however merely modulate rather than weaken the argument for engagement. With explosion in scale came diversification of institutional type. There are now many competing and changing typologies of universities. For some institutional types working with and within local regions is natural and essential; for others the opposite may apply.

Such an increase in volume and variety has posed new questions about the meaning and purposes of HE and its financing. It has opened and deepened philosophical and ideological rifts within the higher education policy community about the purpose and quality of higher education, opposing relevance and utility against an older liberal idea of higher education and the university. The undergraduate curriculum in particular comes under public scrutiny as to its utility and relevance to the needs of the society and economy and for the employment of its graduates. Similar questions arise about the subject-matter and utility of the rising research budget and output. Who reads and uses what is published, with what effect?

Whole systems are assessed, audited and judged for their national cost and utility. A new armoury of measuring tools and audit devices tests for quality, efficiency and value for money. With massification in a neo-liberal yet paradoxically tighter audit era, the autonomy of individual universities comes under question in countries where it was traditionally high. Meanwhile in an opposite trend, universities which have been virtually departments of state staffed by civil servants, in much of continental Europe and other world regions, are being pushed towards 'freedom' in the sense of needing to become entrepreneurial and make money rather than rely upon state subsidy. A European Universities Association (EUA) report in 2009 argued that in most countries universities were under threat because of lack of autonomy that limited their ability to plan and to operate in a market environment (*THE*, 30 December 2009).

In the UK these trends, together with the requirement for far tighter internal management, suggested the expression 'three Ms', meaning massification, marketisation and managerialism (Tapper and Palfreyman 2000).[4] An evocative book title from the same country referred to the decline of 'donnish dominion' (Halsey 1992). Many titles use the term 'crisis' about the university (see for example Scott 1984, also Readings 1996). Halsey's title finds more recent echo in Ginsberg's *The Fall of the Faculty*. This attacks the increase in 20 years in US universities in numbers of administrative and their attendant staff by 85 per cent (66 per cent in the state and 135 per cent in the supposedly more efficient private sector) and 240 per cent, respectively while faculty increased by 50 per cent (Ginsberg 2011).

The 'three Ms' use a modern language offensive to many scholars and increasingly vigorously challenged, as management consultants operating with a business imperative argue that higher education must change tune to a neo-liberal paradigm or die: there 'will need to be a radical transformation in the way tertiary institutions do business', transforming management systems, faculty and curricula, according to Deloitte's *Making the Grade* (2011, p. 3) which drew on consultants in twelve countries. As to the threat of for-profit universities favoured by the government, the same consultants assert that faced with competition for market share, they and public universities will act just the same (*THE*, 4 August 2011, p. 17; 24 November 2011, p. 16). Many speakers at a year-end Conference on Universities under Attack indicated that the sector must reject neo-liberal business-speak to defend its values (*THE*, 1 December 2011, p. 8).

Diverse curriculum innovations are intended to make universities more competitively distinctive, attracting students and diversifying income. Higher education, once a meld of charitable and low-cost self-financed study to complete the coming-of-age and life preparation of a mainly class-bounded clientele, has become a big-ticket item in industrialised countries. This has moved it towards central direction and control. Controversially, curriculum and research agendas are aligned with what are thought to be national priorities. Many of the institutions originally created at least in part with local-region funds and purposes, like the US land grants institutions and the English industrial city civics, abandoned their local roots and allegiances, looking globally for identity and acclaim. The proportion of government funding for HEIs fell from country to country at different rates. This too has become almost universal. Alongside it, private sector provision, whether for-profit or not-for-profit, has become hugely significant in many world regions, from the USA to Western Europe and Latin America to East and South-East Asia.

These consequences of massive system expansion provide an immediate context for universities' involvement in regional development, Anglo-Saxon-led but fast-emulated in post-Soviet Eastern Europe, Latin America and parts of Asia. Especially with the GFC, governments attempt to reduce the direct role and expenditure of the state in health, education and welfare, with more privatisation and changed institutional and individual reward systems.[5]

For individual universities but also for ever more national governments, globalisation means competing globally for staff, students, performance and acclaim. A new driver has become the several competing world university ratings. Having highly placed universities in these rankings is a source of national pride and self-respect; not having any a cause for shame. This may distort resource allocation to the country's universities, disadvantaging newer and more local in favour of more established institutions. We return to this question in the concluding Chapter 14.

The pressures of global competition and status transform the behaviour of many prestigious universities. They threaten the sustainability of some and offer new opportunities for others. Skills-oriented tertiary colleges as well as universities may think and recruit internationally; seeking market niches where they can do well. In some countries they also influence national policy and behaviour for whole tertiary systems across all institutional types. Some of these rapid and dramatic changes incline institutions to look again, and to seek to engage or re-engage with their local region and its diverse 'stakeholders'.[6] Others pull them away from their localities, none more so than world ratings and league tables, now much debated and increasingly criticised.

Ratings and tables disproportionately favour English-language and pure research output. They are shifting the egalitarian character of the Netherlands as reflected in its higher education.[7] Globalisation has meant serious erosion of Dutch as a medium of teaching and scholarship in the universities of the Netherlands, characterised as an Anglo-Saxon takeover. A new type of lecturer 'performs in a global market of knowledge consumers'. Dutch history has become at best 'local history', as Dutch-written scholarly articles and books were abandoned in favour of 'the much higher-valued "international peer-reviewed articles" (ie. in English)'. In France there are radical plans to create a French 'Ivy League' or 'Sorbonne League' to create a world-class elite of universities by merging *grandes écoles* and smaller universities and increase French presence in the world's top-rated 200 (*THE*, 8 September 2011, p. 23; 6 October 2011, p. 10; 3 November 2011, pp. 20–21).

In 2011 the EUA criticised the impact of ranking on politicians who use them to favour elite research institutions, 'making funding decisions for entire higher education systems based on the ranking performance of a small number of universities'. Different global rankings cover only 1–3 per cent of the world's 17,000 universities, while creating problems for 'the thousands of normal universities' that simply do their job' (*THE*, 23 June 2011, p. 10). In the UK the allocation of funds in 2011 following the quality rating of research further concentrated resources to the research-intensive universities. Spokespersons for this sector criticise the EC-commissioned U-Multirank feasibility study and call for still more competitiveness, and exclusive concentration of research funds to no more than thirty universities (*THE*, 17 March 2011, pp. 6–7; 30; 24 March 2011, p. 20; 8 December 2011, p. 11). John Summers makes a savage indictment of the US academy's greatness and the US Department of Education's 'Race to the Top' reform programme. He refers to privileged universities' 'catastrophic failure' apropos the Great Crash (GFC), and the exposure of elite universities following the Wall Street implosion (*THE*, 24 March 2011, pp. 46–49).

'Glocal' is an optimistic neologism. Combining world stature with effective regional engagement is problematic. The Chief Executive of the UK Royal Society for the Arts argues that 'elite institutions should help create a more equal society', (Taylor 2010) with civic advisers to help local administrations and communities facing GFC difficulties; but gained the understanding, interviewing a Russell Group Vice-Chancellor, that as a 'global player' it was above local concerns.[8] The President of Universities UK argued the importance of R&D to knowledge-econo-mies 'in the international competitive environment', given the costly national dilemma about concentrating to remain in the world's top five R&D nations. The problem for regions is that intense national concentration deprives most of them of this asset which is seen as essential to them also (*THE*, 25 November 2010, p. 16; 24 March 2011, p. 27).

The role of higher education – two missions or three?

In terms of engagement one central question stands out: does the modern univer-sity have two main 'missions', teaching and research, or three? If the latter, should the additional one be referred to as the 'third mission'? It is necessary at this point to make a distinction between so-called 'third mission' and engagement in regional development. In Steve Garlick's word, 'they are not necessarily the same where the former can really mean either everything or alternatively very little at all'; there may be lacking 'any clear policy connection between higher education and processes of regional development' (Garlick 2010).

Histories of the university identify periods when teaching was the central and effectively the only recognised task. Sociologists also recognise such functions as social reproduction, and the conservation and transmission of knowledge. Other phases gave prominence to the university as a creator of knowledge in the form of research, and its dissemination as scholarship. Today it is universally accepted that universities have two central responsibilities: teaching, sometimes simply called education, and research. Each can be qualified, sub-divided and classified, as can the institutions that undertake them. We speak now of research-led and teaching-only institutions; and in terms of student admission, of selective and access institutions. These categories carry strong status connotations. The idea of 'teaching-only' may be hotly contested by such institutions, and by staff unions seeking the status and rewards of research for their members.

In some countries a further core responsibility has been recognised, often called simply service, or perhaps civic engagement. This refers to engaging with the communities and regions with which the institution connects, normally and mainly by virtue of proximity. This third leg or strand was recognised in the founding conditions of mid-nineteenth century US land grant universities; its fortunes have waxed and waned over the decades and in different countries. Terms such as development, engagement, extension, outreach and partnership are or have been used, as well as service. Many terms are disputed for their connota-tions – for example the unidirectional and perhaps patrician flavour of outreach and extension; too humble or servile an innuendo in service; the smack of social engineering in (community) development. Partnership is more neutral and favoured, except when the partner has doubtful morals or credentials, as with some unelected political regimes and the manufacturers of unacceptable products such as cluster-bombs or nowadays cigarettes. Engagement has been taken up widely as the more acceptable term, as relevant titles demonstrate (Gibbons 2001; Bjarnason and Coldstream 2003; OECD 2007; Watson 2007; Beere, Votruba and Wells 2011; Watson et al. 2011).

The term 'third mission' has obvious logic when set against the historical evolution of universities. Now widely used, it was a source of discomfort for some PURE project participants. Also identified as a 'third leg' of knowledge transfer, it appears to invite universities to choose which legs to stand on, rather than imply that all three legs are required for good balance. Making such a choice harmonises with the tendency to differentiate the mission of HEIs, from teaching-only to 'top-end' theoretical research-oriented. Government instrumentalities in many countries incline this way. Not only is the principle of diversity attractive, allowing specialisation within what has become the very wide mission spread for HE overall. By separating a large part of mass-HE teaching from higher-cost research-based institutions and using new ICT methods it promises to lower the total cost of HE education while protecting up-market research.

The problem is that separating research (knowledge generation) from engagement for knowledge dissemination outside the classroom removes the nexus between research and its application to the direct benefit of regions, businesses and communities. This 'third mission' cannot sensibly be hived off into other institutions if it is to draw on the research of the more wealthy universities. The tendency for engagement to be identified with and practised by the newer, more regionally oriented, often more vocational, institutions automatically too easily defines it as third in status, esteem and in importance. This conundrum could not be resolved at the big OECD review meeting in Valencia in 2007 (OECD 2008). It continues to hover around new cycles of OECD work and that of PURE.

There are several aspects of this. First, the separation of research (and indeed of more traditional undergraduate teaching and curriculum) from dissemination, engagement and service deprives society locally of direct connection with heartland HE endeavour. What is available, and by what institutional channels HE is engaged, becomes limited to lower-status and less-well-resourced institutions. Secondly, this form of thinking is unhelpful for the anyway difficult task of organising or re-organising the institution internally to favour engagement alongside teaching and research. Engagement requires and is about the mainstream teaching and research of the university. Separating it into a separate portfolio with different internal accountability weakens or negates its capacity. A related third dimension has to do with the contemporary thesis that learning and teaching should be more self-directed and oriented to real work, while research should be more applied. A number at least of more technologically grounded and oriented universities see such forms of engagement as at the heart of their research strategy, while curriculum becomes more workplace-based as well as grounded and work-related.

This leads to another consequence, no less serious. The more a tripartite sense of mission is employed, the less likely it is that 'Mode Two knowledge production' will be valued and practised. Research remains a separated mystique, not understandable or accessible to ordinary organisations and ordinary people. This may matter less for highly specialised laboratory science and technology. For many fields of scholarship, including health and medicine as well as the creative arts, humanities and social sciences, the loss can be grave. Economic development agencies may look first to science and technology. Yet balanced and sustainable development and well-being require a wider range of academic knowledge and skills than sci-tech alone can offer.

These issues underlie many of the regional studies of engagement, if not always recognised and formulated in this way. To anticipate what follows later: it may be time to abandon the tripartite notion of mission and accept that teaching or education, and research or knowledge creation, whatever terms are preferred, are still the central activities of all higher and even perhaps tertiary institutions. *Engagement, application and utilisation are not a third option, but an informing principle for all teaching and all research.* Studies of the impact of research, and of students' after-graduation experiences, already attempt to address this. A better model than third mission, stream or leg might be holistic impact analysis. This might be on the lines of the environmental impact studies required of planning proposals, and even stress tests such as post-GFC banking is coming to require. We return below to the consequences in terms of how HEIs equip themselves to engage, learn with and from, and help their regions; and also to policy implications for national and regional tertiary-HE *systems*.

The discussion in this chapter shows why *crisis in higher education* and *the demise of the public university* are so much in the air. The entrepreneurial university, the spread of privatisation, the 'three Ms' of massification, managerialism and marketisation, are feared to herald the demise of the public university dedicated to public good. Some meanwhile fear that new ICT threatens the survival of the on-campus university in an era of mass provision. Liberal ideas of a deeper and more general lifelong learning approach to higher education are affronted by demands for more vocational education and training before graduating into the changing labour market. What, it is asked, remains special and higher about higher education in a world of how-to training?

In an economic-fixated era other sociological functions of universities may be overlooked. Social differentiation and reproduction require a part-elite system set against a liberal equity and widening access agenda. The access agenda can be paraded in economic terms to win Treasury support – 'we cannot afford to waste the human resources needed to be competitive'. Even then it does not address questions about the quality of life and active civil – and civilised – society.

The engagement of higher education in regional development

The change from traditional to neo-liberal-modern traumatises some national cultural and higher education systems more than others. Anglo-Saxon nations led by the US moved faster and sooner in a market direction; a belated backlash in the UK ramped up dramatically during 2011. Much critical literature was generated about what is being lost. Nations and systems in other more recently emergent regions less steeped in liberal tradition and with more unhappy histories to leave behind them may find modern trends easier to accept. Continental Europe has a strong tradition of faculty-level academic autonomy and a weak institutional centre, married to overall state direction and control. It struggles with large cultural changes. New economic and social needs and crises are generated globally and experienced locally. As these intensify they pile demands and pressures on HEIs and systems. Institutions and systems find themselves culturally divided, pulled simultaneously in old and new directions. The call to relevance, partnership and regional engagement may feel more like interference than an opportunity.

Some countries have changed the name as well as function of the ministry or department administering higher education, some frequently. Universities and the rest of the post-secondary sector – community, further or technical colleges – are handled separately. The UK manifests this in extreme form. The language of skills has partly displaced that of education. In Australia technical and further education has become vocational education and training. Continuing binary separation dividing tertiary between further and higher, while refocusing both higher and further education into a skills agenda, mirrors a general cultural shift from the broadly social to the more narrowly and functional economic in a policy arena where post-GFC indebtedness and short-term 'return to growth' command the stage.

Countries exhorted to adopt lifelong learning across the lifespan struggle to integrate administration of the many levels and phases of education (learning and training), yet also to link post-school education to business and the economy. The seemingly insoluble problem of reconciling greater specialisation with cross-portfolio integration is exacerbated on the public policy side by the high number of departments having a stake in regional development outside the education portfolio. The predicament that universities in particular have discovered is not dissimilar. Many academic sub-specialisms proudly guard separation, distinctiveness and freedom to pursue their craft.

It is hard for a rector, president or vice-chancellor to lead a fully engaged university. As university leaders and managers they must cope with many often conflicting demands: multiple 'market' needs; rising accountability; new indicators including worldwide rankings; and limited or declining resources. They need courage as well as clear purpose to take and sustain direction. They need to persuade their own internal communities, for example that engaging strongly in regional development is a valued aspect of their work which carries tangible as well as feel-good rewards and benefits. In these circumstances, which were essentially similar despite national variation across most regions taking part in the PASCAL PURE project, the task of engaging for regional development with so many conflicting demands looks at least as tough for the HEI as for the region.

Research and teaching, the commonly identified main business of higher education, are both relevant to regional needs. Engagement means orienting them to external needs, local and regional as well as wider. Universities may be expected to contribute to place-based regional as well as global and national well-being: creating and applying new knowledge as well as teaching what is thought to be relevant and urgent. Regional innovation systems call for creative and innovative product design, process development and problem-solving. They require the application and use of new knowledge. The broader post-secondary college level of tertiary-higher education has if anything a still larger and more direct contribution to make to regional development in meeting the growing and changing human resource and skills needs of a changing regional economy.

In a difficult time of rapid change and shaken foundations, student numbers are still rising. However, public funds are static or declining in many countries, especially in the West, and competition for students can be fierce. The idea of engagement with a region and its future may seem one challenge too many. It may on the other hand be seen as a road to salvation, especially for regional universities. The membership of the Talloires network of engaged universities and of OECD's older IMHE reflects this, with more regional and teaching-oriented and fewer research-intensive universities. Universitas 21 (U21), a self-selected international club of elite institutions, has supported a modest project on engagement, but few U21 members have shown interest. Some leaders of highly prestigious universities (London University's UCL for example at the OECD IMHE Biennial Conference in 2010) have been scathing about the distorting damage caused by world rankings. But most leaders of prestigious universities and their governing bodies remain mesmerised by rankings. Here regional engagement has really no place.

In summary, the global and national policy environments of the early twenty-first century have generally become less hospitable to regional engagement, even while the need becomes more pressing. A large OECD conference policy review of its work in fourteen regions as recently as 2007 noted that the nineteenth century (as we would now say research-led) Humboldtian university was in effect 'a denial of place': 'the university had to have a mission that transcended its actual location' for its credibility and legitimacy. Modern trends in broadening regional policy place higher expectation on HEIs by cities and regions, supported by the expansion into mass HE mainly through new institutions (OECD 2007, pp. 33–36). On the one hand, universities with strong local links and identity see their future as increasingly interwoven with the futures of these regions. Mainly rural Nordic PURE regions are good examples. Elsewhere, especially in city regions, some universities took a keen interest in forms of local partnership; others with their eyes fixed elsewhere proved largely or entirely indifferent.

Are collaboration and 'cooperation' sustainable? Local tertiary systems

In concluding this consideration of higher education, let us return to tertiary education and the idea of regional higher-tertiary *systems*. So far we have considered the individual HEI and its region, its public administration and its diverse private and civil society partners, in isolation. We have noted a tendency for established, prestigious and research-rich universities to look and to recruit globally rather than locally for reputation and success, undermining any regional aspiration to tap into the richest intellectual resource in its locality.

Thinking in terms of *national systems* is gaining currency in many countries, if only in national HE policy and resource management, whether binary separation or tertiary integration is favoured. It may go in hand with distinguishing between different *types* of institutions, seeking to specialise and fund their different roles and contributions at different levels and in different ways. Some may be 'teaching-only', some 'research-led', some 'world class', scoring high in global league tables.

It might be possible to secure a strong and effective regional contribution to the knowledge society and economy by planning for and supporting regionally based higher or *tertiary systems*. Such an approach would value, pay for and respect different strengths and identities. It would aim to secure *for a region* that all elements of a balanced and engaged teaching and research mission are somehow fulfilled *for that region* by its tertiary-HE system. 'Somehow' would require a clear national policy steer, and a stake by each institution from the most grand to the most humble. This could ensure that the full 'mission spread' is somehow met collectively, whatever local division of labour is used between institutions. Institutions scoring high for research in world rankings could flourish in such a system. But they would share a duty to see that regional innovation and development needs are also somehow met by and within the regional consortium, sharing a penalty if they are not.

In terms of arrangements for engaging regionally, many elements are required, working fluently together. Examples can be found in the OECD and PURE studies of different elements in the local mix. It is not so easy to find the necessary full set of requirements. Different country histories, cultures and ways of working, inside and beyond HE, mean that different combinations, for example centrally controlled or dispersed, formal–informal and top-down or bottom-up, may work better in different places and at different times. Individual staff members may be brilliant in one or another context, but universities are not often familiar with or very good at engaging with other kinds of partners across the three sectors. They need what are sometimes called boundary-spanners, who can speak in the different tongues of public, private and community as well as academic discourse. Institutions also need clear and confident leadership, appropriate internal structures and reward systems congruent with such a mission (Beere, Votruba and Wells 2011); and powers of persuasion to see to it that the academic community believes in the value and validity of this direction of travel.

No less intransigent is universities' propensity to compete, often ruthlessly, with their HE neighbours while collaborating amiably and productively with more distant institutions. There are many examples of attempted local collaboration via consortia, but few of sustained success. More often the story is one of suspicious and well-guarded separatism, with joint activity only in closely bounded areas. In England, Greater Manchester has attempted sustained partnership several times, with limited success. The English 'Northern Alliance' may have more hope: the region is larger, and united by lobbying hostility to the privileges of London and the South-East. The same could apply to southern Italy where dissonance with the north might provide a bond; but collaboration at regional level in the Puglia region struggles with local histories and rivalries. A longer-lasting example featured in an OECD study in North-East England, which has a strong historical sense of identity. Here collaboration among the region's several universities has been sustained under one or another name (from HEIs into Universities for the

North-East) over several decades, though without the effective inclusion of the wider further education sector.

Inter-university collaboration working with city authorities in PURE proved a struggle in Glasgow, Helsinki and Puglia. Dublin's universities have recently formed a consortium, untimely in the sense of confronting severe post-GFC cutbacks as well as natural local rivalries. Most interesting among the PURE cases is Greater Melbourne, which took part concurrently in PURE and OECD studies. For a brief period Melbourne City Council's Office of Knowledge Capital (OKC) enjoyed the partnership of all the State of Victoria's universities. However, some dissonance about its priorities and about the boundaries of the region then arose (see Chapter 3), especially given that the Council's own boundaries were limited to little more than the Central Business District. In little more than two years, the OKC was pulled back by the City of Melbourne. After a series of conversations with key stakeholders, including the vice-chancellors or their nominees of each of the universities, it was resolved that its two major activities, a 'welcome desk' for international students and a focus on the knowledge needs of the City, would continue, but be supported by core Council officers. What looked to be a very promising and ambitious attempt at HE collaboration with State and City authorities for joint regional planning and development proved short-lived. This might serve as a metaphor for the difficulties confronting engagement which this book examines.

Part I, then, has provided an overview of the crossroads which the world now faces. It sets the context in particular within which the PASCAL project on universities and their regions has been undertaken. To what extent do our universities constitute part of the way forward from the contemporary crossroads? That is the story to which we now turn.

Notes

1 The difference between HEIs and universities is important. For example, in 2011 Canada was rated first among nations for the proportion of people holding a post-secondary qualification by the OECD, but eighth when only university degrees were considered (*THE*, 21 July 2011, pp. 20–21).

2 In the UK, where a new government introduced fundamental changes to the funding of English higher education, the sense of crisis in the identity of the public university was shown by the wider and deeper debate as well as more familiar lobbying that ensued in 2011.

3 We use this term for convenience. It refers to the (mainly) non-HE part of tertiary education, public and private, using different terms such as community college, college of further education, technical college, technical and further education, or simply vocational education and training. 'Mainly' because the boundaries between HE and sub-HE are themselves fuzzy, shifting and contested, as is the defining characteristic of HE – 'what makes higher education higher'?

4 And yet a 2011 report *University Autonomy in Europe* by the European University Association shows England to enjoy still the greatest freedom from state interference of twenty-six European countries (*THE*, 17 November 2011, p. 6).

5 This raises the important speculative question not addressed in this study of whether these emergent world regions will break away from the soft neo-imperialism of Western-derived and globally triumphant capitalisms and develop different models of both governance and management.

6 David Watson has commented reflectively on the initial meaning of this term, when backers put their stake on the table which was held in security for them and wagered against the outcome of a fight. The analogy to regional partnership is thought-provoking – which local parties really commit by means of a stake and who stands surety for them as action proceeds (Watson 2010, p. 402)?

7 See also 'Striving to be first among equals', *THE*, 15 December 2011, pp. 32–37. For a discussion of the UK debate on a new policy to fund research partly for its impact outside the world of scholarship, at times more passionate than balanced, see Duke 2012b.

8 On the other hand a colleague on a research post at the same University advises that she is working on a project designed to inform the preparation of future changes for 'sustainable food consumption' (Darmon 2012). This, if not exclusively local, certainly has potential local utility, illustrating what is surely well known: that much takes place in such an institution about which the chief executive may lack knowledge as well as interest.

PART II

PURE findings: leading policy issues

5

PASCAL and the PURE Project

The genesis and purpose of this volume

This chapter explains what led to a book drawing on the work of the PASCAL PURE project as a main source: action-research field-experience intended to enhance good practice, which involved regions participating on four continents. It sketches the PURE project and foreshadows the chapters that follow. These examine and draw lessons from different dimensions of the work of the project.

When the book was planned the intention was to write something accessible to the diffuse and diverse people implicated in engagement: in universities, in regional and national policy communities and also in the private sector and civil society, as well as consultants. By then the impact of the global financial crisis had become evident in terms of austerity and fiscal consolidation, with persisting weak economies in most developed countries increasingly also affecting other economies and societies globally. In the search for new sources of growth universities and regions have to look with greater care at specific local assets as these become more important, relatively speaking, in the overall theme of things. The issue of engagement between regions and universities had been on the agenda for decades rather than years; yet efforts to improve the limited interaction between universities and regions, to their mutual benefit, continued to disappoint.

During the subsequent year until the book was finalised in mid-2012, things became significantly worse, with the 'Euro crisis' all but dominating the international agenda. Growth however remains unchallenged, faith in the 'neo-liberal project' seemingly unshaken. In our conclusion we look beyond 'new sources of growth' to ask whether it is time after four such years to look elsewhere – for enhanced well-being on a different ethical base. Innovation is a universally proclaimed value and necessity for national and regional prosperity. Much effort goes into seeking new sources of growth, constantly redesigning education and training systems and creating regional innovation systems, with economic and cultural frameworks supportive of innovation. New partnerships might now better channel these energies into finding new solutions.

Regional development is taken to mean economic growth, but in the new world discussed in Part I, it might equally mean adapting for more healthy and sustainable development, managing the transition to a more viable and balanced regional socio-economic system, looking more deeply locally as well as globally for new kinds of resources. Steve Garlick expresses a different and increasingly wide-shared point of view about innovation and development, in referring to David Suzuki (the well-known environmental scientist and broadcaster), biocentrism and sustainability: 'history shows us that it is the educated people, and the institutions that generate these educated people ... that have created the mess with the unsustainable cities that we now have. The argument that there is no limit to human creativity is flawed ... Perhaps it is time the 'learning city' learned from others on this planet (some ... have been here for much longer) rather than from the very folk that got us into this mess!' (Garlick 2011).

The idea of the PURE project arose from OECD work reported and reviewed at a large international meeting in Valencia (OECD 2007); and immediately after that at PASCAL's own international conference at Pécs in Hungary. It was launched late in 2008, following international consultations first in Limerick in May, then in Glasgow in September. The project was to run through 2009–10, with the possibility of extension thereafter. The acronym *PURE* comes from the project title – PASCAL Universities and Regional Engagement. A period of two years was chosen, albeit reluctantly, in full recognition that the kind of partnership, development and progressive change visualised needed longer – more realistically a five-year rather than a two-year initial term. PASCAL's original intention was to work with at least some of the fourteen regions involved in the OECD cycle, and connect them with other regions new to such work. In the event only one of the original fourteen, Värmland in rural Sweden, signed up to PURE. The reasons why 'despite keen interest' others did not itself illuminates some of the difficulties that regions encounter in attempting such work. Some emanate from local changes, some from changes of national government and policy, some from changes of personnel, and some from contextual changes, notably the GFC.

6

Social inclusion and active citizenship

A deep-felt need

It is perhaps not surprising that social inclusion and active citizenship should have been identified as a key theme by several of the regions participating in the PURE project. Even without the impact of the GFC, the past two decades have been a period of considerable change as countries throughout the world, North and South, have come to terms with the implications of new technologies which have transformed the working environment as we have known it, and have led to what David Harvey (1989) has described as the 'collapse of time and space'.

The earlier chapters have described the significance of changes which have occurred in people's lives; what has been perhaps less clear so far has been the implicit social disjunction and cultural turmoil which have surrounded significant unemployment, overall restructuring of labour markets, new forms of relationships mediated by online social networking, and dislocated communities.

At the same time, universities have also been seen as part of the solution, through research, student action, policy support and community engagement initiatives to address social exclusion. Indeed, there has been no shortage of examples of university engagement with communities around initiatives to support social inclusion and cohesion, and active engagement with community decision-making. However, much of this has been undertaken by individuals acting out of their own agendas, whatever they might be. Less common have been programmes or initiatives which have been at the heart of university strategy. Where it has worked well, a strong emphasis on partnerships, rather than charitable activity, has strengthened marginal communities' capacities not only to improve their quality of life and standard of living, but also to engage more effectively as citizens. Programs to address local environmental issues or to offer children opportunities to connect with professional sporting programmes are examples of this kind of initiative.

Alongside this, and at least partly because of it, we have seen a massive increase in participation in higher education over the past forty years, initially in the United States and then England, Australia and Europe. An arena of education once the preserve of the religious or the wealthy has become much more open to a broader social cross-section of social classes. A university education has been seen not only as an alternative to prospective unemployment, but also as a means of enhancing one's position in the national and international labour market. Increasing professionalisation has occurred in some sectors, so that a range of occupations which had depended historically on vocational training, such as some fields of engineering, teaching and nursing, have been reframed as higher education studies.

This chapter explores the significance of the possible contribution by universities to social inclusion and active citizenship. It notes the influence of different policy agendas and acknowledges the insights of other studies. However, it draws particularly on the learning from the PURE studies across several regions to highlight the different kinds of contributions which can be made by universities. Several issues which undermine the potential effectiveness of these initiatives are noted.

Government policy for social inclusion

Governments establish diverse policy settings within which their higher education institutions must then operate. These policies typically focus in particular on access for students and on research. Countries such as Finland offer free access to universities even for international students. They also see higher education as a key part of their efforts to build stronger international partnerships. The Cameron government reshaped the financial costs in the English higher education landscape significantly after it was elected in 2010, in order to reduce its budget deficit. The Australian government has for some twenty years charged university students a significant fee, typically deferred and paid as part of the taxation system. This has funded the expansion of the system while keeping federal expenditure within budget limits. It also sees research and development as being integral to the nation's innovation system.

However, governments also have wider policy expectations of higher education. In the United Kingdom, there has been a specific allocation of funding to encourage universities to engage in 'knowledge and exchange' activities in which their expertise is shared with key stakeholders. Industry as well as community partners have benefited from this funding commitment. Nordic countries such as Sweden and Finland have implemented a statutory requirement for universities to undertake a third mission of service to community, encompassing lifelong learning. In late 2007, the Australian government appointed the Australian Social Inclusion Board. Its membership brought together a range of people who had spent much of their lives working to address the circumstances of marginality, poverty and disadvantage which different communities have faced. They adopted a set of priorities for social inclusion policy and programmes to address:

- supporting children at greatest risk of long-term disadvantage by providing health, education and family relationships services;
- helping jobless families with children and the vulnerable unemployed by helping the unemployed into sustainable employment and their children into a good start in life;
- focusing on the locations of greatest disadvantage by tailoring place-based approaches in partnership with the community;

- assisting in the employment of people with disability or mental illness by creating employment opportunities and building community support;
- addressing the incidence of homelessness by providing more housing and support services;
- closing the gap for Indigenous Australians with respect to life expectancy, child mortality, access to early childhood education, educational achievement and employment outcomes.

Clearly, these priorities have direct implications for the higher education sector, not only in Australia but in any nation where these issues arise. Indirectly, it is apparent that there is expertise within the sector that can contribute both through research and application of learning to supporting the implementation of relevant initiatives. Not only staff, but higher education students can be a wonderful resource for programmes where the engagement is supported appropriately.

The drive for increased participation

Irrespective of overall policy directions, it is accepted widely that higher education institutions play a direct role in mediating people's access to the labour market, and especially to the better remunerated and higher-status occupations. It has taken on another layer of significance as governments in many countries have struggled with the twin challenges of increasing the aggregated levels of skills achievement (required by the 'knowledge' economy) and with the growing social polarisation associated with industry restructuring (the decline of manufacturing and the rise of financial and business services, for example). There have been pressures and incentives for higher education to increase the number of students which they enrol, especially those from low socio-economic status backgrounds. This reflects the growth in significance of higher education as a means of sorting job applicants in the labour market, and of providing the more abstract learning needed in contemporary work processes.

In many parts of the world the disproportionately low representation of poor students has a distinct regional dimension, even in countries such as Finland where higher education is free. Tony Vinson's work on the spatial distribution of inequality in Australia demonstrates that:

> when social disadvantage becomes entrenched within a limited number of localities, the restorative potential of standard services in spheres like education and health can diminish. A disabling social climate can develop that is more than the sum of individual and household disadvantages and the prospect is increased of disadvantage being passed from one generation to the next. (Vinson 2007, p. ix).

Efforts to understand this pattern have considered the historic exclusion which social class has fostered as well as the more practical and immediate factors of cost and travel. Among education scholars and government officers, enormous effort and debate have been invested in exploring the ways in which educational processes at all levels have been affected by, and contributed to, unequal social experiences and outcomes. Flowing from this, a range of approaches has been developed in all parts of the world owards achieving more equitable outcomes. These responses have in some instances been very broadly based, emphasising the importance of early childhood learning. Others have been more specific, addressing issues arising in secondary school curriculum activity, vocational pathway articulation, scholarships, higher education recruitment and selection, and more diverse forms of delivery. The OECD has been a prolific source of reports exploring these issues and promoting greater sharing of perspectives across different international settings, not least through its sponsorship of PISA, the attempt to compare educational standards internationally (see OECD 2012, for example).

These were significant issues for Thames Gateway, in south-east London. There are twelve higher education and further education institutions in the region, and together they had identified a number of emphases necessary for higher education to become more accessible. These included:

- appropriate infrastructure in non-traditional buildings;
- placed at the centre of communities to encourage participation and support for local business;
- partnership (the multi-versity) between HEIs (and between HEIs and further education colleges), allowing each to develop their particular strengths in close collaboration with others;
- clear pathways through further education, and to HE; and
- meeting the needs of the economy through improved skilled labour.

In the Melbourne PURE project, the universities focused more specifically on questions of aspirations and access. The questions have been framed in terms of encouraging more young people to consider entering higher education, and on how to ensure that 'school to university' selection processes enable a more socially representative range of matriculates to gain university places while maintaining principles of merit. These initiatives appear to have had a strong regional dimension, as institutions have begun to explore various forms of cooperation with schools in specific regions to raise aspirations among school students. The University of Melbourne has worked with Melbourne City Council to offer students the opportunity to work as volunteer learning mentors, while La Trobe University has focused on refugee communities. While this work is obviously important, initiatives and policies also need to focus on ensuring that young people do accept appropriate opportunities to enter higher education.

Buskerud University College in Norway offered a more holistic approach, where it was involved in the development of a Science Centre which would link 'cutting edge' health science care and R&D and introduce children in primary and secondary schools to health issues. While the approach would deliver immediate health benefits, part of the motivation for the University College was to attract well-prepared students into study.

A different structure and process emerged in Northern Illinois, where the PURE project supported stronger collaboration among Northern Illinois University (NIU) and the community colleges in the surrounding region. Here, the community colleges and NIU have been developing new pathways for students, with the pilot of an Associate degree in the colleges that can articulate into a Bachelor degree offered by the University. NIU also offers an outreach program directed at people with Latino backgrounds.

These kinds of initiatives have clearly been intended to enhance social inclusion. Their focus has several dimensions:

- enlarging students' frames of reference so that attendance at a higher education institution becomes a feasible option;
- enhancing their skill and capability to perform successfully in higher education;
- providing alternative forms of entry which enable students from poor backgrounds with appropriate opportunities to have their capability recognised; and
- bringing higher education closer to students' homes so that the costs and regional inaccessibility of higher education are lessened, at least in the first year or so.

Their insights are shared across a number of the countries involved in PURE. Further education in the UK, TAFE in Australia and university colleges in Nordic countries play an important intermediary role that is largely devalued (a subsequent book in this series will address this issue).

Do these initiatives work? In many instances, it is too soon to tell. However, there is no doubt that over the past two decades there has been massive expansion in higher education participation across all continents. The challenge is to achieve a socio-economic spread of student enrolments which matches the proportionality of the wider population.

In other regions, such as Värmland, Jämtland and Kent, similar views about the importance of the accessibility of higher education were articulated in the PURE reports where the Consultative Development Groups made strong calls for clearer human capital planning. Regional authorities can make an important contribution to longer-term regional development through identifying from early childhood onwards the learning needs of people in the region, including higher education, and exploring how appropriate provision can be made.

Emerging pedagogy and delivery

Beyond access, however, the focus on participation needs to be complemented by more innovative thinking and action around where higher education is delivered, and the pedagogy which is used. Online delivery is of increasing importance, and in Northern Illinois the PURE project identified the importance of network learning which offers various means of gaining access to information. A regionally oriented outlook, such as that which NIU and the community colleges were exploring, offered an opportunity to develop a shared platform for network learning which would facilitate greater transparency and coordination.

At the same time, the 'civilising benefits' of the experience of university life involve much more than the delivery of the courses. Notwithstanding the impact of part-time work and an increasingly electronic mode of relationship, the significance of opportunities for developing extra-curricular interests and relationships cannot be neglected. This suggests that place will continue to be an important consideration in how higher education opportunities will be extended to new participants.

With respect to pedagogy, the concept of partnership is integral. 'Service learning' has long been an important part of the higher education scene in the United States, where formal components of service can be undertaken and receive credit towards the completion of the program. Similarly, a growing number of Australian universities are committing students to a distinct component of work-based learning as a formal credit-bearing part of their degrees. While not a new idea, especially in North America, the recent interest in Australia in developing much more systematic arrangements which link learning in university classes with real community and workplace settings has much to suggest with respect to future innovation in university pedagogy.

As part of the Thames Gateway focus on partnership and community connectedness, four innovative campus developments had occurred. In Medway, there were three higher education institutions sharing a campus. Each had its own building but with some shared facilities including the library and a single students' union. They had also signed non-competition agreements with each other. Other interesting examples of new forms of higher education provision had been established at Grays, Southend and Whitechapel.

From Melbourne PURE, Hume City Council developed the idea of a 'multiversity' (drawing on experience in Medway in the Thames Gateway) as a means of enticing universities based in other parts of Melbourne to offer higher education programmes in the Council's own, rather well-designed and -equipped facilities. This municipality has residents of among the lowest socio-economic status in Australia, with significant concentrations of people speaking a language other than English. Rather than a university taking on the challenge of establishing its own facilities and meeting the threshold for viability from its own resources, the proposal was that Melbourne universities be invited to offer programmes in a complementary manner, using existing and proposed learning facilities. The actual mix of programmes would reflect analysis of demographic data, emerging information about industry and occupational trends, and local citizen demand. Victoria and Deakin Universities, as well as the local further education institution, have responded to this invitation and are beginning to implement this initiative.

The other important diversification relates to lifelong learning. As its importance is recognised, there is increasing effort to acknowledge that learning occurs in many different settings, and that this knowledge should be accredited. The Northern Illinois PURE team identified this as an important opportunity for various regional stakeholders to become better connected, with a focus on longer-term regional development.

Higher education, community engagement and active citizenship

While many university administrations (and governments) are preoccupied with the questions of research and tertiary participation, universities play a much broader role in promoting social justice and active participation. This is apparent in the work of a growing number of international networks, including GUNI (Global University Network for Innovation) and GACER (Global Alliance on Community-Engaged Research). There are large networks such as Talloires and national associations such as the Australian Universities Community Engagement Association (AUCEA). All of these promote actively the greater involvement of universities with their communities. In the case of the predominantly US-based Talloires, the emphasis on 'service learning' clearly reflects the importance of social inclusion.

In short, the PURE project has demonstrated an ordinary array of regional and community engagement activities, many of which are aimed in one way or another at contributing to social justice, increasing social cohesion and strengthening democracy. These initiatives range from a professor of social work becoming a member of the governing board of a welfare organisation, to encouraging students to contribute to community projects as a means of learning by doing (service learning or work-integrated learning), through undertaking student projects of one kind or another, staff consultancy, collaborative research or formal partnerships.

However, the vast majority of engagement activity is undertaken or sponsored by individuals, even in their own time and on top of their campus commitments. Research-related activity might have more formal recognition, especially if some kind of funding contract is involved. Service learning and work-integrated learning might be endorsed more formally as part of a university's offer to students or the community, but a clear strategic commitment by a university to engagement for socially inclusive and just purposes is rare. Such examples do exist, however. Christchurch University in Kent, which has strong community partnerships, undertakes more active planning, has a close relationship with the Kent public sector and is involved with community regeneration and lifelong learning projects.

Not surprisingly, perhaps, the National University of Lesotho in Africa has a number of projects which are multidisciplinary and involve direct engagement with communities at 'grassroots' level. One example described in the PURE project was efforts to improve agricultural skills, enhance understanding of HIV/AIDS and sanitation issues, and advance community and economic development. Another focused on understanding the importance of 'African values', and how the spirit of traditional values could be sustained while exploring opportunities for innovation and adaptation.

Another is the Victoria University of Technology, which is based in the industrially focused western region of Melbourne. Its role and commitment as a large institution in the west have seen it partner with another iconic western suburbs organisation, the Western Bulldogs Football Club. The subject of a 'good practice' case study for the Melbourne PURE project, these two institutions have formed a partnership to lead a range of education and training initiatives which are intended to promote greater inclusiveness, improved health and more effective pathways for the multiculturally diverse population of the west.

There are many examples, however, where a particular university department or unit has stepped into a community partnership, or where there has been a willingness by a university to contribute to a major project. University representatives in Puglia have supported the regeneration of an abandoned factory in an urban area into a major cultural centre; this could enable the Lecce region to become a major centre for cultural industries. In Helsinki, the Active Life Village was sponsored by the City of Espoo and the Laurea University of Applied Sciences, with a range of service and technology companies as partners. It supports new businesses, drawing on technological innovation to provide new opportunities in the welfare sector. Both Laurea University and Aalto University of Technology have been involved, with significant implications for student engagement. Glasgow universities have community outreach programmes which encompass arts, culture, lifelong learning and work with poor communities.

A 'mid-range' example of a strategic approach involving a particular university faculty came from Buskerud University College in Norway, which has participated in the development of a county-wide structure for innovation in health care. The proposal for a Science Centre with a sector cluster approach encompasses a focus on R&D, development of new businesses, education in schools (mentioned earlier in connection with preparation for future student attraction), professional development and encouraging 'consumer-oriented innovation'. The scale of this project depended on close cooperation among several key, major stakeholders, not least the University College. Several disciplines from the College would have integral roles to play.

Opportunities and challenges

Taken together, the case studies indicate that social inclusion is a significant regional priority to which higher education can contribute. In many ways, this is a good story. Universities can and do make a difference in their regions through the direct and indirect contribution that they make to social objectives, whether inclusion or greater social cohesion and justice.

However, the uneven attention to social inclusion initiatives, reflected in university decisions about priorities in research appointments and funding, in areas of student recruitment, in the speed with which universities respond to emerging social circumstances, has led to frustration in many communities with the ways in which universities take their places as key regional stakeholders and as drivers of social inclusion and cohesion. To some degree, the role that is played reflects national context, and specifically government policy, in framing the ways in which universities have thought historically about their role and how best they might contribute to social inclusion.

England and Australia represent two distinct examples, as 'third stream' funding has been a clear component of the allocations of the HEFCE throughout the past decade. In Australia, on the other hand, the Bradley Review (2008) of higher education in Australia chose not to recommend specific funding for this purpose, despite having given it some consideration. Indeed, the model of competition for students that was recommended has hindered the capacity of universities to work together in a strategic and coordinated way on social inclusion issues.

Another source of incoherent practice is fragmentation within universities, even where there is an academic infrastructure to support social policy work or student service/field placement. Hence, several research units or perhaps school groups might work in parallel with community or government organisations, rather than collaboratively. This pattern arises even more commonly where there are multiple universities within a region.

The issue is two-fold: achieving collaboration among universities; but even more so, enabling regional authorities to see universities as constructive allies in addressing social injustice. Furthermore, regional authorities have demonstrated variable capacity to engage universities in social justice initiatives. As often as not, social researchers are regarded as critics of policy, sometimes welcomed but more typically to be contained.

Some of the specific learnings from the case studies have included:

- engagement with the broader community, and not just students, helps make universities accessible and safe to all of the community, in addition to the specific benefits for students and policy and program development;
- access to the university for those in outer metropolitan or remote areas can be explored through new models (such as the multiversity approach);
- joint partnerships with community organisations enable better utilisation of resources for cross-fertilisation of ideas, knowledge and resources;
- benefit is derived from core partners of programmes understanding each other better, which assists greater participation and sharing of ideas and actions;
- communication pathways need to remain open throughout the university structure to enable buy-in and consistency across faculties, thus avoiding duplication and missed opportunities to leverage participation; and
- a central 'driver' within the HEI can help link interactions and build cross-disciplinary support, to prevent duplication or missed opportunities.

With the exception of Northern Illinois and Thames Gateway, it has been rare to find examples of inter-institutional collaboration on initiatives to enhance social inclusion. While academic staff are engaged regularly in projects involving colleagues from other institutions, some with a regional focus, it is rare for such initiatives to occur at an institutional level. At the very least, the underlying framework of competition seems to determine that it is easier to collaborate formally with bodies in other states or even internationally than with others from the same region.

Government policy settings can shape institutional behaviour in direct ways, especially where funding hinges on institutional responsiveness. The very nature of academic work, both student learning and staff research, can separate those at the computer screen of university life from community stakeholders. This can result from differing perceptions of knowledge, contrasting languages, timelines and interests. Unless government policy specifically encourages a focus on social inclusion as a direct (and funded) objective (such as had occurred with the question of access in Australia), higher education efforts are likely to be subordinated to those objectives which do have deliberate funding implications.

Nevertheless, the importance which is placed on social inclusion by regional and national governments should not be underestimated. These authorities, almost universally it would seem, regard social inclusion as a key goal. Furthermore, their expectation is that their higher education institutions will be involved integrally in their efforts to achieve such goals. At the very least, this involves provision of pathways for young people from all backgrounds within the region to gain skills, a rounded appreciation of citizenship, and the capacity to contribute to the economic and social life of the region.

Furthermore, there is widespread expectation that HEIs can contribute directly to initiatives which help to understand the circumstances of privilege, inequality and disadvantage within a region, and to advise on the levers for change. Research, service learning and community initiatives can all mitigate the local circumstances of social exclusion.

Conclusion

While there are wonderful examples of higher education contributions to greater social inclusion, cohesion and social justice, the overall picture is that they tend to be fragmented, lacking overall strategic vision, and dependent on the particular efforts of individuals and of units within universities, rather than part of a comprehensive institutional approach. Until these policy issues of strategy and partnership can be addressed, and appropriate internal planning and reward arrangements introduced, the universities' capacity to contribute to social inclusion initiatives within their regions will be deeply undermined.

7

The new ecological imperative
– green skills and jobs

The second *GreenMetric Ranking* of World Universities was announced in December 2011 by Universitas Indonesia with the described objective of allowing 'universities in both the developed and developing world to compare their efforts towards campus sustainability and environment friendly university management'.[1] The university ranked first was the University of Nottingham in England. There must be something particularly green about the city of Nottingham since Nottingham Trent University, for the second time in three years, topped the UK's *People and Plant Green League*,[2] a ranking produced in collaboration with *The Guardian* newspaper.

The *GreenMetric Ranking* uses five metrics with variable weighting (shown in parenthesis): green statistics (24 per cent), energy and climate change (28 per cent), waste management (15 per cent), water usage (15 per cent) and transportation (18 per cent). It is based on 178 university responses across 42 countries.

The *People and Planet Green League* ranks 142 UK universities, awarding them a 'degree classification' of First, 2:1, 2:2, Third, or Fail, against 13 weighted criteria: publicly available environmental policy, environmental management staff, environmental auditing systems, ethical investment policy, carbon management ethical procurement and fairtrade, sustainable food, staff and student engagement, curriculum, energy resources, waste and recycling, carbon reduction and water reduction.[3] It combines data obtained directly from universities through the UK Freedom of Information Act with Estates Management Statistics data obtained from the UK's Higher Education Statistics Agency.

Around the world there are many other league tables and measurement mechanisms. The Association for the Advancement of Sustainability in Higher Education in the US offers a Sustainability Tracking, Assessment and Rating System[4] for the self-reporting of sustainability performance, and the College Sustainability Report Card[5] provides reports for over 300 HEIs in the US and Canada.

As with all metric-based ranking systems, there are questions about the validity of league tables that are based to a greater or lesser extent on self-reporting by universities (directly or indirectly via an agency) and on the justification for the choice of particular indicators and weighting given to these. That will not be our focus, but two examples are illustrative of the balance in the indicators used. In the UK's *People and Planet Green League*, just three points out of a possible seventy are given to staff and student engagement and two points to curriculum. In the North American College Sustainability Report Card there are fifty-two indicators, but these are focused on campus operations and endowment policies with little or no focus on external engagement.

Attention within the sets of metrics that have been highlighted, and many others, focuses largely on the behaviours of universities as they impact on their internal functions rather than on external matters, although clearly internal policies and practices have external impacts. This is evident, for example, in choices of supply of energy. In the US, the Environmental Protection Agency publishes a Top 20 College and University list as part of its Green Power Partnership. This is a measure of green power purchases and part of an aim to 'reduce the environmental impacts of electricity use and support the development of new renewable generation capacity'.[6] Of the Top 20, some universities are producing more than 100 per cent of their needed electrical energy and selling on the excess.

In our work within the PURE project many of the criteria found in green league tables are found in the analytical framework that we use. This is evident from the elements found within section 7 of the benchmarking tool that we utilised, which lists the following benchmarks:

- universities leading societal responses to the challenges of sustainabilit;
- sustainability at the heart of university governance;
- universities managing research to focus on core societal challenges;
- universities creating new models for sustainable societies;
- promoting sustainability through the curriculum;
- promoting education for sustainable development;
- performance against environmental management systems.

As with similar instruments such as that used for benchmarking community engagement by the AUCEA (Langworthy 2009), the purpose is not to create league tables but to allow universities to reflect on their own practice, making comparisons with practices elsewhere in order to develop strategies to improve their own.

As will be evident, the focus is not simply on 'greening the campus' which, as Tilbury (2012, p. 19) within a comprehensive publication of the GUNI argues, has been the preoccupation of universities. This is of course a laudable ambition, which few universities ignore, but sustainability is about much more, and starts with leadership and challenging existing ways of doing things both within and beyond academia.

Greening is of course an issue for cities and regions as well as universities, as is evident in the work of the OECD's Green Cities programme.[7] This 'seeks to assess how urban green growth and sustainability policies can contribute to improve the economic performance and environmental quality of metropolitan areas and thus enhance the contribution of urban areas to national growth, quality of life and competitiveness';[8] several case studies have been published recently (OECD 2011a). There are also a number of current international events focused on these issues, including the OECD LEED (Local Economic and Employment

Development) Programme – CEDEFOP (European Centre for the Development of Vocational Training) conference in Paris on *Skills for a Low Carbon Economy*[9] in February 2012. The potential for cities to be leaders in green growth is also the subject of the Fourth Meeting of the OECD Roundtable of Mayors and Ministers hosted by the City of Chicago in March 2012. The LEED programme at the OECD is also working on a number of other related projects at a local and regional level, including work on climate change, employment and local development (involving Extremadura, London, Podlaskie/Pomorskie and Sydney in the study); indicators of local transition to a green economy; and improving the effectiveness of green local development initiatives, all within the framework of the OECD's Green Growth Strategy (OECD 2011b).

Societal leaders

The role of universities in sustainable development was cited in Chapter 36 (Promoting Education, Public Awareness and Training) of Agenda 21, the Action Plan of the 1992 United Nations Conference on Environment and Development. Furthermore, the Rio + 20 United Nations conference on sustainable develop-ment[10] seeks to secure renewed political commitment to perhaps the most pressing challenge that the world faces: its own survival. The ever-increasing use of energy and the stresses to our ecosystem are accepted widely as bringing the earth to the point of catastrophe (Matthews, Garlick and Smith 2009; Rockström *et al.* 2009; Brown 2011). It would be strange if universities did not play a significant role in creating a greater awareness of the political urgency that concerns sustain-able development. The university is perhaps best equipped in its locality to place the possible solutions in their wider context and in so doing persuade local and regional partners of the need to begin implementing a transition to a sustainable society. To paraphrase Boyer (1996), there can hardly be a more significant civic purpose for universities. As the G8 University Summit of 2008 states in the Joint Affirmation and Action 3 of its Sapporo Sustainability Declaration, 'the role played by universities is changing and becoming increasingly critical, since universities, being neutral and objective, are best situated to inform political and social change toward a sustainable society'.[11] It also implies that there is a role for universities to be models of sustainable practices. A number of universities describe themselves as 'green' and set themselves apart in all aspects of their behaviour. This is evident in the green league tables that were introduced at the begining of this chapter, though the translation of internal behaviours to create change in external commu-nities through replication is not self-evident in most rankings.

In terms of benchmarks, the following were identified as manifestations of practice in this area. The university would have a clear institutional statement of the importance of sustainable development as part of its wider societal contri-butions. The university would use its institutional leverage to provoke political responses to the urgency of the challenge, firmly embedding that activity within high-quality scientific work. The university would educate the next generation of leaders with an understanding of the imperative of an effective societal response to emerging problems. The university would work with other regional partners in demanding responses to the challenges of sustainable development, and helping to realise those responses within their regional context.

While a number of universities in the PURE study had strong internal procedures, as seen below, it was rarer to find examples of how they take a lead in advocacy in this domain. A limited number of examples of how universities provide models and offer a lead to their communities emerged in the PURE studies. These include activities such as hosting Fair Trade days, community garden development and encouraging the community onto the campus along green trails to develop awareness of sustainability issues.

Governance

Commitments to sustainability as a core value which is operationalised in goverance structures are perhaps rarer than the statements by university presidents and laudable statements in missions. From a starting number of 20 in 1990, as of May 2012 440 signatory institutions had signed The Talloires Declaration,[12] a ten point action plan of university leaders for a sustainable future. This declaration is comprehensive and importantly makes a commitment in Action 5 to practise institutional ecology and in Action 6 to involve all stakeholders in government, foundations, industry, community and NGOs in finding solutions to environmental problems. Other declarations have followed, including, as reported by Roberts and Roberts (2007, p. 318), the *Halifax Action Plan for Universities: 'Creating a Common Future'* (1991), the *Swansea Declaration of the Association of Commonwealth Universities* (1993), the *Copernicus University Charter for Sustainable Development of the Conference of European Rectors* (1993) and the *Kyoto Declaration of the International Association of Universities* (1993). Additionally there have been the *Lüneburg Declaration on Higher Education for Sustainable Development* of 2001 and the *Ubuntu Declaration on Education and Science and Technology for Sustainable Development* of 2002 with a specific North–South orientation. The list could be continued since, according to Grindsted (2011, p. 29) a total of thirty-one Sustainability in Higher Education declarations have emerged, of which fifteen have been made by the university sector and sixteen by inter-governmental institutions, mainly UNESCO.

It is however perhaps necessary to go one step further beyond declarations, and not only to give commitments but also to create mechanisms by which internal and external communities can hold universities to account. As in many endeavours the signing of a declaration does not mean implementation of its principles. This has been shown in the field of sustainability by studies such as those of Clugston and Calder (1999) and Bekessy, Samson and Clarkson (2007).

Our benchmark in this area therefore suggests that a university with sustainable development central to its purposes will:

- have a firm commitment to sustainability in the corporate plan;
- have a sustainable development group with members from across services

and academic and external relations departments;

- communicate its activities to stakeholders, including employees, students, local residents, suppliers and local authorities;
- have a performance monitoring system which goes beyond service departments (e.g. transport, procurement);
- have modules which all students can take which develop civic, social and professional/ vocational aspects of sustainable development;
- encourage all its clubs, societies and unions to adopt an active approach to sustainable development.

A number of the universities that were included in the PURE studies had elements of these types of structure, but by no means all institutions and even more rarely in all areas of activity. Notable among universities within the study was the University of Plymouth in Devon, UK, where sustainability is clearly being embedded within the university in what was described as a holistic model of change, a '4C model' of Campus, Curriculum, Community and Culture. Thus sustainability was being located in internal behaviours and in commitments through quality labels such as ISO14001 (although we argue later that this has some limitations). Externally the University of Plymouth ranks highly in the UK *People and Planet Green League*, having been number 1 in 2010. The challenge is to link sustainability and enterprise effectively, and to match internal developments with external engagement.

One outcome of the work in some regions was to increase awareness of the importance of formal structures. Benchmarking had a marked effect especially on the University of Bari in Puglia. Here a growing network of professors with environmental interests found that they were doing rather poorly. They welcomed a baseline against which to measure progress. In this large and highly decentralised university typical of the Italian system, as a result of the PURE work, the Rector set up a cross-faculty committee on environment and sustainability to continue this monitoring.

Managing research

The role of research towards achieving sustainability was part of the Talloires Declaration in 1990 and is an obvious contribution for the sector. In practice this might involve a number of disciplines making a contribution to mitigating the impact of current and future developments in cities and regions on the environment through offering research and consultancy services to industry, infrastructure projects and the like to reduce ecological footprint. These could involve specific departments making contributions, but many of today's problems require an offer that transcends disciplinary boundaries and an engagement with external communities that allows for collaborative inquiry with beneficiaries and collaboration with knowledge creators beyond universities' walls. This notion of course incorporates ideas of Mode Two knowledge production (Gibbons *et al.* 2004) focusing on specific problems in a multidisciplinary fashion, and doing so with regard to implications for society (Novotny, Scott and Gibbons 2001) and co-construction of knowledge with communities.

The elements of the benchmarks within this area are that universities have reconfigured their research processes to support high-quality and fundamental research strongly oriented towards addressing the challenges of sustainable development. Further they have developed innovative techniques for engaging with local and regional partners to understand the societal context of these problems. Finally they have a shared programme of multidisciplinary co-inquiry drawing across university and external expertises, supporting high-quality research and effective exploitation of that knowledge.

Developing university research expertise in renewable energy, climate change, carbon reduction and technologies that utilise resources more efficiently was evident *inter alia* in PURE in the studies of both Devon and Cornwall and Melbourne. An example is PRIMARE, the Marine Institute, a joint University of Exeter and Plymouth initiative in innovative research to develop marine renewable energy, most notably through work on wave power at Hayle in Cornwall, funded by the South-West RDA. It also offers environmental monitoring and impact services, expertise on marine electrical systems, resource characterisation, marine operations, and safe and economic operations, as well as giving attention to socio-economic issues. In the same region, the University of Exeter's research expertise in environmentally sustainable building was cited by the RDA, and the University was recognised by Devon County Council during the PURE study for its skills for renewable energy, agriculture and climate change, and in zero carbon development.

Sustainable societies

The challenge of the shift to long-term sustainability is as much a question of a social transition as one of technical innovation. The way that university research encourages and creates opportunities for new behavioural forms and norms within society will determine the impacts of that scientific activity as much as its intrinsic worth. The way in which universities are able to work with local and regional communities to explore the socio-technical diffusion of new technologies and innovations is a vital contribution to building a sustainable society. Such micro-communities can act as laboratories for the shaping of research to maximise its subsequent diffusion, and hence maximise universities' contributions to promoting regional sustainability.

Universities invest as much effort and strategy priority in understanding the societal diffusion of transition technologies as in the creation of those technologies themselves. Universities develop exemplar communities as demonstrators for new technologies, gaining wider recognition (e.g. awards) and understanding of transition pathways towards sustainable development and embedding those in regulations, standards and norms. The university co-creates knowledge and helps to diffuse new technologies, techniques and behaviours sensitive and appropriate to the wider regional situation. Universities work with regional partners to help them understand and incentivise through innovation, entrepreneurship, environmental, and industrial and infrastructure policies, a transition to a sustainable economy. A particular societal role in assisting in mitigating the impact of development on the environment was evident in the PURE region of the county of Kent in the UK.

Curriculum

It has been recognised for some considerable time by those involved in environmental education that sustainability is not an added extra. Orr (1992) was one of the first to argue that for the challenges of sustainable development to be addressed ecological literacy must be embedded across the curriculum and into all university operations. This is perhaps the most obvious way in which a university can adopt an agenda of sustainability and has been a major facet of environmental education initiatives in higher education. A range of initiatives can be put into place, including an offer of discrete modules concerned with sustainable development available to all students and the integration of the concept into discipline-specific content. The university could also strengthen regional capacity in the field by developing placement opportunities with external agencies.

This links to offering core university teaching and learning that addresses sustainability issues in flexible forms to a variety of communities. In this context issues that arise relate to the generic skills associated with a commitment to sustainable practices; the new intellectual and technical skills which might be required for green occupations and industries; and the extent to which they might be internationalised?

The benchmarks utilised for a university providing sustainability education to its students were to:

- ensure students have opportunities to receive some academic and practical sustainability education;
- link sustainability education to research activities within departments/faculties;
- institute continuous improvement in existing modules to identify where there is potential to introduce sustainability;
- allow students to take responsibility in practical course components to develop ideas of sustainability, for example placements and marketing course;
- work with professional and vocational bodies to ensure that students are aware of the sustainability requirements of their future employers ; and
- ensure departments' own practices do not provide conflicting signals to students in areas such as transport, waste management and procurement.

Offering core university teaching and learning that addresses sustainability issues is evident within many PURE regions. For example in Flanders there were many examples of courses ranging from post-initial BA and MA programmes for the chemical industry to promote more environmentally sustainable production methods, through the advanced technical competences of process operators, and the maintenance of heavy machinery, to laser welding technologies.

Perhaps the most important aspect, however, is tackling the twin imperatives of combating economic decline and creating new jobs. New employment opportunities are associated with green technology transfer and commercialisation. These are associated with developing university research expertise in renewable energy, climate change and carbon reduction and capture, technologies that utilise resources more efficiently and using sustainable practices to anchor regeneration opportunities, as was evident in the PURE study in Kent. Here, associated with the regeneration of the Thames Gateway, the Universities of Kent and Greenwich have participated in the development of the Institute for Sustainability, which seeks to promote sustainable construction and development. This is also linked to one of the eight themes of *Vision for Kent* (the county-wide strategy for the social, economic and environmental well-being of Kent's communities), namely 'Environmental Excellence', where the countryside, coast, natural resources, wildlife and heritage are protected and enhanced for their own sake and for the enjoyment of current and future generations, and are valued as the key to a high quality of life in both urban and rural areas.

There is still little clarity about what constitutes the distinctiveness of a 'green job' (UNCSD 2011, p. 1). One key report from CEDEFOP and the International Labour Organisation (ILO) (CEDEFOP and ILO 2010) argues that all jobs have the potential to be greener and that perhaps all future jobs will be green. Other observers have argued against the very notion of a green jobs sector, noting that it is a malleable concept that encompasses such vastly different jobs as to have little practical utility. Pinderhughes (2006), in a California study, provides twenty-two categories of jobs, and includes green building, organic agriculture, installation of solar panels, and building of wind turbines and electric cars. The analysis also includes other less self-evident jobs, like bicycle shop workers, furniture makers using sustainable sourced products and petrol station attendants who pump biofuels. The UNCSD in its analysis prefers to use the net employment impacts economy-wide of policies and measures taken to 'green' the economy rather than focusing exclusively on 'green jobs' per se.

A United Nations Environment Programme/ILO/International Organisation of Employers/International Trade Union Confederence (UNEP/ILO/IOE/ITUC) (2008) report has argued that the number of green jobs across the world could increase from 2.3 million to 20 million during the period 2006 to 2030. It uses the notion that 'not all green jobs are equally green' and the term 'shades of green' to indicate that some policies will yield greater environmental benefits than others (*ibid.*, p. 299).

Whatever their distinctiveness, many of these jobs rely on skills gained in higher education. The UNEP/ILO report argues that skills profiles will change, and that 'there is clear evidence that much of the green employment of the future will be high skilled' (*ibid.*, p. 308). The report also suggests, quoting from a 2007 survey of Germany's renewables industry that 'companies in this field are already suffering from a shortage of qualified employees, and especially those needed in knowledge-intensive positions. There is thus a need to put appropriate education and training arrangements in place' (*ibid.*, pp. 308–309). The report continues that 'for universities this may mean at the cutting edge of technology development for wind turbine or solar PV design, for instance, that specialisation has progressed to the point where universities need to consider offering entirely new study fields and majors' (*ibid.*, p. 308). In the studies of CEDEFOP (2010) and ILO (Srietska-Ilina *et al.* 2011), there are a number of examples of the university role and the role of the vocational sector in skills development for the green economy among some twenty-one country studies.[13]

One example of the impetus in the direction of green jobs is in the USA where governors in both California and Massachusetts have signed bills funding the creation of a green workforce, while think-tanks are projecting millions of new green jobs. Part of President Obama's $787 billion stimulus package included roughly $90 billion in green spending on energy and infrastructure, for boosting energy efficiency in federal buildings, increasing investment in mass transit and creating a smarter energy grid.

A number of insights into the issue of green jobs and green skills emerged in particular during the PURE study in the city of Melbourne. The city's *Green Jobs Study Report* (PURE 2010) has relevance for many regions (see also Thomas, Sandri and Hegarty 2010). Insights include:

1. While there is extensive discussion about green jobs, there is little clarity about the concept.
2. New green skill policy is needed to address incentives, shape industry performance, and develop effective skills and training programmes.
3. There is no evidence yet of developmental work in which clear sustainable outcomes have been achieved.
4. There is no forum or opportunity for partners (i.e. government, business, unions, the third sector and higher education) to work collaboratively on either the job or skill dimensions related to the challenges of environmental sustainability.
5. Connection is needed among the sites where the conversations are occurring, to reduce fragmentation and achieve critical mass.

That being said Melbourne did provide an example of how new employment opportunities associated with green technology transfer and commercialisation can be generated. The Monash University's Centre for Green Chemistry had over the eight years preceding the study in 2010 engaged approximately sixty doctoral students in its work, with a large majority being employed in high-skilled industrial jobs.

Education for sustainable development

The United Nations in *Agenda 21*, the voluntary action plan on sustainability developed with national governments at the 1992 Rio Earth Summit and thereafter, and beyond argues that universities have a wider societal responsibility in education for sustainable development beyond their walls. They have a role therefore in facilitating education for sustainable development within the wider community both in other formal educational institutions and in the non-formal and informal arena.

The United Nations University Institute for Advanced Studies (UNU-IAS) leads in this regard with two flagship initiatives within its Education for Sustainable Development programme. These are its Regional Centres of Expertise (RCEs) and the Promotion of Sustainability in Postgraduate Education and Research Network (ProSPER.Net). RCEs form a network that spans formal, non-formal and informal education, with the purpose of delivering education for sustainable development at local and regional level. Some 100 RCEs exist across the world and as a network are described by UNU-IAS as the basis for 'the Global Learning Space for Sustainable Development'. They are charged with translating the global objectives of the UN Decade of Education for Sustainable Development into localities.[14] In many ways the RCEs parallel in their structures the concept of a learning city or region, and seek as one of their principal objectives to coordinate and harness the capacities of all stakeholders in education, business, the public sector and civil society around the unifying principle of lifelong learning (Longworth and Osborne 2010). The RCEs are doing this in the particular domain of sustainable development.

Analysis of the objectives of the specific RCEs shows universities working with a wide range of stakeholders in their regions. Being part of an RCE in itself requires universities to have provided evidence of a strong commitment in practice to engagement and interaction with the field, and offers a template to universities of what might be. The benchmark in this area therefore has strong parallels to these principles and measures the extent to which universities support the wider principles of sustainable development in their own regions.

The sorts of activities within this domain are extensive. They include fostering citizen participation around sustainable development policies that support learning regions while protecting natural resources (e.g. water conservation and quality, waste management, zero-energy building, energy conservation including insulation and reduction of air conditioning, use of renewable energy and developing sustainable, people-friendly public transportation). Here the focus is on the greening of daily life, and on universalising and popularising 'green economics'.

Enhancing community awareness about green issues through public education for the greening of values, expectations and behaviour is a dimension of lifelong learning and active citizenship. Arguably, within the debate on lifelong learning concerns about the challenge of climate change have been largely ignored, with environmental education rather a niche area for universities connected almost solely to schooling. Within the PURE study, the region of Puglia in Italy is engaging its citizenry in policy discussions addressing water conservation, managing the waste system, and sustainable public transportation specifically for the city of Bari. The region's concern relates to what practices are proving the most effective in using environmental protection and sustainability to support the development of learning regions. Here huge opportunities were presented to the university sector to help provide solutions.

There is also a role in helping businesses, including SMEs, to become more green, especially in the useage of water, energy and transport fuel through training programmes and individual consultancy, and thus contributing to general environmental improvement in regions. Training can also be provided for alternative and localised agricultural systems for food production and to contribute to pressing needs to ensure food security. Helping SMEs in these ways was, for example, identified within the PURE study of the city of Melbourne. And although it was not a focus of the PURE study in Northern Illinois even in that region in the most prosperous country in the world there are signs that food security has become a major agenda item. A recent report for nearby suburban Cook County in Illinois details the severity of fresh food scarcity and links to obesity (Inman and Davidson 2012).

A notable example of the support for localised agriculture was found in South Trans-Danubia in Hungary. Here community activists such as the Mayor of Karasz animate and manage a variety of tradition-restoring and income-generating activities. They serve as visiting faculty to the University of Pécs, and enable student work experience and research project placement in the villages mainly by home-stay. They draw on university expertise, mainly from Pécs but also from Kaposvár (forestry management) and at least two other universities with relevant specialisms, particularly in truffles and fungi. The village fruit-juicing facility even includes Kaposvár University apples along with those from surrounding subsistence and small growers. The fruit is brought in for processing in a cooperative-style multi-supplier activity which spreads the benefit widely; part of the value-added finished product is marketed in places such as Budapest.

In Gaborone, the University of Botswana's Department of Environmental Science and *Somarelang Tikologo* (Environmental Watch) provided a variety of environmental projects in which the University has been engaged, including city and eco-park development, schools projects in water harvesting and household solar energy trials.

Environmental management systems

An important element of a sustainability strategy in universities is the outcome as measured by performance indicators. In the benchmarking activity of PURE, it was considered that traditional environmental management systems (EMSs) such as ISO 14000 would not be entirely suitable for the higher education sector, because of the diffuse nature of decisionmaking and the inappropriateness of a uniform approach to research management and teaching. Thus best practice would go beyond a successful implementation of a particular EMS tool to include the contribution which academic and research activities make to sustainable development.

The benchmarks for a university with an effective EMS policy would:

- identify and implement an EMS system covering the services used and delivered by the HEI, continuous staff development, and feeding back results to senior management;

- have a communications strategy for its EMS report to ensure local participation and scrutiny of aims, performance and conclusions;
- build on the formal EMS to ensure teaching and research activities complement service department activities;
- offer accountable annual reporting on suggested improvements from previous performance reviews.

A number of the universities within PURE regions utilised ISO 14000, but we did not identify a more holistic approach as suggested by these benchmarks.

Conclusion

Overall the actions of universities in sustainable development in PURE regions cover a multiplicity of areas. Some can be categorised as being directly about job creation given the new employment opportunities associated with green technology transfer and commercialisation. Others tend towards green skill development in various populations: within the general community, at the post-secondary level, or by business and industry. Each may have an indirect impact on employment. Some of these are linked to issues within the domain of active citizenship (Chapter 6); others relate to eco-tourism, for example mountain tourism in Buskerud County in Norway, nature and culture-based tourism, indigenous people tourism, and local food, as well as the sport and adventure themes in Jämtland in Sweden (Chapter 8); and nine others related to the creation of niche businesses, especially SMEs in the environment field and their training and development needs (Chapter 9).

From our work in this area six opportunities to shape constructive conversation and action around green jobs and green skills were explicitly suggested or implied by the PURE regions:

1. *Green skill identification.* What generic skills are associated with a commitment to sustainable practices? What new intellectual and technical skills are required for green occupations and industries and to what extent might they be internationalised? Industry Skills Councils could be important partners with higher education in this enterprise. Some regions in our study, such as the now defunct Thames Gateway, had aspirations to become an eco/environmental region and this may be an aspiration elsewhere to secure both inward investment and to promote export of green technologies. In such cases there would clearly be a need to develop new skills and practices.

2. *Regional needs analysis.* What are the processes by which the range of regional partners are being brought together to agree on green priorities and strategies to systematically carry them out? What is the role of higher education in convening, conducting, supporting and implementing this work? This includes issues of future strategic development of regions; for instance in Värmland a key question is how universities can advise and work with regions to promote internationally promising high-level environmental technologies.

3. *Green-focused learning regions.* Puglia is engaging its citizenry in policy discussions addressing water conservation, managing the waste system and sustainable public transportation. What practices are proving the most effective in using environmental protection and sustainability to support the development of learning regions? This is not new territory in as much as the idea of sustainable learning communities has been posited by Morris (2001) among others. Furthermore, cities such as Rosario in Argentina have focused on sustainability as an outcome of being an Educating City and Okayama in Japan has described itself as a 'Sustainable Learning City'. However, this has yet to find a momentum on a large scale. The same might be said of initiatives in Canada, for example the aim of establishing the learning city as a legacy of the 2006 World Urban Forum in Vancouver, including through the then emerging Great Northern Way Campus, and the involvement of British Columbia Institute of Technology, Emily Carr Institute of Art and Design, Simon Fraser University and the University of British Columbia (Holden and Connelly 2004).

4. *Green entrepreneurship.* Higher education can play an instrumental role in supporting green entrepreneurship. Opportunities range from providing research support and technical assistance to small and medium local enterprises to commercialising green technologies and providing international markets for green services.

5. *Sustainable regeneration practices.* Mitigating the impact of development on the natural environment and promoting sustainable construction practices require the adoption of green skills and are likely to result in the creation of green jobs.

6. *Greening higher education.* What is the role of higher education in connecting and responding to the green agenda? There are 'greening the campus' and energy conservation activities in universities in a number of countries, but what re-organisation is occurring in curriculum, research and innovation? Has there been recognition that fundamentally new courses are needed for tomorrow's green jobs?

We end this chapter with an observation following the PURE review in Melbourne. The disastrous Victorian bushfires midway through the project led every university to place climate change on its agenda. If we wait for the next disaster to happen, which surely it will, it may be too late to have an impact. Universities should be better placed than most organisations to anticipate future scenarios rather than being simply reactive.

Notes

1 See http://greenmetric.ui.ac.id/ (last accessed 24 December 2012).
2 In 2011; see http://peopleandplanet.org/greenleague (last accessed 24 December 2012).
3 http://peopleandplanet.org/greenleague/methodology (last accessed 23 December 2012).
4 See https://stars.aashe.org/ (last accessed 24 December 2012).
5 www.greenreportcard.org/ (last accessed 24 December 2012).

6 See www.epa.gov/greenpower/toplists/top20ed.htm (last accessed 24 December 2012).

7 See www.oecd.org/dataoecd/44/37/49318965.pdf (last accessed 24 December 2012).

8 See Green Cities Programme, www.oecd.org/gov/regionaldevelopement/49318965.pdf (last accessed 24 December 2012).

9 See www.oecd.org/document/56/0,3746,en_2649_37465_48874552_1_1_1_37465,00. html (last accessed 24 December 2012).

10 See www.uncsd2012.org/rio20/index.html (last accessed 24 December 2012).

11 http://g8u-summit.jp/english/ssd/index.html (last accessed 24 December 2012).

12 See www.ulsf.org/pdf/TD.pdf (last accessed 24 December 2012).

13 These reports cover Australia, Bangladesh, Brazil, China, Costa Rica, Denmark, Egypt, Estonia, France, Germany, India, Indonesia, the Republic of Korea, Mali, the Philippines, South Africa, Spain, Thailand, Uganda, the UK and the US.

14 The full list of RCEs can be found at www.ias.unu.edu/sub_page.aspx?catID=1849 &ddlID=661 (last accessed 24 December 2012).

8

Culture and creativity

In January 2012, it was announced that the UK's Heritage Lottery Fund had given its support to a project that would 'breathe new life into Glasgow's vast Victorian Kelvin Hall' (University of Glasgow 2012). The plans, if they come to fruition, would involve the University of Glasgow and Glasgow Life working collaboratively to develop the building as a shared museum collections facility. Not only would this permit greater public access to the many exhibits in the various museums of the city, many currently now in store, but the aim is also to use the collections for research, learning and training, and public engagement.

This may become an example of where the cultural presence of universities can enhance and invigorate 'a whole way of life' (Duke et al. 2006)or, as Hamilton and Sneddon (2004) have suggested, to create a buzz. It is one of many initiatives from regions involved in PURE of the role of culture in the engagement of universities with their cities and regions.

There are, however, many other facets to the work of HEIs in this area. Charles and Benneworth (2002), whose model of benchmarking engagement was used at the starting point of PURE, speak in this context about the 'creation, enhancement and reproduction of regional cultures … interpreting culture both as activities that enrich the quality of life and as patterns of social conventions, norms and values that constitute regional identities'. In this regard, Duke et al. (2006) argue that universities are 'straddling' two aspects of culture. The first of these views culture as facilitating indirect economic benefit by attracting and retaining the creative classes: Florida (2002) would suggest that this encourages other, more productive workers into cities and regions. The second views culture as an end in itself, with economic development as the means of improving quality and richness of life (Duke et al. 2006). In this analysis, universities play a role in 'reflecting the region's history, culture and identity back to itself and to newcomers as a place of interest and a place to be' (Duke et al. 2006).

The potential activities that make contributions in the cultural domain are extensive, and authors such as Clover and Sanford (2011 p. 1) remind us that these are not simply economic. They argue that innovative approaches in 'arts-based education and research in civil society, universities, communities and social movements … uncover social and environmental equalities'. Knox (2011, p. 108) 'drawing on over fifty years of experience in adult education in US universities', indicates how adult education can help enhance creativity. He points to the role of universities in 'raising the consciousness of the general public about the nature and importance of creativity in various artistic, scientific, scholarly and professional domains', and suggests that 'a deepened understanding and appreciation of the process and products of creativity can contribute to their decisions as consumers and producers'. As is evident from the PURE studies in Puglia and South Trans-danubia, culture is not only about creating attractive and innovative ways of selling products, but it is a manifestation of the traditional, and of the indigenous knowledge and wisdom of individuals and communities. It also links to issues of diversity and social inclusion.

At the most basic level this is achieved at universities by offering specific courses with a cultural content delivered for local audiences at all levels from non-accredited adult education to post-graduate. However, more broadly the field also includes contributions through research, development and consultancy to heritage and cultural tourism, including sport, innovation and entrepreneurship, art and design, eco-tourism, crafts and food production, and the promotion of traditions of all ethnic groups and minority languages.

The cultural impact of universities on their regions across these domains has been the subject of a number of previous studies, and was a feature, for example, of work undertaken by the OECD in its programme, *Supporting the Contribution of Higher Education to Regional Development*. However, the extent of this activity and its benefit for many HEIs is somewhat of a mystery. For example, an Economic and Social Research Council study (Brennan *et al.* 2006), which among other things assessed the impact of UK universities' 'cultural presence' on disadvantaged communities, found that even where HEIs gathered data on their activities, it was difficult to actually locate the activities within the institutions. This was true in respect of their cultural presence in their immediate vicinities and even more so when the inquiry was extended out further to a regional sphere of influence' (Doyle 2007). Further, it is difficult in many cases to distinguish the cultural from other areas of development. As Doyle has also reported in a preliminary analysis of our own work in the field of culture in PURE, there are 'different interpretations and emphases placed on cultural engagement not only between countries but between regions within countries and "cultural development" frequently overlaps with other areas of development, for example business, industry, community and human and social capital'. She further argues that there emerges from the PURE cases both 'a distinction but also an overlap between cultural development and cultural engagement' of universities, and that 'it is sometimes necessary to delve into the particular political and/or administrative concerns of individual regions' (2010, p. 467).

Course provision

One of the principal roles of higher education has been to offer access to culture. As well expressed by Yanming: 'Higher education has the venerable mission of transmitting and developing culture, promoting individual and social advancement, and offers learners a cultural environment full of rationality and humanism' (2011, p. 200). Delanty (2001), expressing this sentiment in a more reciprocal fashion, sees the university as a key institution of modernity and as the place where knowledge, culture and society interconnect.

Such traditions and sentiments have been well expressed for over a century in the US, UK and some other Anglophone countries through the offer of adult education in the liberal tradition and through extension studies offered through university continuing education. This is a territory that two of the authors of this book have known very well over the last few decades as well as charting its decline (Osborne 2003; Duke 2009; Osborne and Houston 2012). In other countries, activity in the cultural arena has been no less prominent, but expressed in other ways, for example via popular adult education linked to social change in Latin America (Kane 2001) and through folk high schools in Nordic countries (Borish 1991) drawing on Dewey, Freire, Grundtwig, Horton, Knowles, Lindemann and Rogers among other influential figures in adult education.

This tradition does still survive to a limited degree in the UK universities, and most particularly in Scotland because of the different funding regulations of the devolved government in Edinburgh. In the Glasgow region, therefore, there is still thriving provision in this field at the Universities of Strathclyde and Glasgow, including a very well-known *Learning in Later Life*[1] programme and Senior Studies Institute at the former of these HEIs. It is interesting to note that while there is significant course provision in the cultural and creative sector, in parallel there are links to work in employability for the 50+ age group, and to the role of volunteering for this age group within and beyond the University as part of its community engagement strategy. At both Universities this reflects pressure for adult education to more closely fit with institutional mission and to align itself to regional concerns.[2]

Also in the realm of adult education in Lesotho, there is a rather different form of provision in the area of cultural engagement. The Winter/Summer Institute for *Theatre for Development* is a collaborative initiative between the National University of Lesotho Theatre Unit and Medicins sans Frontières (Lesotho), using techniques that initially emerged from Nigeria (Ewu 2007). The objective is to use popular performance to encourage community participation in development, and in this case the focus is on health issues in a country with a high prevalence of HIV/AIDS.

Another facet of the course offer is the design and delivery of core undergraduate provision to meet regional needs. This is of particular interest when implemented in an interdisciplinary manner linking the arts to other disciplines. In PURE perhaps the most notable example of such practice is at the new Aalto University in Helsinki formed from the merger of Helsinki University of Technology, the Helsinki School of Economics and the University of Art and Design. This carries great hopes that it can lead Finnish science and technology into a new era of global competitiveness and it seeks to do so by offering teaching and research that is genuinely interdisciplinary and oriented towards enhancing innovation for global markets. Its activities are structured around three 'Factories' in Service, Design and Media, to build a strong culture of application of science in partnership with industry.

Earlier studies of the role of culture have provided examples of customised provision in the field. For example, in a study for the European Commission (KEA European Affairs 2006) the Popakademie[3] was highlighted as the first art school in Germany to offer academic education in pop music. More interesting perhaps is that Universal Music, the largest music company in Germany, moved all of its trainee education programme from Berlin to the Popakademie in Mannheim. Furthermore, some of the company's executives teach finance, management and marketing at the institution. The Popakademie has also other collaborations, for example with Sony BMG, AOL and MTV.

Such examples did not emerge in PURE regions, but a good example of how provision in the creative field can be offered by a range of institutions in collaboration was demonstrated by the *Creative Way* in the Thames Gateway. Here through one web space, both employment, and education and training opportunities are highlighted. It is a good example of partnership between universities, colleges and private training providers to establish routes through education and training to employment and enterprise in the creative and cultural sectors, and was highlighted in our study of the region as a model potentially transferable practice.

Heritage and cultural tourism

The preservation of cultural environments and turning cultural heritage into visitor attractions are important factors for regional development and growth. This was highlighted on a number of occasions within PURE studies, when there was a particular focus on cultural assets linked to a specific designation, for example when a city is a European Capital of Culture (ECoC), has a UNESCO badging as a Heritage City or City of Literature or Music.

Within the PURE set of studies, the cultural event that stood out was in the city of Pécs within the South Danubian region of Hungary which was an ECoC in 2010. One of the main objectives of the ECoC was to create a Zsolnay cultural quarter in the city, at the site of the Zsolnay ceramics factory, thus making the area the biggest brownfield development of the region. Apart from retaining a factory building still in operation, it was planned to include an exhibition centre on Zsolnay ceramics and porcelain, to install the Faculty of Arts and some Departments of the Faculty of Humanities, and create an incubator house for creative industries, thus attracting artists as well as fostering cultural tourism. This was just one example of the very strong linkages that existed between the region, city and university in the context of the ECoC, which were strongly emphasised by the City Council. As with many other ECoCs, the challenge will be sustainability as highlighted, for example, by Chambers (2011) using the example of Liverpool from 2008, where there have been very extensive links between the city's three universities, Liverpool City Council and the Liverpool Culture Campus.

Glasgow also has a longstanding history of hosting significant events. For example, in 1988 it hosted the National Garden Festival, attracting 4.3 million visitors. However, the city's cultural revival is linked most closely to it being awarded the status of a European Cultural Capital in 1990 during which time there were over 3,000 events and the opening of a major new concert hall. In 1999 it was UK City of Architecture and Design, in 2008 it was named a UNESCO City of Music and it will be the host city for the Commonwealth Games in 2014. The city has built on the profile afforded by these events through the work of the Glasgow City Convention Centre, which in turn works with its universities and others to bring major conferences to the city. As is evident in its ambassador programme,[4] which prioritises the profiling of key academics, it is the existence of universities that is the key to success. Being made European City of the Year by the Academy of Urbanism in 2010 adds further to its profile. Given the enormous industrial decline in the latter part of the twentieth century in a city that had been dependent on shipbuilding, coal mining and steel, it is the new service economy created by culture, tourism and associated leisure pursuits alongside retailing and international finance that now provides the basis of the city's prosperity.

Cultural tourism can lead to development of infrastructure, and various services. It is also a spin-off from mega-events such as the Olympic Games and World Cup, which can be the basis for a range of potential benefits with long-term legacy. Benefits identified as being important in the context of the hosting of a mega-event include security, employment, health, personal safety, housing conditions, physical environment and recreational opportunities (Hall 1992), but it is tourism that is most often cited as having the biggest social and economic impact (Brown and Massey, 2001).

A number of the regions within PURE had been or will be host cities for such events, for example the Thames Gateway for the London Olympics and, as mentioned above, Glasgow for the 2014 Commonwealth Games. Melbourne hosted the latter games in 2006, and like most events of this kind emphasised that the games were about more than just sport, utilising a cultural programme to engage a wider community. The 2012 Cultural Olympiad in London is reported to be the largest of its kind, with over 16 million people having attended performances, its culmination being the London Festival.[5] Malfas, Theodoraki and Houlihan (2004) argue that raising local interest and participation in sporting activities can strengthen regional traditions and values and local pride and community spirit. Further, they suggest that increased sports participation can lead to significant contributions in the quality of life of the individual and the community. Using Barcelona as an example, they argue that this can translate into increased opportunities for those people who are normally socially excluded in active sports participation in the years following the Olympics Games. The synergy between sport and culture, not to mention health and well-being, educational participation by under-represented groups, improvement in social justice and social inclusion (Ruiz 2004), and the concomitant opportunities for universities to contribute, is substantial.

However, impacts of such events are sometimes far from positive (Newman 1999; Jones 2001; Kim, Gursoy and Lee 2006), and social impacts are under-researched. One of the huge opportunities that exist for universities is therefore to contribute to studies of the impact of mega-events, especially the social impacts, which are often relegated to a minor role in analyses, typically made by private consultancies which focus on the bottom-line. Ohmann, Jones and Wilkes (2006), for example, argue that research on the social impact of sports events is limited and the lack of empirical evidence on these impacts makes it difficult to identify any patterns. Small, Edwards and Sheridan (2005) argue that because of the unique interaction between tourists and a destination, it is important to examine these socio-cultural impacts.

In the Thames Gateway region, the delivery of the 2012 Olympics is intended by the organisers to contribute to major regeneration of the surrounding areas, and to deliver a long-term legacy to the area. HEIs in the Thames Gateway clearly recognise that this mega-event presents an opportunity for them not only to contribute to the securing of such a legacy for the community, but also as presenting opportunities for their own institutional development. Possibilities are extensive and not just about direct links to sporting events. The University of East London's strategic direction is linked to building on the Games to promote access to its local facilities and its sports science courses, and it is validating courses in sports and events management. It is also building on its proximity to major exhibition centres, such as the Edexcel Exhibition Centre and the O2 Arena, by developing short-cycle provision (Foundation Degrees) in visitor management related to retail, exhibitions, tourism and hospitality. Further, it is also developing multi-level training in support of the booming construction industry associated with the Games, through strong links with further education, which is recognised as a key part of the student supply chain.

In Glasgow, members of the University of the West of Scotland have contributed to the development of regional and national strategies on the potential impact of the 2014 Commonwealth Games. The University has part-funded a post within the Games Organising Committee with a particular focus on the development of the further and higher education strategy in securing the Games legacy.

There are also opportunities that link tourism with the research offerings of universities. An example from the Swedish region of Jämtland within the elite sports performance testing laboratory centre at the Östersund campus of Mid-Sweden University is illustrative of the potential. The centre works with elite skiers and companies seeking to assess the performance of athletes or the products and equipment they use such as shoes. During the Consultative Development Group's (CDG's) first visit it was identified that potentially such services could be offered to cross country skiers before competitions such as the Vasaloppet with its 35,000 or so participants. The objective of the University with other regional actors was to build an innovation system around the development of sports equipment. During the course of the two-year study it was noticeable that tourism had become an area where the Mid-Sweden University had built its teaching and research strength at Östersund through ETOUR (the European Tourism Research Institute). This showed good convergence with the strategic importance that the region has placed on tourism for its future.

Last and not least, some cultural assets of regions are longstanding, notably their museums and galleries. These can be supported in their education and training endeavours by universities. In turn universities can use such facilities for outreach work within the wider community, for research (e.g. though use of archives), and of course universities have their own museums, galleries and arts centres, which provide many opportunities for public engagement. However, Zipsane (2011) warns us that a gap has emerged between museums and universities. He argues that museums had not recognised that in academia disciplines such as history, archaeology, art and ethnology had lost their belief 'in the great narratives based upon unchallengeable interpretations of material and immaterial traces from the past'. However, even so, museums are not simply a vehicle for reinforcement of a particular take on the nation or region, but might also challenge a particular interpretation of the past. Collaboration with their university neighbours provides such opportunities.

Innovation and entrepreneurship

As Guile (2009) has noted, the creative and cultural can be defined in terms of the outputs achieved by twelve industries: Crafts, Design, Fashion, Film, Music, Performing Arts, Publishing, Research and Development, Software, Toys, TV and Radio, and Video Games (Howkins 2001). Florida (2002, 2004, 2005) talks about a range of occupational areas that include artists and software designers (the 'super-creative core') and management and legal experts (the 'creative professionals'). He suggests that these occupations in turn attract high-technology and high-growth companies, with those who work in these companies looking for tolerant communities and work environments. Pratt (2008, p. 4) describes this as 'an exercise in place marketing', with the creative classes being used as a magnet, and challenges this model. Most importantly, he points out that the creative industries do not simply play a proxy role but are in themselves an important economic force, citing a pan-European report from KEA European Affairs (2006) for the EC. That study, from the then EU25 countries, reported that some 4.7 million people worked in the cultural and creative sector (around 2.5 per cent of those actively employed), with another almost 1.2 million working in cultural tourism. Further statistics from the report show that 46.8 per cent of workers in the cultural sector have at least a university degree in comparison with only 25.7 per cent in the employed population as a whole. So whether cultural and creative industries are direct or indirect creators of economic development, it is clear that the university sector is creating almost half of their workers. This is certainly reflected in some of the PURE regions. For example in Kent, England, the creative industries are the fastest-growing section, and in an Action Plan generated by the county following our initial visit it was proposed that the sector should be a priority for further development, given its role in generating new jobs and aiding graduate retention.

A more nuanced analysis would distinguish between the 'cultural sector', breaking it down into non-industrial and industrial sectors, and the 'creative' sector within which culture is a creative contribution to the production of non-cultural goods.[6] This is a distinction within one European-wide study within which a further link is then made between creativity and innovation (KEA European Affairs 2006,

p. 2). In this analysis, creativity is presented as 'the use of cultural resources as an intermediate consumption in the production process of non-cultural sectors, and thereby as a source of innovation'. It is then but a small step to entrepreneurship since so many of the businesses in the sector are SMEs, including many start-up companies.

The importance of establishing ways for people to turn their creative ideas into successful and sustainable businesses is an important component of regional growth, and links to Chapter 9 since the focus concerns the contribution of individuals in this field to regional innovation systems. Universities can play an important role in providing knowledge and education for potential entrepreneurs in this area. A number of examples in which universities facilitate such activity in the creative industries emerged within PURE. For instance, a Creative Industries incubator at the University of Plymouth in Devon was supported by the RDA with funding from the European Regional Development Fund. In this model individuals were provided with work-spaces and a virtual office package to support business development in this field, the overall objective being to create both new businesses and new jobs.

In most other regions we found recognition of the importance of stimulating a 'creative economy'. For instance in Flanders in Belgium, a number of local authorities saw such a development being associated with the existence of a strong ICT structure and the creative arts, drawing upon the local university colleges in particular to offer provision in music, fashion and the visual arts. The CDG reported that activities in this field also look to innovation in architecture, design and broadband-based ICTs as the networking sources of new forms of employment in creative cities. HEIs are regarded as drivers in this area of job creation. This can be regarded as the 'spatial branding' of the local community in order, on the one hand, to attract students, and, on the other hand, to develop creative and dynamic cities. On a broader front, local authorities can promote, stimulate, inspire, create and, above all, facilitate such processes. This can involve establishing agreements between the city and educational institutions on demographic, economic, social and cultural developments that are of great importance to the sustainability of cities.

It is particularly important to realise that no one sector really operates in isolation. Värmland region in Sweden, which has been very successful in constructing a regional innovation system, achieving widespread recognition of its success, provides a good example of the need to recognise this issue with respect to the creative sector. During its visits, the CDG identified that the main challenge was how to implement the system. Cluster organisations and platforms would seem to be the essential instrument in making it happen. However, horizontal links between different clusters and platform organisations need to be promoted in order to encourage new innovation and entrepreneurship. This was particularly relevant for the creative industry sector, which was already trying new ways of connecting clusters, developing entrepreneurship and competences which would need to be explored, including developing international linkages.

Art and design

Longstanding traditions within arts, crafts and design have developed in many regions into national and in some cases world famous brands. Fine art can be an important contribution to a region's character. Some regions become magnets for artists of world repute with concomitant spin-offs through tourism as galleries are established, as is the case with the Tate Gallery in St Ives (Devon and Cornwall region of PURE) and the Turner Gallery in Margate (Kent region). As was indicated earlier, other regions have had numerous longstanding galleries, some located in universities themselves, providing educational functions for local populations and in themselves attracting visitors, as in Glasgow.

Universities can also assist in developing brands through supporting businesses in art and design, and in maximising a range of cultural spin-offs. Many universities have Fine Art and Design departments, and in many regions there exist specialist institutions. These can both provide specialist domain-specific advice and can contribute regionally through the service learning of their students.

Eco-tourism, crafts and food production

Many regions, especially in rural areas, focus on eco-tourism or tourism that features local crafts, foods and drinks. Many food producers who work on a small scale also have a strong connection to eco-friendly production and sustainable development. This in turn connects with the issue of green jobs and food security highlighted in Chapter 7 and the development and strengthening of skills for sustainable development. In some regions such as Puglia, our visits identified opportunities that had not been exploited in part because of a weak link between the regional innovation system and the university sector. Real opportunities existed for HEIs to develop the knowledge and skills of communities in the region for new markets in eco-tourism, and organic and other specialised foods, in a connected way.

There were many examples within the PURE project related to eco-tourism, and the role of the university sector. Just one in the Norwegian county of Buskerud illustrates the sorts of discussions that have occurred as a result of the visits by our CDGs. In this county a partnership agreement, which the region has had with Buskerud University College since 2009, sets out the overall role that the College should play in competence development for business and industry, regional development, innovation, leadership, entrepreneurship and tourism. The agreement looks to the College to conduct R&D and business development projects which address the key issues for the region, and the county wishes to support the establishment of a centre for tourism leadership. Much of the discussion in a second visit to the region focused on strategic matters and how to capitalise on Buskerud's competitive edge, namely its natural and cultural heritage, its stunning scenery and its proximity to Oslo. The PURE team were not only able to comment on plans but also to advise on national (in Lillehammer and Stavanger) and international (such as in nearby Scotland) comparators and focus on the potential contributions to overall regional strategy that could be made by the University College. This included the integration of specific components in degree programmes such as Visual Communication Studies and the merits of setting up an Institute for Tourism.

In some regions major tourist attractions have strong environmental orientation. For example in Cornwall, UK, the Eden Project is an eco-attraction of world renown. This represents an opportunity as it has relatively few links with the universities in the region.

Promotion of traditions of all ethnic groups and minority languages

Promoting the traditions, culture and languages of various ethnic groups is a prominent part of the work of many regions. Working within an inclusive multicultural society is an important facet of almost all governments' policies. It is linked to issues raised in Chapter 6. For universities predominantly their role in inclusion has been to improve their attractiveness to traditionally excluded ethnic groups, and thereby create improved access to mainstream undergraduate degrees. However, inclusion can occur in other ways, such as through building on the interest created by large-scale events. Such is the case for the 2012 Olympic Games in the Thames Gateway, where at least one of the universities in the region is linking part of its widening participation efforts to the event. Universities can also work directly with the cultural sector in order to improve social inclusion for those culturally excluded through a range of less formal outreach activities.

Many examples from PURE studies could be cited but two are illustrative approaches. The first is from the City of Pécs (the 'Borderless City'), in South Transdanubia. Here the City Council and its partners identified its multicultural heritage as the main characteristic of the region, emphasising its position as the cultural gateway to the Balkans. There are nine minority local governments working in Pécs (German, Romani, Croatian, Serbian, Bulgarian, Polish, Greek, Ukrainian and Ruthenian); of particular significance, it is the only Hungarian city where the Roma population (the majority belonging to the Boyash branch and the rest to the Romanian Gypsies) is able to study in its own language, from kindergarten to university. This occurs through the Romany educational institutions such as the Ghandi grammar school, the Collegium Martineum and the Department of Romology at the University (40 per cent of its permanent staff being from the Roma community). A second example, in the city of Glasgow, is the links between the University of Glasgow and Glasgow Life that were mentioned at the beginning of this chapter. There are very high levels of unemployment in the city, with pockets of severe deprivation in wards displaying multiple indicators of poverty. High concentrations of migrants and asylum seekers in some areas also present challenges but offer a rich cultural diversity to the city. The project involving the Kelvin Hall is at the apex of a number of collaborative ventures in a city with very significant commitment to ensuring that a more representative range of its population encounters its cultural collections.

In other cities there is no less concern or ambition in relation to culture, but less movement in this direction. For example, during our review in Gaborone,

Botswana many possibilities arose in the arts and culture area. These included engagement as a means of contributing to the evocation of a cultural consciousness, the marketing of cultural assets and the development of cultural industries. Pockets of possibility at the University of Botswana were identified in many discipline areas that formed a strong basis for collaboration with the city. Representatives of the City Council, however, spoke of Gaborone as a 'silent city' – there is little visibility of its history, its culture or its industry, and the University could advise on these matters. Up to the point of our first visit, while the University's strategy document for Arts and Culture engagement was well crafted, the perspective of the city was that it, as a stakeholder, had not been involved. However, the PURE study created the awareness of possibilities and the creation within the University of a 'culture' team.

Conclusion

Culture and creativity covers a wide range of activities that can be the basis for contributions by universities to their cities and regions. These range from those that are very small in scale, such as offering courses focused on the interests of particular communities, to research and development support for events of the highest international significance. The initiatives can support social inclusion for excluded groups, and can be the catalyst for innovation and be a very significant part of the economic future of many regions. Our cases in PURE illustrate a remarkably diverse range of actions and opportunities.

This leads, of course, into discussion about the broader role of universities in regional economic development, particularly in relation to small and medium enterprises. The next chapter provides an overview of some of the key examples which emerged during the PURE project.

Notes

1 See www.strath.ac.uk/cll/llp/ (last accessed 14 December 2012).
2 It is interesting to note that during the PURE review of the Glasgow region, this provision at the University of Glasgow was considered for cutbacks, but ultimately arguments based around locating the offer within a framework of regional as well as international engagement led to its survival.
3 See www.popakademie.de (last accessed 14 December 2012).
4 See http://conventions.seeglasgow.com/glasgow-conference-ambassador-programme/ (last accessed 14 December 2012).
5 See www.london2012.com/cultural-olympiad (last accessed 14 December 2012).
6 The cultural sector includes:
   Non-industrial sectors producing non-reproducible goods and services aimed at being 'consumed' on the spot (a concert, an art fair, an exhibition). These are the arts field (visual arts including paintings, sculpture, craft, photography; the arts and antique markets; performing arts including opera, orchestra, theatre, dance, circus; and heritage including museums, heritage sites, archaeological sites, libraries and archives).

Industrial sectors producing cultural products aimed at mass reproduction, mass-dissemination and exports (for example, a book, a film, a sound recording). These are 'cultural industries' including film and video, video-games, broadcasting, music, book and press publishing.

The creative sector includes 'activities such as design (fashion design, interior design, and product design), architecture, and advertising' (KEA European Affairs 2006, p. 2).

9

Entrepreneurship and SMEs
– regions and innovation systems

An interest in regions as a critical focus of economic policy has been growing in importance for two decades. While the OECD played a key role in promoting this interest through its early work on learning regions, it has been regional agencies throughout the world, responding to circumstances of industrial decline (collapse, in some cases), which have resolved to work with their own inherent human capital and local resources to forge new futures for themselves. A new spirit of entrepreneurship has characterised many of these initiatives, typically taking shape as small and medium-sized enterprises, and often working in a collaborative spirit as part of new networks. Large companies (and employers) continue, of course, to be important and an integral part of supply chains.

An even sharper focus on regions, regional development and regional innovation has emerged in the last few years. Part I of this book explored a range of issues arising from the economic and financial crisis which has precipitated so much distress for so many people, particularly in North America and Europe. Old policy prescriptions and presumptions are in dispute, as there has been increasing recognition that 'one size does not fit all'. While there is widespread emphasis on the importance of the 'knowledge economy', there is much less consensus about what it means, or about its implications for policy and programme. 'Innovation' is promoted and regional action is seen to be advantageous in this regard (after all, 'knowledge walks on two legs'), but far from easy. Similarly, while higher education institutions might be anticipated to be a key part of a regional innovation system, the evidence has been that they are less effective than might have been expected (see OECD 2007).

Indeed, the typical story of university engagement with regional development is one of missed opportunity. It is not hard to find disgruntled industry representatives who register a range of stories about the difficulties of working with universities. There are regional authority representatives who are disappointed that university leadership appears more interested in the university's institutional status than the broader framework of regional interests. Nevertheless, the PURE project has revealed many examples of university support for, and collaboration with, not only individual firms, but regional efforts to improve their economic base and to develop innovation systems.

Across the diversity of the PURE regions, 'regional innovation' became the language which best linked the various threads which related to industrial change, regional development and emerging occupational opportunities. It is not surprising that this idea recurred so clearly as part of the discussions about universities and regional engagement, given the degree of economic dislocation which has affected all participating regions, and the priority which has been given to innovation as a key focus of discussions about how to move forward. Given the priority on knowledge as the critical ingredient in emerging industrial sectors, universities have become significant resources for enterprises and authorities, and it is not surprising if they have looked first to those closest to home.

Before sharing some of these stories, an overview of the priority given to regional innovation systems thinking across OECD countries can be found in a series of reports produced in recent years (see for example Cooke 2001; Benneworth and Dassen 2011; and a series of OECD reviews from 2008–2012). While the research began during boom times, the key insights were presented in the heart of the economic and financial crisis (OECD 2009) and indicate the hopefulness which has been placed in regional-level action.

OECD thinking about regions

The focus on regional-level action reflects a change in focus from subsidies and transfers to stimulate growth in one region or another, to an emphasis on competitive advantage and on mobilising resources to promote innovative practices. As the report's title, *Regions Matter*, indicates, national governments are not as well placed as 'lower' level governments to understand opportunities for growth, nor to facilitate partnerships between key economic and political actors.

For the OECD, its eye was on how national governments can benefit from greater attention to regional policy issues. From this perspective, regional policies could contribute in a number of ways:

- accelerating and maximising the impact of public investment;
- combining different types of investment to maximise their impact on sustainable growth;
- effectively targeting regions in need;
- ensuring coordination at the central level;
- harnessing the experience of regional development agencies;
- ensuring that local and regional knowledge, funds and capacity are mobilised (Ssee OECD 2009, p. 13).

In its growing interest in a more discerning approach to regional economic performance, the OECD has echoed developments in the design and implementation of Regional Policy in the European Union. Over the past two decades, EU Regional Policy has grown in importance to involve now more than a third of EU budget expenditure. Largely focused on infrastructure and skills formation, it has moved from subsidising poorer regions in the EU to a more positive approach on competitiveness. Regional Policy has been identified as a key mechanism for the comprehensive EU strategy, Europe 2020, which promotes 'smart, sustainable and inclusive growth'.[2]

More generally, regional innovation systems have become an increasingly significant focus of research and of policy over the last two decades. This has arisen from the view that interaction is critical to knowledge exchange and learning, which in turn are significant elements of innovation processes. Notwithstanding the communication possibilities now available and the emergence of 'virtual communities', regional environments and spatial proximity have been seen as critical resources for understanding the formation of clusters and their potential significance in facilitating the kinds of interactions that lead to innovation and hence to increased economic activity. SMEs are critical in these processes, as they often constitute key links in supply chains; yet, over time, efforts to enhance their involvement in innovation processes have often been frustrating (see European Commission, Enterprise and Industry Directorate General 2009).

While there are a number of prominent writers whose work has received a lot of public attention (Porter 1990, 1998; Florida 2002, for example), there is now a very substantial body of research which encompasses all kinds of theoretical perspectives, industries and locations which illuminates the importance of locality in framing opportunities for innovation and enhanced economic performance. The research shows great variety in clusters and how organisations network, depending on historical, industry, cyclical, cultural and regional circumstances. Much of it has focused particularly on small and medium enterprises, their relationships with large organisations, and the potential value of collaboration in enhancing their prospects for growth and increased profitability.

Across different national settings and industry sectors, the studies also raise as many questions as they answer, about such issues as scale, diversity in type of organisation, the roles of intermediaries, variations according to industry sector and cultural influences. Frames of reference vary so often in many of the studies that it can be very difficult to develop a coherent perspective on many of these issues.

Two key themes recur in the debates about the regional character of innovation processes, and particularly about the relationships among organisations within a region: the importance of knowledge exchange, especially where it is tacit, not codified in an easily transferable form; and collaborative action to invent, design, produce and distribute competitive products and services. In these respects, at least, regions matter and 'news about the death of geography is much exaggerated' (Berry 2003, p. 55). This seems to be relevant particularly where proximity can enhance innovation at different points in supply chains.

Underpinning much of this research has been the question of whether policy or other interventions can influence the development and effectiveness of regional innovation systems. This is a critical question for governments and for HEIs, in understanding how best to develop their relationships with particular companies, industry sectors and regional clusters – and local government and community networks. As almost all studies of innovation suggest, implementation of innovation is framed increasingly by a much more inclusive understanding of partnerships, much more than science and technology. Access to skilled labour, reliable regulation standards, logistics and collaborative marketing are examples of factors which can have important influence on innovation processes. Furthermore, this raises questions about how higher education institutions can support a framework for innovation that is broader than a focus on science and technology alone. This is particularly important where there is growing interest in public sector innovation, and in elaborating a more coherent approach to economic, social, cultural and environmental development.

The role of higher education institutions in regional innovation systems has been articulated most clearly in the report of the OECD (2007) Review of this topic. Based on studies in fourteen regions, the review concluded that higher education is important not only in the provision of new graduates entering local labour markets, but also the provision of professional development and contribution to lifelong learning. It also described the ways in which universities can engage in partnerships with other regional stakeholders to address a range of local development opportunities in social, cultural and environmental domains.

More generally, the specific studies of regional innovation systems draw attention regularly to the ways in which key university resources can be critical to new developments. Just as often, they report on the lack of accessibility of universities to external organisations, especially SMEs.

Stories from the PURE regions

Not surprisingly, given the issues articulated around regional policy and innovation, most PURE regions had a high priority on economic development issues, and were interested in how their universities and further education colleges could support that objective. At the very least, there was an expectation about support for skill development and the supply of labour necessary for new firms and for industry regeneration. This was a fundamental issue in Glasgow. However, many regions offer more sophisticated examples of regional innovation in which their higher education institutions were involved. This section presents some of those stories.

Värmland has been recognised widely for its work over some years in developing a regional innovation system which has established appropriate structures. These have included regional cluster organisations and other architecture to link different strategic players. The development of a 'Packaging Arena' has contributed enormously to inter-cluster interactions, acting as a platform linking researchers and facilitating international collaboration. It is anticipated that global connections will enable another phase of regional innovation. Locally, the regional authority's emphasis is on embedding an ongoing spirit of innovation and entrepreneurship.

The region has financed partly the appointments of professors at the Karlstad University, creating close links with the clusters. There is a Memorandum of Understanding (MOU) between the region and the University, and the University has opened a one-stop shop for small and medium enterprises to enhance accessibility. This will help to broaden the academic culture at the University and support a more systematic approach to lifelong learning and competence-building. Another key role of the University will be monitoring regional trends, specifically economic and labour market data, so that decision-making by stakeholders will be informed adequately. A similar role has also been foreshadowed for Northern Illinois University in its region.

Thames Gateway, which straddles the River Thames on the eastern side of London, is a particularly interesting story because its regional authority was created specifically in 1995 by the United Kingdom government to drive development of a region which has experienced a period of decline and now has relatively high unemployment and a lower skills base. It is the site of the London Olympics in 2012, and its growth strategy is focused on investment in infrastructure, housing and retail developments. There are twelve further and higher education institutes in the area and, given the skills shortages, there has also been some emphasis on an 'education-led regeneration'.

The twelve institutions differed widely, yet each was expected to play a role and be visible in the regeneration process. Various initiatives around skills development were a key action, with impressive work to develop guaranteed progression pathways from further into higher education. This was identified as valuable in itself, but it had also enabled colleges to promote a positive aspirational atmosphere.

Apart from a shared institutional effort to set up a knowledge exchange, Knowledge East, most other examples of entrepreneurial engagement were undertaken by individual institutes. These included provision of specialist equipment to a local business, a business incubator and the Thames Gateway Knowledge Platform, an analytical resource which provided economic development evidence on local boroughs, monitoring the impacts of change at the local level.

In Buskerud, by way of contrast, there was a strongly locally based approach to developing a regional research and development strategy. A foresight process involving a strong contribution from the business sector had resulted in the formation of a strong regional partnership which had identified five areas of focus: tourism, systems engineering, health, environment and green energy technologies. Buskerud University College has a role to play in each of these, apart from the supply of skilled labour. Mention was made in Chapter 6 of the proposal for a multifaceted Science Centre which would adopt a sector cluster approach, and there was a proposal also for an Institute of Tourism. Already, Innovation Papirbredden is facilitating linkages between health researchers and businesses.

A third model was found in Helsinki, where innovation and competitiveness policies were another important dimension of national and municipal policy. The current policies build on continued strength in science and technology development, and promote decentralised Centres of Expertise, and strategic centres for science, technology and innovation. The Centres of Expertise are now focused as regionally based national competence clusters. Helsinki is involved in nine of the Centres of Expertise, and coordinates three of them. While there is a clear emphasis on creating a national critical mass in each Centre of Expertise, they are also seen as key resources for regional development.

Alongside the national innovation framework, the Helsinki Metropolitan Area (HMA) has adopted a competitiveness strategy: *Prosperous Metropolis: Competitiveness Strategy for the Helsinki Metropolitan Area.* The Strategy identifies four priorities:

- improving top-quality education and know-how;
- building good quality of life as well as a pleasant and secure living environment;
- strengthening user-driven innovation environments and developing public procurements; and
- internationalisation of the metropolitan area and its connection to global networks.

The strategy then spells out a number of 'actions' to be undertaken in relation to the four priorities. Universities and polytechnics are integral to these actions, and there is a clear intent to channel much activity through Culminatum, a key agency in which the higher education institutions are clear stakeholders.

A consistent theme here was breaking down traditional barriers and building cooperative relationships among the large and traditionally separate municipal organisations, as well as with higher education institutions. One means of doing this was various specific-purpose companies that might have municipal, university, business or other stakeholders represented in their ownership, management and operation. Culminatum is one very good example of this type of collaborative forum, but this seemed to be a common arrangement, whether on a regional or city basis. Culminatum was a company formed by the three participating cities, the Uusimaa Regional Council, universities, polytechnics and businesses to manage the Centre of Expertise programme in the Helsinki region. Formed in 1995, Culminatum coordinates three of the national competence clusters, and plays a key role in coordinating funding and expertise from various sources in the interests of business and job development. As a longstanding intermediary that is crucial to the implementation of the HMA competitiveness strategy, Culminatum is an extremely interesting example of collaboration in PURE Helsinki.

Melbourne was another region in which the role of intermediaries was again important. The PURE project was itself sponsored by the OKC, formed by a partnership among Melbourne City Council, the Committee for Melbourne and eight metropolitan universities. PURE Melbourne undertook case studies of four agencies which played key roles in supporting and developing regional innovation systems within the metropolitan area and in a large provincial city. In a context where local government areas are relatively small units, considerably less significant than State governments, it was striking that local government authorities played an important role in the formation of each of these agencies. For example, in the case of G21, five local government authorities (LGAs) took the initiative because of their social and economic interdependence with each other. Similarly, seven LGAs had played a key role in the formation of NORTHLink, a regional partnership of industry, education and government established in 1995 in Melbourne's northern region.

G21, for example, is the largest and most comprehensive of these agencies. It has facilitated innovation in a range of local sectors, including well-being and health, not only education and economy. It was established in 2002 in recognition of the need for much greater coordination among the various municipalities. G21 describes itself as an alliance of a variety of independent organisations with a shared vision for the future of Geelong. It has eight pillars: Arts and Culture, Education and Training, Health and Well-Being, Economic Development, Planning and Services, Transport; Environment, and Sport and Recreation. Each pillar draws together a significant network from diverse organisations with an interest in that area.

Deakin University and Gordon TAFE College, as the two key, local HEIs, have been integral contributors to G21 since its inception. The Deakin Vice-Chancellor was the first Chair of the Board, and senior Deakin staff have been involved consistently since. Deakin has also funded a very interesting relationship with Enterprise Connect, where an Enterprise Connect staff member has been seconded to the University to work on a series of projects to build relationships between government, business and university.

Many other examples emerged across the PURE regions. In South Transdanubia, the European Capital of Culture project required a strong city–university partnership, but there were also examples of a biotechnology innovation, and heritage and creative industries clusters, none of which could have happened without university support. On a smaller scale, a village agricultural endeavour has had support from universities in both Pécs and Kaspovar. In Flanders, there was great anticipation early in the PURE project following the Flemish government's plans to develop Flanders as a dynamic regional knowledge economy, with significant implications. However, political struggles within Belgium impeded the fuller development of these ideas.

Themes and issues emerging across the PURE regions

A number of significant themes emerged from the various examples drawn from looking across the PURE regions. A report to a PURE regions conference in Ostersund in June 2010 indicated that all regions appreciated the role that their HEIs could play in the generation of knowledge as the basis for innovation. The two-way transfer of knowledge in local economies and regions was seen as a foundation for regional renewal and regeneration. The report distinguished three levels of development of this contribution across the PURE regions:

1. *Foundation*, in which the higher education institutions were developing their capabilities and capacity to support innovation through knowledge generation and transfer. This level focuses specifically on the HEIs, their resources and how they can be linked more effectively with regional economies.
2. *Transitional*, in which the mechanisms for knowledge transfer included skills and workforce development. This level focuses more on the relationship between HEIs and regional economies, exploiting the knowledge resources for organisational and product development purposes.

3. *Advanced*, which involved frameworks and integrated approaches to leverage knowledge assets from various sources in order to secure the competitive economic base of the region. This represents a more systemic development of HEIs as central to regional innovation, and part of complex regional economic relationships in which two-way exchange is increasingly common.

Regions are at different stages of development across this continuum, reflecting their history and settings. A common thread across most regions was the need to develop local enterprises, especially at the SME level, and to develop a skilled and knowledgeable workforce and society. Only rarely, however, did this mean support for spin-offs; the greater emphasis was on enhancing the competitiveness of existing SMEs. The need for leadership at both government and industry levels and the setting of a clear vision and regional plans was also apparent, and varied considerably in terms of examples and success.

In Melbourne PURE, a number of critical success factors in engagement around regional innovation were identified. Most of these seem to be pertinent to the successful examples in other regions:

- strong and persistent champions, with strong local networks;
- a holistic approach to strategy;
- bringing government, industry and education together;
- a consistent emphasis on sharing knowledge about broad regional issues and learning about technology;
- sufficient resources for the tangible outcomes which they set themselves to achieve; and
- supporting networking and collaboration as a foundation for ongoing activity.

There are a range of other insights from the conversation and investigations in the PURE regions which warrant further mention. Perhaps most importantly, there is widespread agreement about the importance of higher education institutions in regional capability-building. This typically implies a focus on skills formation, in supporting the development of a labour force which can enable local industry to respond and grow as new opportunities emerge. Underlying this expectation is a generalised anticipation that the 'knowledge economy' is arriving and requiring a new type of worker that embodies more than specific technical capacity.

While the PURE evidence indicates some clear examples where this occurs, it is apparent that there is rarely a direct or linear relationship between emerging opportunities and the specific skills supply which results from higher education programmes. Two other aspects of the skills strategy are necessary. First, an understanding of the depth and parameters of a region's capability is enhanced immeasurably when the key stakeholders engage in the development of a 'human capital' plan, where grounded understanding of the prospective industry cluster developments for the longer term is linked with detailed commitments around education and skills formation, from early childhood onwards. Second, so much of workplace requirements depends on tacit and abstract knowledge, that the more students' learning is linked with workplace experience and practice, the more effective their contribution is likely to be, once employed.

Frequently, collaboration is undermined by widespread misunderstanding about innovation, and the kinds of contributions which can be made by university researchers. Clearly, scientific investigation is a major activity for many research universities, and those involved in key sectors (such as pharmaceuticals, for example) are alert to opportunities for commercialising their discoveries. However, the kinds of regional partnerships which grow around local innovation systems and development of knowledge industries do not necessarily need insights from 'patented' science but rather with business and logistical issues such as supply chain problem-solving. These are the circumstances in which small and medium enterprises, in particular, often struggle to find relevant support from universities. Some in universities argue that it is not their job; yet it is where they have expertise which can be very valuable for the development of the local innovation system.

As has been commented in other places, the impediments to building effective and ongoing collaboration between university researchers and departments have several dimensions. The key actors can speak different languages (public discourse rather than academic), they have different priorities (market development versus publication of research funding), timelines (short-term production pressures, in contrast with the time required for thorough research) and funding (preparedness to pay, when effective research can be very expensive). The stronger orientation of researchers towards publication in esteemed international journals, rather than cross-sectoral collaboration and industry problem-solving, is a key example of this tension.

In this respect, several regions demonstrate the important role of intermediaries. This insight has been confirmed also in other studies in which a 'core' group can offer an overview independent of any specific interest groups (see International Regions Benchmarking Consortium 2010). Intermediaries play a key role in recognising the perspective, expectations and needs of each stakeholder, and offer a forum to bring stakeholders together. Across the PURE regions, there are different examples of intermediary groups, some of which have been led by local or city government, others by key business groups. Typically, they attract significant public resources because of the contribution that they make to framing a more holistic view of the regional innovation system, and facilitating more efficient interaction among key stakeholders who might otherwise struggle in sustaining their relationship.

Typically, the formal intermediaries have begun with one or two key people seeing an opportunity and then enlisting other organisations and stakeholders in the development phase. Their aims have focused on economic, environmental and social action without any specific mention of innovation, yet there has been a clear desire, even hunger, for knowledge transfer and skills development.

The evidence from the PURE project would be that intermediaries work best when there is a genuine inclusiveness of different interest groups, with sufficient resources to support their agreed responsibilities. Less predictably, their effectiveness can depend on their legitimacy with the different stakeholder groups – and their legitimacy itself can depend on their effectiveness! Few of the intermediaries identified in the PURE regions could assume a long-term existence.

Regions vary also in the extent to which there is a spirit of entrepreneurship. This depends on cultural context, and it has proved challenging to encourage entrepreneurship where there is no history. Just as important have been the practical issues of access to capital, and management of risk. Some universities are much more effective than others at generating spin-offs from university research, and typically these have been managed from institutional rather than collaborative resources. Overall, the circumstances in the PURE regions where research universities have made a significant contribution to the regional economy through spin-offs have been limited – there has been no Silicon Valley!

In all regions, governance, whether of an overall system or of specific initiatives within that region, has been an issue. In the first place, regional economies rarely coincide neatly with established governmental administrative boundaries. Among the PURE regions, the Thames Gateway was perhaps the sharpest example of a governance problem, in that a specific authority had to be created to manage the overall development of the area. This authority was clearly a creation of the national government, and not subject to any form of democratic accountability. In Helsinki, there were various examples of city governments coming together to co-sponsor organisations or initiatives to perform designated regional responsibilities, while the kinds of intermediaries which were identified in Melbourne were a response to inadequate governance arrangements.

Collaboration among different governments is clearly contingent on the coherence of their policy objectives, their approaches and their resource capacity. There were examples in some PURE regions even of competing policies held by different agencies within the same government. The complexity of these governance issues has been recognised by the OECD. It commented that:

> Collaboration (vertical and horizontal) between different government and non-government bodies exists in the great majority of countries. It brings about coherence and greater impact from public investments (more appropriate selection, funding and implementation monitoring). The key issue is the lack of co-ordination between different policies, as well as between their different providers and constituencies. Fragmented approaches mean that many countries face problems of overlapping or even conflicting policies, all aimed at having a regional impact. This fragmentation has consequences for the regional effectiveness of public policies, as well as for their national impact. The question is how to find a coherent and effective approach. (OECD 2009, p. 108)

This has led to work on 'multi-level governance', which can address problems arising from different layers of government, but not the silos that can be associated with different agencies, or local or city-regional governments working alongside each other. Infrastructure projects represent a major challenge because of the scale of the resources involved, yet they also offer more tangible examples around which negotiations can be managed. Ironically, it is the less tangible but arguably important dimensions of regional innovation systems, such as human capital or land use policies, which can be challenging for efforts to collaborate.

Opportunities and challenges

There are many opportunities for HEIs to contribute to regional innovation systems, if the challenges can be addressed. This depends on clarity of regional visions and policies and resolution of contradictory expectations on the higher education sector. Some of the opportunities which emerged were:

- The need for models and resources to support effective interaction between HEIs and the SME sector is an ongoing challenge. The challenge is to ensure that the relationship has a systemic base, rather than depending on individual efforts.
- The need for resourcing mechanisms which address the persistent difference in the timeframes expected by industry and that are required typically for formal research. This is necessary for industry to be able to deliver quick responses to rapidly changing technologies, yet also freeing academics from the fear that they will be punished for not publishing straight away.
- The development of more explicit yet adaptable models of multidisciplinary cross-sectoral engagement with representatives throughout the supply chain, to identify critical design, production and distribution issues which can be enhanced by learning and knowledge exchange. This would help to deliver appropriate and effective approaches and skills for problem-solving.
- The development of a clear model for the secondment of academic staff to economic development bodies.

While the focus of this analysis has been very much on regional activities and collaboration, the regional innovation systems are open and are heavily dependent on state, national and international economic systems. Greater sharing of perspectives across regional entities might be a useful foundation for policy advice to state and national governments.

Conclusion

This chapter has focused insights generated in the PURE regions into the possibilities for effective higher education engagement in and support for regional innovation systems, particularly those which involve small and medium enterprises and seek to foster greater entrepreneurship. In conjunction with the other chapters in this part of the PURE story, it has demonstrated the breadth and complexity of engagement. A consistent part of this story has been the tension for universities in seeking to balance their primary focus on teaching and research with possibilities for regional engagement which are conceived regularly as being additional to the core work.

Part of the PURE project sought to focus on the extent to which universities were able to engage at a regional level in their internal planning and strategic development. 'Benchmarking' instruments were offered to both regional authorities and universities in participating regions as a means of enabling them to reflect on their own arrangements and to learn from others involved with PURE. The experience with benchmarking is discussed in the next chapter.

Notes

1 www.oecd-ilibrary.org/urban-rural-and-regional-development/oecd-reviews-of-regional- innovation_19976585 (last accessed 14 December 2012)
2 http://ec.europa.eu/europe/2020/ (last accessed 14 December 2012)

10

The audit era and organisational learning – benchmarking and impact

Context

The increasing internationalisation of higher education markets has led to a surge in interest in the development of the measures which allow universities to measure themselves against each other, and to claim a relative pre-eminence of one kind or another that they can then use in marketing. 'League tables', as they are sometimes described, have proliferated in the last decade.

At this point, there are no fewer than thirty noteworthy rankings, ranging from broad rankings of national universities, such as Maclean's and US News and World Report, to comprehensive international rankings, such as *The Times Higher Education Supplement* and Shanghai Jiao Tong University, to research-specific rankings, such as those of New Zealand and the United Kingdom, and even to idiosyncratic rankings such as those that claim to identify the most wired or most politically active campuses. (Salmi and Saroyan 2007, p. 2; see also Hazelkorn 2011).

As the notion of league tables suggests, these kinds of rankings typically imply that there are winners and losers. It has led to an ambivalent culture of measurement, in which institutions choose to take part, even though they recognise that the results might well be counterproductive to their ambitions. One reason is that research output and its perceived quality has been a key indicator in the more highly regarded rankings, even though student programmes continue to be the primary focus of so many institutions. Regional engagement has featured rarely although perceived relationships with industry have been included in some rating frameworks.

As Hazelkorn has noted, there has been extensive debate over questions of methodology and perceived benefits. She has drawn attention to three areas of concern:

1. Technical and methodological processes.
2. The usefulness of the results as consumer information.
3. The comparability of complex institutions with different missions and goals. (Hazelkorn 2007, pp. 4–5).

She believes that worldwide comparisons will become even more important for institutions in the future (2007, p. 21). However, the problem with the contemporary 'audit' era is that it is more concerned with ranking organisations or institutions, rather than understanding why one is doing better than another, and focusing on the points of leverage which could make a difference. This can not only be unhelpful but also destructive insofar as it leads to organisational decision-making which focuses on the criteria rather than organisational vision and purposes.

This is quite different from the earlier era in which 'benchmarking' was proposed as a resource for learning in corporations. Even though it relied on data and on a comparative process, looking across institutions and regions, its purpose was not the relative rating of one institution as being better or worse than another, but on facilitating a process of identifying the areas where one institution might look to learn from the outstanding performance of another on a particular indicator.

Hence, the PURE project used university and regional benchmarking instruments to complement the more directly qualitative processes of CDGs and associated project activities. The focus of the benchmarking was on seeking to build a dataset which could be used to share learning among institutions and regions, a method for facilitating a consistent conversation across different regional and national settings.

This chapter presents an overview of the thinking underpinning the benchmarking activity and an overview of the learning which occurred in different regions. While there was some resistance in many regions, many people came to find it a very useful activity.

Benchmarking, higher education and regional engagement

Benchmarking relies on the comparison of statistical data about various dimensions of organisational performance. As a resource for learning, the data become a resource for comparative assessment, as a means to set goals for a continuous improvement process (see Camp 1989). Spendolini (1992) examined the meanings attributed to benchmarking in more than fifty companies in the United States and constructed a definition which emphasised certain key elements and processes:

> Benchmarking, a method for organisational improvement that involves continuous, systematic evaluation of the products, services and processes of organisations that are recognised as representing best practices. (Spendolini 1992, p. 9)

It is based on the assumption that factual data collected in different sites can be used comparatively to understand organisational strengths and weaknesses, and to identify areas in which change ought to be a priority. Macneil *et al.* (1994) distinguished between three types of benchmarking:

1. *Internal*, which involves benchmarking of internal operations, between divisions or sites of the same organisation.
2. *Industry* or *competitive*, against other companies in the same industry, which has the advantage of comparing firms with common technological and market characteristics.
3. *Generic* or *process*, which involves comparisons of specific processes (e.g. billing, or perhaps debt collection) with international leaders irrespective of industry.

The use of apparently objective data is a key feature of benchmarking. It provides a basis for identifying which unit or partner is showing the best results on a particular process, and then analysing why. Other organisations can learn about what was working and see whether it would work for them. Some consulting firms have played a key role in facilitating benchmarking, and over time, have built up databases which enable an organisation to compare itself against aggregated data. Governments, on the other hand, have encouraged comparative benchmarking as a means of driving cultural change within workplaces, enabling their public sector agencies or private enterprises to understand better their own processes, and encouraging a strong external focus.

There has been increased research activity on benchmarking in higher education. The OECD initiated one project while another was sponsored by the European Commission. The latter initiative began in 2006, with a focus on using benchmarking more effectively to modernise European higher education management. The project is now reaching the end of its second phase, having moved in 2008 to a strong focus on implementation of better practices.[1] However, none of these projects or initiatives has paid attention specifically to questions of engagement, nor specifically to the regional context.

Benchmarking in PURE

Why use benchmarking as a method? The PURE project incorporated this resource partly to assist the key stakeholders *within* a region to explore their universities' current approach to regional engagement, and to provide a common language and framework for grounded comparison of university approaches to regional engagement *across* regions.

The higher education and the regions instruments were designed first and foremost as learning resources, to facilitate reflection and discussion both within institutions and comparatively about their current aspirations and arrangements, and how they might be enhanced. In this sense, the conversations were more important than the ratings themselves. The two instruments were quite discrete. One was designed for universities, with extensive experience behind it in the form of an instrument which had been used since 2002 to inform decision-making about third-stream funding by the HEFCE in the United Kingdom (see Charles and Benneworth 2002).

The other was for regions, a completely new instrument that was really treated as a prototype and was likely to require further development. The regional benchmarking was focused not on universities but on regions' own progress towards regional goals. The idea was that the resulting analysis would point to regional needs towards which universities could then target assistance. This has been confused with an alternative process, namely regional authorities rating their university(ies)' performance and practice.

The universities benchmarking instrument required stakeholders to self-assess their institutions' engagement across eight domains which research has shown to be important for developing regional competitiveness. These domains are shown in Table 10.1.

Table 10.1 Domains for benchmarking university engagement with regions (from Charles and Benneworth 2002)

Enhancing regional infrastructure	Community development processes
Human capital development processes	Cultural development processes
Business development processes	Promoting sustainability
Interactive learning and social capital development processes	Promoting engagement

Associated with each domain were a number of more specific areas of engagement on which people assessed performance by locating their institutions on a five point scale, using the indicators provided. Based on these ratings, judgements could be made about the institution's performance on each domain, and an overall profile of regional engagement produced which indicated those aspects where practice was strong and those where it was less so. The profiles could be compared with other local HEIs, and, perhaps more significantly, with benchmarking by regional authorities on these same domains.

'Engagement' spanned a wide range of different kinds of activities and contacts with the business community, public policy and service organisations, and community groups. These included formal institutional or departmental initiatives, problem-solving with local firms and agencies, participation in and support for public and community events, and ad hoc assistance offered by individuals with particular skills or interests. HEIs are large organisations, and it was unlikely that systematic appreciation of this range of engagement activity would be held in any one place.

Use of benchmarking instruments in the PURE regions

In many regions, it was a struggle to get the universities to participate fully in the benchmarking process. The Melbourne region, led by the project auspice, the Office of Knowledge Capital (an independent broker), was the first to make significant progress, and not without serious debate and firm assurances about confidentiality and how the results would be used.

Over time, most regions used the instruments one way or another, and typically with valuable learning. As an overview, a number of key insights have been derived from the benchmarking method.

Priority-setting

In a project like PURE, with multiple stakeholders and an agenda which seeks to link local projects with comparable interests and initiatives in divergent regional settings, there is a clear need to establish points of focus for bringing the parties together. Getting universities and regional stakeholders to become involved with the benchmarking required significant energy from the Regional Coordinating

Group (RCG) and especially the Regional Link Person but, once achieved, it provided a focus for discussion and priority-setting that proved important in generating subsequent project activities. A critical issue in many regions was the challenge of building sufficient trust in each other and in the process for participants to share their ratings with each other and to engage openly in the subsequent discussion. Formal commitment of confidentiality helped to achieve trust.

The instruments and implementation

The intent of the universities benchmarking instrument was that it focused on the contribution that the HEI made to the region, based as much as possible on reasonably objective criteria. In practice, that usually meant the criteria as viewed by a variety of different groups within the university. If a university did involve a diversity of internal people then a good debate might result; if only senior management took part, a degree of positive spin might result. It was more valuable if external stakeholders were involved in the exercise.

It became apparent that the instrument itself would benefit from ongoing refinement. The consistent message was the need to ensure simplicity, clarity and ease of use, especially in 'non-Anglo-Saxon' settings. It became apparent also that it was important to ensure quality assurance through not only the design of the benchmarking instrument, but a consistent methodology in application across a cohort of universities.

Through engaging with the key concepts, the response to the instrument in most regions was generally favourable. It was recognised as a resource which universities (and regions) could use for their own benefit, adapting the task to suit their own circumstances.

Not surprisingly with a prototype, some questions and answer options in the regional instrument were somewhat difficult to understand and/or to interpret due to local conditions. Again not surprisingly, the concepts in many questions were seen as representations of an Anglo-Saxon operating environment, instead of a large, public Welfare State model as in the Nordic countries.

The regional questionnaire was intended to indicate the areas of weakness in the region so that the universities could give priority to those aspects of regional development. If the regional tool indicated that the region was particularly weak on human capital and culture, then the region might expect the universities to make some efforts in those areas as identified through the HEI questionnaire. If the universities were performing poorly in those areas where the region was weak then there would be some clear policy recommendations and identified areas for intervention.

Difference in university practices and achievement

Many universities were concerned about how differences in ratings would be interpreted. Conceptually, the design of the instrument assumed that universities would perform differently, reflecting their own strategic priorities and their locations. Furthermore, it was anticipated that there would be significant contrast between those circumstances where there was a single university in a region (Värmland or Darling Downs), compared with 'multi-university' regions (such as Melbourne or Flanders, for example).

This has particular implications for the analysis and interpretation of the benchmarking data. The simple dictum to describe the PURE approach is: 'you can't compare, but you can share'. In the end, Melbourne was the only region to use a numerical template and produce a mean rating on each of the indicators which were covered in the benchmarking instrument. It was also the only region in which several institutions undertook the benchmarking twice, allowing some comparison across the two years. However, the differences in implementation in the various institutions mean that the data are indicative, rather than carrying numerical significance.

Melbourne's aggregated data were helpful in prompting discussion among the RCG members about the reasons why the universities did deliver the results which emerged. It was interesting also that more or less the same result was achieved across the two years, even when individual universities refined their rating method and fewer took part.

Regional aspirations and university priorities

The regional benchmarking instrument required regional stakeholders to consider their achievement in a number of areas that are central to regional development. In some settings, there was confusion over whether the instrument was designed to enable regions to offer their rating of the universities' engagement or the state of development in the region.

In Helsinki, the regional instrument was the focus rather than that for universities. The Helsinki RCG brought together a group of representatives from the cities and from regional development companies.

In Melbourne, the Victorian government provided an extensive body of formal reports, but found the political sensitivity which would have been associated with the rating element of the benchmarking to be rather difficult to manage. Two other regional stakeholders did complete the instrument, demonstrating reasonable consistency in their responses. Comparison of the regional ratings with the university ratings was also interesting, raising the question of whether the areas in which the regional stakeholders identified relative weakness could be seen as areas that should be priorities for the universities. Overall, the regional results in Flanders, Glasgow, Helsinki and Melbourne generated interesting discussion about the patterns in those regions, prompting a range of thoughts about potential opportunities for more effective engagement.

University strategy

The instrument provides extensive descriptors which assist an institution to explore carefully where its current performance is positioned, and whether its policy and strategic orientation supports effective regional engagement. In several universities, the process generated internal initiatives in which they refined their overall strategy to engagement.

Results in regional settings

Melbourne

All nine universities participated in the process in the first year, and five in the second. This provided some opportunity for identifying both patterns across the higher education sector and differences within it, and, following the second iteration, to do so with the benefit of a year's transition. Three regional stakeholders responded to the regional benchmarking instrument in the first year, one of which provided formal quantitative data, while two provided ratings as required by the instrument.

All of the Victorian universities bar one have their base in metropolitan Melbourne and multiple campuses, while three also have a strong provincial presence. As a simple summary, the results are shown in Table 10.2.

Table 10.2 University benchmarking in Melbourne

Indicator Groups	Mean ratings		Lowest ratings		Highest ratings	
	2009	2010	2009	2010	2009	2010
Enhancing regional infrastructure	3.3	3.6	2.5	2.8	2.8	4.2
Human capital development processes	3.7	3.9	3.4	3.8	3.8	4.3
Business development processes	3.0	3.2	1.6	2.6	3.8	3.5
Interactive learning and social capital development processes	3.4	3.6	2.6	3.1	3.9	4.0
Community development processes	3.7	3.6	3.2	2.9	4.3	4.5
Cultural development	3.0	3.1	1.7	2.6	3.7	3.7
Promoting sustainability	3.2	3.6	1.7	3.1	4.1	4.5
Promoting engagement	3.8	4.1	3.0	3.9	4.7	4.7

Note: Nine responses in 2009; four responses in 2010. Detail provided for information, not for statistical purposes.

In both years, the strongest ratings were given to the work of promoting engagement within the universities, and lesser scores to the other dimensions of contribution to regional development. This in itself was an intriguing finding which raised questions about the effectiveness or the orientation of the engagement focus.

With respect to the regional stakeholder benchmarking in 2009, the strongest ratings were given to cultural development, while enhancing regional infrastructure received the lowest rating. The relative ratings were:

- cultural development (4.9);
- human capital development processes (4.3);
- interactive learning and social capital development processes (3.9);

- business development processes (3.6);
- promoting engagement (3.5);
- promoting sustainability (3.5); and
- enhancing regional infrastructure (3.2).

Flanders, Belgium

The distinctive feature of the use of the instrument in Flanders was the adaptation of the instrument to an online format. Its design enabled the higher education institutions in Flanders to provide detailed, somewhat general but very grounded responses to each of the indicators. However, they did not provide specific rankings, making it difficult to get a clear picture of relative areas of strength in engagement. A number of institutions provided responses, providing a rich overview of the kinds of practices supported in different institutions.

It was hoped that the online version might be used in other regions which had been tardy in embracing the benchmarking activity. However, this did not eventuate.

Glasgow, UK

Initially, only the University of Glasgow provided an assessment (rather than ratings). Its assessment showed that human capital, business development and social capital processes were high-engagement priorities for Glasgow.

Its initiative led to five regional bodies, led by Skills Development Scotland, and six universities and colleges taking part. With support from the Glasgow PASCAL office, reports were prepared for each participating institution. All participants were invited to a seminar which explored the broader patterns in the data.

Whereas there was a generally high level of commitment to engagement from mission statements and from senior management, and a clear commitment to human capital, there was more variation across providers when it came to cultural and community development, and to business development. Sustainability was rated lowest.

Some interesting observations resulted from the Glasgow experience. PASCAL Associate, John Tibbett, observed that the distinctive profiles of each institution's engagement resulted from an interplay of regional, market and institutional factors. This suggested four different profiles of engagement:

1. Specialist institutions which engage on the basis of their specialised capability.
2. Regional institutions whose mission is shaped strongly by a commitment to engagement.
3. 'Short-cycle' colleges that are strong on regional needs in relation to human capital and community development.
4. Research-intensive universities which emphasise their international linkages as much as their regional identity.

The conversations prompted by benchmarking in Glasgow pointed to a number of engagement issues. These included:

- universities hold interesting views about how their international profile and linkages can have regional benefits;
- working effectively with SMEs continued to be a challenge;
- institutions differed in whether they sought to manage engagement from a central or a decentralised perspective;
- there continue to be greater opportunities for universities to contribute to business innovation; and
- Glasgow universities, like those in Melbourne, grappled with the challenge of 'co-opetition', finding ways to collaborate within the context of an environment in which they were also competitors.

Jämtland, Sweden

During the second CDG visit, both university and regional representatives realised that benchmarking could be useful within their organisations if an appropriate group of people were gathered. It became clear that there were some differences between the region's and the university's views on their cooperation and involvement in regional development. The benefit of the benchmarking was that it created discussion on each partner's view of things and some self-reflection.

Lesotho

In Lesotho, benchmarking was used as a basis for assessing the nature and extent of community service activity being undertaken. The university's involvement in community service was assessed across five levels. Level one indicated that the main form of activity was through isolated individuals 'acting from a mixture of altruism and desire to access resources'. Level three indicated 'Some institutional commitment but tends to be restricted to key departments and focused around core research roles'. Level five indicated 'Strong institutional commitment with wide-ranging involvement from across the University, including students. The University is a key stakeholder in the initiative and seeks to enrol other agencies and facilitate collaboration across traditional boundaries.'

On this basis the RCG was able to make some initial assessments about the current level of activity in the university. This could be broadly categorised under four headings: individual initiatives to set up community-based organisations (e.g. setting up a pre-school or self-help HIV/AIDS support group); departmental activities involving students in capacity-building or discipline-specific education projects (such as new farming techniques or family health assessment and diagnosis; Theatre for Development project); ad hoc involvement by departments when requested by external agents (such as participating in cultural activities, assisting in environmental policy formulation); and, finally, community-focused research (such as action research into learning support for vulnerable children; a survey of the financial activities of pension recipients). None of these activities was identified as multidisciplinary, though some were directly linked to teaching programmes. Their level, in benchmarking terms, therefore, ranged from level one to level three.

Gaborone, Botswana

The benchmarking tools were extremely helpful, albeit adapted to fit local situations. For example, they were useful:

- to identify the four areas for action in the PURE project;
- as a reference point when constructing data collection instruments for the self-reflection and needs assessment study; and
- as resource material for the stakeholders' workshops and research teams' training workshops.

Helsinki, Finland

Regional benchmarking was the focus of an expert discussion group in summer 2010. The other benchmarking tool, targeted at higher education institutes, was not used. The memo of the regional benchmarking discussion translated into Finnish, has been delivered to the board of a regional development company, Culminatum Ltd. These results might also have a role in future seminars or workshops concerning societal interaction between regions and HEIs.

The group evaluated especially the following four thematic topics: (1) understanding the region, (2) human capital development, (3) business development processes and (4) interactive learning and social capital. The conclusion was that the actors in the different fields in the region generally know each other well; centres of expertise and clusters were far advanced. However, the discussion revealed also that interaction among the different regional partners could be increased. This would make the grassroots level more visible in decision-making. It could also be possible to draw up a regional strategy for learning regions.

The following issues were seen as challenges: the small market, and high taxation and low wage level of executives as compared with international benchmarks. The education level of immigrants needs to be improved. It is also important to make it easier for immigrants to be recognised for their prior education and degrees. The discussions at Helsinki were a very good example also of how the instrument could prompt conversation and discussions which led into further initiatives.

Puglia, Italy

Puglia was slow to take an interest in benchmarking, and universities were very reluctant. In 2010 a dramatic change occurred and the universities, notably the 'naturally conservative' University of Bari, used the benchmarking instrument and found it valuable. It was almost a 'road to Damascus' experience. If the universities, Bari especially, can sustain momentum, the benefits will be important.

Conclusion

With the benefit of hindsight, the inclusion of benchmarking as such a key part of the PURE methodology was ambitious and was always going to be problematic. The diversity of regions, and of agendas and resources within those regions, posed considerable obstacles to the aim of being able to generate sufficient insights to share learning on a systematic and comprehensive basis.

Nevertheless, the experience in several regions has demonstrated that the instruments themselves have considerable potential to assist regions and universities to enhance their understanding of opportunities for greater engagement. This indicates something of the enthusiasm of both university and regional stakeholders to use a resource which provides them, at the very least, with opportunities for reflection on their own arrangements and practice, and for seeing how the experiences of others might be useful.

Three key principles seem to be essential in the ongoing implementation of benchmarking, as a general strategy by universities. These are:

1. Developing trust among the participants is crucial to achieving the commitment to use the instrument, and to engage fully in the subsequent discussion of the analysis.
2. The value is not just in the 1–2 year application through the PURE project, but ongoing application as part of self-assessment and continuous improvement.
3. One of the key values of benchmarking is the emphasis on data and on evidence-based examples of good practice to assist in communication of university contribution and engagement.

Of course, in the current stage of development of the methodology, the process has relied heavily on the self-perceptions of stakeholders and participants, whether in the universities or the regional authorities. Where the benchmarking has been implemented with serious intent, the issue of self-perception has been a strength, insofar as it has engendered a degree of commitment on the part of the stakeholders, and hence some commitment to subsequent action.

With the benefit of the experience of the past few years, it seems likely that this method requires more than the two years nominally available for the PURE project. It takes time to build the level of trust among partners for genuine sharing of data and then to have one's ratings scrutinised, given the possible reflection on performance. However, once the trust develops, it is clear that fruitful conversations can occur. With regional stakeholder benchmarking, it seems that there could be useful scope for regional representatives to share their ratings and to explore the reasons for the difference.

The chapters in Part II have provided an overview of the experience and the learning in PURE regions. Facilitating learning within universities and regions has been a key theme of this final chapter, which has suggested that 'learning' rather than audit is the valuable dimension of efforts at benchmarking across the higher education sector. In the next and final part of this volume, we return more generally to questions of learning and engagement, policy and practice, for universities and for regional authorities.

Note

1 See www.educationbenchmarking.org/projectbackground. html (last accessed 14 December 2012).

PART III

Learning and partnership processes
– wider policy reflections

11

The PURE Project and inter-regional learning

Introduction – the nature and spread of learning

The universal talent for learning was assumed by the organised community many eras ago to belong in part beyond the family group. Schooling began as organised learning required by the young. It was extended over time through young and into early adult years. Informally in recent centuries, and in formal and at times mandatory ways more recently, it has extended through much of the lifespan to include the education and training of adults; in their own interest, and in a wider, often political and economic, interest. This recognition and evolution is celebrated and rationalised as the *lifelong learning* of the individual.

Learning occurs in many places and ways unfamiliar to classrooms, teachers' colleges, even university departments of education. It includes the learning that takes place in individuals' heads, hearts and skill-sets as they work and live, self-employed or paid through organisations, and in civic regional and community settings. It also includes the learning and resultant changed behaviour that can happen in and by those organisations, communities, and systems of governance and administration. Indeed, whole cities and regions are now said to learn, hence the expressions *learning cities, communities and regions*. This very notion may arouse alarm and anxiety in those who value traditions of liberal individualism and are watchful of any collectivity that appears to invest man-made structures with animate powers, or elevate structures above people.

Liberal individualism can be two-edged: individuals are blamed in an econom-ically 'free and competitive' neo-liberal era for failing, for not learning and getting on by their own efforts. It is as if being a 'learning society' absolves governments and nations from an interest in education, from responsibility for breakdown in the social structure, from the collapse of social inclusion with its attendant ills (see Wilkinson and Pickett 2010). Access to formal education and training and their credentials remains an important public responsibility.

Ultimately learning may be a private matter in each person's head and heart, something on which brain research is beginning to throw new light. Its conse-quences when applied will produce different understanding and new behaviour. At the collective level of a society, an organisation or a region, changes in planning, administration, management, self-evaluation, appraisal and performance are indicators of what is being learned and applied; whether from unprompted self-initiation or, more commonly, in response to changing circumstances. Either may mean new methods and new directions of governance. High-quality governance, 'high on learning', is required if regions are to seize opportunities and shoulder responsibilities in demanding and dangerous times. This is *the new imperative*.

This chapter takes stock of the learning that has taken place through the PURE project, by the partner organisations and regions themselves. There may be lessons having wider applicability: learning includes being able to distinguish what is so particular and unique that it cannot be generalised from lessons having wider application. We begin with the lead partner, PASCAL, before considering what learning may have occurred in and by the regions. We can describe with some confidence what came to light for different parties, and perhaps associate some changes of conduct directly.

Learning for PASCAL – intermediaries and animateurs, impact and appraisal

The international non-governmental organisation that conducted the PURE project is a civil society third sector networking body not yet ten years old: a child of the twenty-first century sharing space with other bodies, both governmental (IGOs) and non-governmental, commercial and private sector. It has some characteristics of the think-tank that has proliferated in these sectors. Like many bodies across and between all three sectors it includes elements of not-for-profit consultancy, in an area where large international companies play a dominant part, and small operators including ex-public servants and former academic scholars, at times collaboratively, jostle for space and business. It is a strongly networked organisation relying on modern communication technologies to manage its affairs and to do its visible work. It was created as and continues to be an 'observatory', giving special attention to the website as a means of sharing knowledge and understanding.

PURE was seen and developed as participatory Mode Two knowledge production. PASCAL and the regions and universities taking part were to collaborate, sharing common learning objectives and setting in addition their own separate agendas: learning from one another through different modes within the PURE project; periodically evaluating what had been done; and generalising what could be learned and shared with others in the PURE network and beyond.

The dimensions of PASCAL learning considered here draw mainly on feedback from the 'client' regions gathered a year after the initial two-year term was over. They address mainly what it means in practice to be an intermediary networking, brokerage and boundary-spanning agency. The PASCAL PURE work was contract-based. This created a dual identity for regions and their HEIs. They were clients in a quasi-consultancy, as well as partners in participatory action research. Some aspects of these identities and of the narrative of the project are particular and accidental to PURE and the way it was managed. Others are more widely shared – 'chronic', and characteristic of such intermediary, brokerage and animation networking generally. A particular and serious characteristic is the short contract duration of almost all such work, manifestly unsuited to the slow process of learning leading to embedded cultural change essential for sustained development.

PASCAL and the regions – lessons from PURE

Part II gave a sense of the several policy areas that featured most strongly in the project; the regions taking part chose them collectively and prioritised them individually. Any claims about their contribution to public understanding of these policy areas would be made cautiously. Part II does, however, indicate their meaning to different regions and their HEIs, and how they are considered and addressed in places with different histories and attributes in different continents and contexts. Here attention shifts to the conduct of projects and processes that may assist the sharing and analysis of experience to lead to action. It is approached in the spirit of learning, as much from failures as from success.

The processes used in PURE were described in the introduction to the project in Chapter 5. Although they were interwoven and influenced one with another, they are separated here for easier understanding.

CDG peer reviewing and reviewers

The groups that normally made two three-day visits to a region a year apart were called Consultative Development Groups. A few weeks after the review visit they presented the region with a draft regional visit review report (RVR 1 and 2). This report was discussed and revised prior to finalisation for general use and follow-up action: first within the region, subsequently by the full PURE network of participants via periodic international meetings and through the website.

Preparation entailed the region's main project leader, host and link person to PASCAL managing the preparation of two background information and briefing papers for the first visit, and normally an update paper prior to the second. It was also meant to include the creation of some kind of local cross-sector steering group. The main project partners in the region would thus share some understanding of the project and its possible benefits, and some common purpose and commitment to the work and its outcomes. This preparatory team-building work was very good in some places, rudimentary in some others, and inadequate in one or two.

The lesson is that impatience and time saved here may cost delay, frustration and poor comprehension further down the way, as the project proceeds and time commitments are required of the parties in the region. One difficulty was the arm's-length and necessarily trust-based form of the region–PASCAL contract partnership. Another was the need to use a window of opportunity when it opened to get the project agreed and started before new obstacles arose. This meant taking on trust that other parties were indeed appraised and involved. In a few places it took most of the two-year life of the project to get all parties to the point of common understanding and interest – ready really to begin almost only as time expired. In some cases, the opportunity to continue was then thwarted by the resource drought of the GFC. For a majority of regions the GFC was a serious blow to the project; for a few it was felt not to have had significant effect on this work so far.

Most regions valued the CDG visits for creating links, strengthening and altering existing ones, and promoting ideas for joint action within the region. Usually the visit was followed by a regional action plan, one focus for the follow-up CDG visit a year later. Pressure of time and scarcity of resources were common concerns; in a few cases a region sought a different CDG review member, or expressed concern about too-academic language. A main success derived from the selection of CDG participants. Where possible these were drawn from among people with relevant expertise in other regions participating in PURE. Direct *in situ* working contact over several days greatly assisted the building of inter-regional links. Sometimes sustained and apparently abiding contact and exchange followed with other regions not always similar in demography and socio-economic profile.

Simply aggregating the number in each team and grossing these up for all the CDG visits, there were in total 130 CDG team members. Many were involved in both visits to a region. Several central PASCAL members were also multiple reviewers; six of the most active seven members were from a participating region. At the time a number of other regions were considering joining or had entered negotiations with PASCAL to do so. In the end they did not, mostly because of GFC-related and other resource constraints. Fourteen CDG review member-visits were from these regions, and eighty from participating regions. Only 36 of the total of 130 were therefore not in a participating or intending region. The term 'peer reviewer' was thus well justified; the practice helped to build multiple strands into the PURE network.

Periodic whole-project planning, review and synthesis events

International meetings were held periodically throughout the project. Workshops at Pécs in 2007, Limerick in 2008, in Vancouver in 2009, and Ostersund and Gaborone in 2010 were in association with the main all-PASCAL international conferences. Others in Glasgow in 2008 for conceiving and co-planning, and Brussels in 2010 and again in May 2011, were exclusively about PURE as part of the planning and review work of the project. These face-to-face events were particularly valued by those able to take part, and important for locating particular 'local stories' on a wider geographical and conceptual map in non-competitive mutual learning.

The newer media – e-mediated learning

Naturally enough, much of the inter-regional learning as well as learning on the part of PASCAL itself used e-mail, group discussion, conference calls and above all the PASCAL website to learn and exchange experience, as well as to plan the work. Even in the short period of time between initial exploratory PURE planning in 2007 and the slow-down in PURE activity during 2011, the social media made huge strides. The PASCAL website began making use of Twitter and Facebook, but the take-up was too late to contribute significantly to PURE.

The importance of these media and especially of the PASCAL Observatory's website was demonstrated by the disruption caused when the site needed a main overhaul midway through the project. In particular the anyway premature effort to activate policy-focused specialist clusters, featured as themes of Chapters 6–9, suffered seriously. Vulnerability to virtual communications failure, and the urge to press too much activity into too little time, and before client-participants are ready, are probably common to many such short-cycle development and R&D projects. This, and the cost of under-preparedness by some regions which were hurried prematurely into making a start, were important lessons learned by PASCAL.

Benchmarking

PASCAL brought expert knowledge and experience of benchmarking the engagement of universities with their communities and regions into PURE. The project also had the opportunity to test and use a new tool designed for PURE to benchmark the behaviour of regions in engaging with higher education. This work is explained, analysed and placed in the context of the recently grown and still changing 'audit culture' in the previous chapter. PASCAL rightly judged that competitive benchmarking with ranking subsequently shared and made public would cause anxiety and meet resistance. Initially, indeed, it was met with a coolness at times approaching hostility, despite the repeated emphasis that it was to be seen and used only by those who were benchmarking themselves. It was to be a tool for learning and voluntary self-improvement, allowing an institution or region to build its own critical self-profile and, if it wished, to repeat the exercise periodically to see where and what change had occurred. It was for institutional self-learning locally rather than for inter-regional, or inter-HEI, exchange.

Some regions devised more user-friendly systems for using the lengthy schedule, or otherwise adapted the tools better to serve their ends. The PURE network then became a vehicle for regions and HEIs which chose to report and exchange experience, not so much of the findings but about the processes and the benefits of using it. With time, other universities elsewhere, and then several regions, became more interested, took heart and used the tools themselves. A post-project review a year on showed that some regions and HEIs still had aspirations to use one or both tools later, well outside the project period. A few also intended to repeat it later, to gain a longitudinal picture of progress. Given more time, more benefit would follow as regions and their HEIs bring together two sets of findings and thereby identify gaps and opportunities to extend what was being done. The lesson for PASCAL was again that such ideas need time for regions and institutions to get used to the idea, exchange views and news, and come at their own pace to taking something up.

A different kind of outcome, new learning and new practice, is implicit in this. However, it requires energy and resources not currently available. This would be to refine and further test tools for both universities and especially regions, building on feedback from PURE and making them more widely available for others to use and to build on. This would be in the collaborative and non-competitive 'developmental' mode employed by PURE to learn and enhance good engagement practice, rather than for external comparison, competing with others.

Meanwhile several other agencies are exploring and testing related questions. Mostly these are less about broad-based engagement than about ways of measuring and comparing the impact of university research and its contribution via dissemination to development, whether local or global. The drive comes from a rampant audit culture and a demand to show value for money; and from the competitive context of national and global rating and ranking of universities, over which fierce controversy has recently built up.

'Good practice exemplars'

When PURE was planned and launched, the initial set of ideas included building up and sharing, via the website and perhaps a manual, a dossier of 'exemplars of good practice in engagement'. Specifically a precise and easily used electronic template system might be adopted to record such examples. This was not pursued; a number of the CDG reports (the documents RVR 1 and 2 on the PASCAL website) call attention to different kinds of good practice in engagement from region to region. As the project, along with its ongoing adaptive management proceeded, it came to be felt that such a compendium could be fruitless or worse in terms of its utility.

Ultimately the view prevailed that any such process and product was likely to fall between two traps. A simplified space-bound set of snapshots would be largely bereft of the context which is vital for adequate understanding of the example. An analytical account with an adequate explanation of the context and circumstances would be too tediously long and detailed for the busy practitioners for whom it would be intended, to study and use. Behind this decision lies an equally important if less obvious difficulty. If such a practice were adopted it would nourish a false belief, giving a misleading sense of what inter-regional and international network learning means, and of where it can be of value and where positively harmful. It risks being taken to imply that there is one best way of doing something, irrespective of the complex legion of particular circumstances that make the example unique, and probably non-replicable in any literal sense.

PURE reminded PASCAL what it already knew from immediate experience and wider knowledge: that differences of history, tradition and culture as well as immediate political and economic circumstances, opportunities and constraints frequently make it hard to communicate well, to understand fully and so to learn effectively, between continents, countries, and even local regions within one country. Dissociated from time and place, apparently general examples of how to do things successfully may not transfer but instead mislead.

Inter-regional networking

Encompassing the different contractual arrangements between PASCAL and each region taking part in PURE, there remains a broader PASCAL meta-agenda: that of fostering international as well as, in the case of PURE, inter-regional learning in the connected policy arenas of place, social capital and learning, as well as mutuality between the worlds of academe and policy-making. Providing rich data in the twenty-first century information-rich Internet era is not difficult. Making it relevant and useful is another matter. Central to this is creating self-sustaining communities of interest and practice that put knowledge to use. This central intent is shared by many major agencies and projects including many conceived and funded by the EU.

In this sense the experience has been important and illuminating: at times a 'syllabus of errors'; at others more encouraging of success. It was hoped to build an innovative and ongoing learning culture in and between the partner regions, such that learning and exchange would continue beyond the life of the project. Such an aspiration calls for perhaps a ten-year timeframe rather than the two to three years represented here.

In formal and contractual terms follow-up beyond the two-year initial project life has been disappointing. Few regions took up the opportunity to make a new contract and continue into a third year: partly because this was not foreshadowed, and therefore not so clearly framed; partly because of the changed global and local fiscal and economic climate. The idea of a distinct, new and separate, cohort of PURE regions rolling on behind the initial fourteen collapsed in this new environment. Three later starters therefore tagged onto the original group along with one of these that needed to defer while local circumstances evolved. (Of these three one was very active and one moderately so, while the third dropped out part-way through.) A reasonable speculation is that for all its expertise and adaptability to local circumstances, PASCAL as a minimally formalised INGO lacked the authority and status of the OECD, which was able to continue with a new cohort of regions pursuing different and well-established track.

Other activities – the invisible iceberg

On the other hand, much has happened by way of ongoing networking through and often outside of what appears on the PASCAL website, among a majority of the PURE regions. Often this is through the main principals in the universities concerned as well as the regional authorities in PURE. Whereas the specialised web-based cluster dimension of the work was premature and disappointing, a range of interactive networking tools have been trialled and are becoming more widely used on the website. Some promise to play much the part that the PURE clusters were seen as playing, with users from PURE regions in evidence in this and other kinds of ongoing networking. This includes opportunistic and locally initiated reciprocal visits between regions.

To conclude this brief scan of what may have been learned by taking part in PURE: network-building has achieved an important success. It has located and animated significant numbers of scholars and practitioners who connect, often not through one of the PASCAL offices but directly between one another. This is indeed a network, rather than spokes of a centralised wheel. How many and what kinds of other exchanges and additional spin-off activities occur, often opportunistically, is unknown; likewise the volume of phone, skype and email traffic among those who met through PURE. As with much work of this kind, what quantum and what sustaining effect and value remain are evasively immeasurable by any kind of meaningful quantitative audit.

A note of caution about learning from others and 'finishing the job' is also in order. A report prepared for the HEFCE in 2010 comparing the 'knowledge exchange systems' of the United States and the United Kingdom concluded that because of the influence of diverse 'internal and external contextual factors' and different legacies there was no convergence on the most efficient organisational models. Community engagement enjoyed higher status in the US than in UK universities and the role of universities in local and regional economic development was better recognised, thanks partly to the land grant legacy and the power and resources of the States in that federal system. UK universities however gave greater recognition via promotions and assessment criteria: 'there is unlikely to be a model of best practice, but rather, the evolution of the system requires a process of learning from the experiences of others in similar circumstances' (HEFCE 2010, p. 32).

More bluntly, Swanson notes the decay globally as well as in the United States of community service or third mission in the absence of institutional incentives and rewards, even among the land grant institutions; rewards are for research and teaching. Universities have become 'islands of higher education' in their regions; in the PURE Northern Illinois region economic development officials had no expectation of universities: 'if they got some help that would be great'. Swanson considers engagement to be an ongoing and never-ending work-in-progress (personal communication, 2 September 2010).

Benefit to the regions

Much of the previous section about lessons learned is also of direct relevance for regions. Many of the dynamics involved in inter-regional collaboration appear to be common, so similar cautions would apply to involvement in other projects. As to sustainability, it is early to know how far efforts expended in the work will continue to influence understanding and behaviour. Two years is too short a time to prompt and embed cultural change within the different parties and their forms of partnership. The trust required for such work to become continuing, natural and automatic builds up over perhaps five or ten years. Värmland region in Sweden has been purposefully involved in such processes for a decade, and it is still developing the work, seeing new changes and benefits arise as it becomes normalised practice.

PASCAL's simple follow-up inquiry a year after the close of the main project period tried to appraise what has been gained in each region. The majority replied openly and with specific comments. Eleven regions reported some change as a result of joining PURE. However, three regions qualified this as being modest in scale; another two reported no discernible ongoing change as a result. One region had the work aborted because the region itself was disbanded following a change of central government: 'there is now no skills partnership of any description'. A non-responding region in the same country experienced too little involvement and too much stress, both political and post-GFC, even to reply. For the latest-starting region it was too early yet to say.

Some extracts illustrate the kinds of changes reported, and the limitations that some suffered. In the case of the Värmland region mentioned above, which has sustained such work via projects for a decade, PURE contributed to the politicians and the university management 'gaining the courage to stick to the strategies of the innovative clusters' such as the OECD project had recommended back in 2004–06. Other regions reported gaining attention and shared interests for engagement; and in another case 'especially in terms of regional partnership by the new "professional" universities. New work was done, and already good relations much strengthened'. It made another region and university talk to each other, with regular meetings several times a year; 'the extension has led to things actually happening as well'. Somewhere else 'as an external catalyst PURE expanded informal relationships and allowed a long-term working group to be set up'.

For the first time in one southern European region, 'the universities met to discuss issues related to the benchmarking activity and to their third mission role … The discussion and analysis between the three universities resulted in a deeper and more structured awareness'. In another 'both universities' formal regional relations have become more intensive and programme-oriented, mutually with their sub-regions'.

Elsewhere 'the process and dialogue are ongoing;[1] in another case 'it was part of the factors which initiated other things, such as the creation of a regional programme for lifelong learning'. Another region reports as an 'accidental benefit' the project timing: a delay to project completion meant that the concluding stages of the PURE project aligned with other relevant policy developments, allowing findings from the PURE project to be used in supporting responses to two policy documents. In another instance 'a set of policy/project proposals was still with the Minister which might yet lead to a concrete initiative to further develop collaboration'.

Not all accidents were fortuitous. In three modulations of disappointment, there was in the first 'unlucky timing (an ongoing crisis in the university) – the project is really timely and needed nationally and continentally, but [it was] not engaged and embedded at a high political level, and over-dependent on one person who left'. Elsewhere 'the work improved partnership and informal cooperation, but failed to involve those at the top on both sides'. In a third region the work was 'less relevant on the regional side: all the activities were interrupted after a good start because of the local Government change'; 'it was impossible to share the results on a larger scale'. The vulnerability to accidents of changing regional as well as national politics and changes of personnel was echoed more recently in a Nordic region. Despite strong commitment by both region and university to continue into a fourth year, without consultation or briefing, new leadership unexpectedly determined that further involvement should cease.

Here are some examples of more qualified and limited gains, with reasons for them. 'Certainly greater appreciation of the role of universities and unfulfilled opportunities for cooperation (it reinforced recognition of the significance of universities); but the opportunities were not pursued because of the competitiveness of the HEIs and limited resources within government.' 'There were specific actions, but these are hard to identify system-wide.' 'It was a catalyst to open up and improve dialogue, but it was not mainstreamed into the work and jobs of the regional authority, and suffered with changes of personnel – too dependent on a few key people.' The phrase 'too dependent on a few key people' was echoed in the same or similar words several times.

To conclude with the point made above about ongoing networking, a year after the project formally ended (and sooner in reality): it is too early to say with vigour how far this networked community of practice will continue; and how far each region will be able to sustain the intentions formed during the time of the project.

Problems and barriers, routes towards solutions

The previous section noted difficulties in the way of purposeful interventions for building region–HEI engagement. Barriers are commonly categorised in three ways: the conduct of national governments, of regional administrations and of universities (or occasionally of higher education more widely; see OECD 2007 and the reports by the OECD on different individual regions). Barriers to inter-regional learning are an alternative issue to this. Another dimension is the variable resistance to or energy for engaging, in relation to different policy arenas. In some, universities may have more that they can obviously offer, and more confidence and prospect of benefit by being involved in the region. Medicine for example has long needed and used the region's communities as an important laboratory. On the other side, public authorities may be more interested in what technology and science have to contribute than in the contribution of the social sciences and humanities, with the exception perhaps of economics and management. In some subject areas private consultants may be seen as more relevant and successful.

As work within PURE well illustrates, problems and barriers include, prominently and partly unpredictably, accidents of changed administrations and new political orientations, national or regional, following an election. Another serious problem is changes in the personnel and personalities who play key leadership roles on all sides, whether as enthusiasts or as obstacles. External crises also play a part – from the GFC to less universal matters. The pressure of the GFC-related and 'small government' policies squeezed people and resources in a number of the PURE regions, and prevented others from joining. For some, participation in PURE and almost all other local constructive initiatives, let alone inter-regional learning, became almost impossible as a sense of crisis prevailed.

126

Some crises including global warming may generate new awareness and urgency about threats and problems that motivate parties to get together in a more systematic and sustained way. For example, the imminence of massively expanded and greatly altered mining (from hard coal to coal seam gas extraction) in South-West Queensland creates new needs and opportunities for a different order of engagement in that region. The solution is simple in principle. It is to embed acceptance and practice of engagement between HEIs and regional administrations, and across the diversity of stakeholders, so thoroughly that they become second nature. Bringing this about takes a lot of time and patience; it has to overcome deeply ingrained habits, stereotypes, and perceptions or misperceptions of self-interest and, more seriously still, of values.

Low confidence, low self-expectation and a disinclination to take an ambitious and long-term view of its own capacity and potential to make a difference may seriously inhibit what a regional administration will attempt. The resulting sense of caution, low trust and defensiveness makes for hesitancy about taking anything that might seem like a risk, or requires trust in unknown or untested partners. This was exemplified in PURE by caution over benchmarking, and fear that the results might be used to compare and punish the region in comparing it with others' performance. This reluctance was less evident among universities, other than possibly in terms of anxiety about discomforting internal comparison, and the sheer time and effort required to do the work properly.

One might expect resistance to international collaboration on engagement, especially in more insular and inward-looking countries, from a view that it would be irrelevant – a 'not-invented-here' tendency to believe that we already know and can do best, the opposite attitude to low self-confidence. There was little evidence of this in PURE, since, as is common to such projects, the regions chose to take part. It might, however, be a factor inhibiting the rolling out of the results of such work to the less innovative; whether they are more cautious about novelty or more confident that they have nothing to learn. More simply, the sheer effort of getting to understand what is different elsewhere can put people off at an early stage, especially if they are not often exposed to different ways of thinking and doing. It is in fact a good way to understand one's own situation better and see what is taken for granted. The cultural dissonance can however be great.

High risk aversion can combine with a tendency under stress to revert to the familiar. Then insularity and xenophobia may triumph, with political conservatism and tightly controlled top-down politically managed change. There may also be prejudicial assumptions about where to look in terms of what kind of region in what kind of country might be relevant and worth a look. PURE demonstrated that some of the strongest inter-regional learning was on the face of it unlikely, counter-intuitive.

The project made evident unequal interest and enthusiasm between partners in some regions. This was partly explicable as shown above, because of haste to start the clock running for the two-year contract period before the opportunity slipped away; and before some significant stakeholders and potentially important partners had become adequately involved and committed to the idea. Funds to pay for the contract came from different sources, and the local link persons and drivers also varied, not always in line with this. This can affect local energy, resources and direction.

In several regions the initiative and leadership were within a university. These had varying success in engaging the region at a sufficiently senior level: very little in some, rather more but still with hesitancy in others. Where the region was the main sponsor and funding partner, the opposite applied: some universities were actively involved from the outset, slow-starting in others, coming fully on board only after two years but continuing to develop the partnership. In one instance the cost was met in full from central government and the project managed from within a prestigious university. Here energy was used to good effect to engage sub-regional authorities as well as the weaker whole-region authority. At the end central political changes led to loss of interest and support, along with dismantling of the weak regional structure itself. Sub-regional engagement with two different universities however continued.

Some obstacles arose from the particular standing and approach of PASCAL as an INGO. The level of direct involvement both in the regional administration and in their HEIs varied: from an occasional courtesy contact with its head at the outset to deeper and more sustained interest and involvement throughout; from the senior political leadership in one region to the administrative head of the ministry responsible for transparency and civic participation in another; and from a token meeting with the rector or vice-chancellor in one university to sustained direct interest in others. PASCAL's NGO status undoubtedly limited the formal standing of the project and its capacity to guarantee the most senior representation by all main parties, compared with the OECD. The skills and staying power of 'second-level' personnel were however vital to the level of impact and practical involvement of the parties in each set of cases.

Some other difficulties also related in part to PASCAL's particular standing and approach, including paradoxically, given its explicitly participatory action research stance, an expectation occasionally that PASCAL should act as a consultant expert and spell out the answers. Inter-governmental organisations tend to be cautious in giving direct guidance and advice, whereas private consultancies expect and are expected to speak more firmly as experts. On the other hand, a positive element that tended to grow as the project proceeded was recognition of the abiding importance of big complex and critical issues requiring long-term integrative planning. If this is grasped regions and indeed HEIs will be more likely to develop a different planning and governance culture, and practices in which engagement is normalised and embedded. Such an approach means, in the old adage, teaching a family to fish so that it can feed itself for life compared with giving it a fish that lasts a day.

The PURE experience shows that action-oriented intervention intended to lead to continuing engagement, as favoured also by the EU, requires committed and stable leadership. It also needs the continuing facilitation on all sides of 'boundary-spanners' who are able to hear and share the language and culture, aspirations and concerns of other parties in the region. Low trust derives from unfamiliarity, often reinforcing stereotypes that obstruct working well together.

A short time allows only so much to be achieved; but it may enable parties to make short-term commitments, the experience of which builds confidence from success in this time. They may then be able to look to a longer period, with a longer-term agenda that assists culture change. Confidence can be built cumulatively through collaboration and tangible gains; it is tactically sound to gather and display low-hanging fruits that encourage wider affiliation to such an approach. It may be sensible to 'play the edge of the board', make small local gains, nurture a groundswell, and trigger a benevolent cycle of cooperation within and between the main organisations.

A number of more obvious solutions to engaging HEIs and regions are well documented in the work of the OECD. The role of national governments and the constraints that they place on effectively devolved regional decision-taking are widely evident (see Chapter 12). Some require new legislation, some a change to cumbersome and interfering bureaucratic control. This may derive from low trust and an urge to micro-manage; or from older and deeper fear of national fragmentation if regions gain too much power and move in diverse directions.

Other and newer aspects of the contemporary regional predicament, shared widely if not universally, are less easy to deal with. Global connectivity can help, through inter-regional learning and the example of others' successes, to induce change at home. However the sheer remoteness and inaccessibility of supernational power, especially the power of corporate industrial, commercial and fiscal interests, is daunting. In the GFC era even national governments appear powerless and half-paralysed; control seems to slip away, to visible agencies like the credit-rating agencies, and to more shadowy power-brokers. Regions need to stick at a long, locally embedded game in an increasingly short-sighted as well as global era; to be flexible and pragmatic in connecting and learning globally; and to continue to recognise, trust and build on local 'indigenous' strengths as special or unique assets.

Conclusion

Inter-regional learning is a powerful means to become more informed and better able to govern locally, using inter-institutional engagement with HE and across and between all three 'sectors'. It has become easier with ever-faster, more sophisticated and user-friendly ICT. The PURE processes and outcomes, despite limitations and severe disruption by forces located outside the region and often too the nation, show the potential gain from international networking and shared activities. Globalisation is seemingly unstoppable, and often destructive. It can however be combated, or turned to advantage. University chief executives and governors can choose to resist rather than adopt the narrow performance criteria used to rank them in world tables that interfere with sensible and fittingly autonomous planning. The same applies to ministries of higher education and their national governments. Regions suffer in identity and status, and from resource deprivation and uncertainty caused by central governments. They can gain influence and power deriving from confidence and success if they play a long game, building on local assets and using whatever room for manoeuvre national governments and other outside forces leave.

A different kind of question concerns not capacity and confidence, but purpose, direction and ethics in engagement. This is considered more directly in the final chapter.

12

Regions, central government power and policy-making

Central policies and vertical authority

The engagement of regions with local higher education institutions implies that those responsible for regional administration have the will and ability to choose partnership. The reality of government power however is such that the degrees of freedom to make and sustain collaborative arrangements are often severely limited: circumscribed by attitudes and policies, political and bureaucratic practices that prevent and frustrate. On the other hand central government can also facilitate. This applies also to regionally based higher education institutions in the context of national HE policies and systems. Whereas regional administrations may be able to create or take part in horizontal relations as partners, albeit within a legislative, regulatory and financial framework set by the state, the reality of hierarchical governmental relations is often very unequal difference in power and authority; the wishes and whims of central government can hamper or prevent engagement within the region.

What can regional administrations do to win from central government the space and resources needed to lead and manage development, sustaining partnership with their cohabiting stakeholders, especially the institutions of higher education? Merely to ask the question points to the difficulty in generalising across continents and countries about this vital relationship. Wilkinson and Pickett well illustrate the diversity and patterns in equilibrium between phenomena in different places and at different times (2010, pp. 131–132 and periodically throughout). There is usually a rough logic and familiarity in the principal division of responsibilities, power and resources between the national and the main regional level. Essential national policies, directions and frameworks are controlled centrally – foreign affairs and security, national budgetary, financial and currency powers and responsibilities. The execution of many other policies and service delivery are commonly delegated to regional and more local levels. Usually there are several levels, with one or more intermediate and lower sub-regional levels of devolution down to the village, parish or commune, in a hierarchical cascade.

The vertical arrangement of governance is often complex and also unstable. It varies greatly around the world and over time in any one place. Central government may relate directly to levels lower than the main region, delegating and funding to different government levels and even to individual institutions in the public and private sectors. It may direct that different methods of appointing or electing and organising regional governments must be adopted; or that a responsibility like policing be removed from regional or city general administration and managed separately. It may move duties up or down between levels: not just between centre and region but between regions and sub-regions, or even from or to more local levels. It may decide to abolish a whole level of government, or to amalgamate or disaggregate at regional and other levels. Where such changes occur, the power to raise revenues and the transfer of central revenue to different levels of administration may or may not follow in equal measure.

In short, as shown in Chapter 3, regional administration is often uncertain, unstable and undermined by interventionist governments, especially where there are centralising tendencies. The relationship with central government is one of unequal power, although two qualifications are needed here. Unequal power does not rule out sustained constructive partnership – 'engagement' between central state and region. More obviously, constitutional arrangements vary between countries. 'The region' may have powerful and assured autonomy in important matters, with a presumption of residual powers favouring the region, much as the principle is held to protect national freedoms within the European Union. In some situations, populist pressure has advanced the cause of regional power even in the face of central opposition.

Central governments and devolution – the PURE project

Among the essentially eclectic and unplanned set of regions that took part in PURE, some were from federal systems. Here the often large and wealthy 'region' of the state in Australia and the USA, likewise in Germany along with the province in Canada in some of the OECD studies, has significant constitutionally assured powers. It can negotiate from a position of relative strength. The PURE regions are diverse. Not all align tidily with formal administrative regions. Their experience can provide quite particular insight into central–regional relations, how these may be obstacles rather than of help to HE–region engagement, and what can be done to ameliorate the situation. The PURE study may indeed suggest that for some purposes 'regions' not matching the constitutional and administrative arrangement of government have advantages for higher education in engaging local–regional development. For individual universities the place, communities and organisations with which it links and does business may not correspond at all closely to a regional authority.

In reality the logical division of governance and executive responsibilities may be overridden by pressing political calculations and concerns. The Thames Gateway special–purpose development authority, an interestingly different UK PURE region sitting across the regular structure of city and local government in the east London and upper Thames estuary area, fell victim to a change of national government and was dismantled. At the same time the nine regular English RDAs, one of which, for the North-East of England, was part of the earlier OECD round of studies, were also abolished. An earlier re-organisation saw two counties in the old English government structure overlapping Gateway have their main towns excised for administrative purposes, while the governance of London was altered in favour of a directly elected and influential mayor.

A Canadian Province or an American or Australian State would not have such matters directed and managed by federal government. However, many of these jurisdictions may be too large to function well as single regions for some aspects of engaging higher education in social and economic development, although the massive California State higher education system may be thought to give the lie to this. Effective engagement and development require intimate connection attuned to the needs and opportunities of locally anchored (sub-) regions. The CDG teams that visited the PURE regions of Puglia in Italy and Melbourne in Australia, regions each small compared with California, recognised viable sub-regions with different sets of HE relationships. Often encompassing several local government authorities with a particular place identity, relationships with local universities are sustained by means of many different local contacts, agreements and mechanisms.

What has been said so far applies to regional governance and devolution in general, and to the effects of different national policies for higher education's engagement in regional development planning. Similarly, national policies affect whether, how and how far HEIs can act as good or poor regional partners. The rest of this chapter considers general matters to do with central–regional relations and devolution, then examines the impact and influence of different policies for and approaches to engaging with higher education.

General lessons and particular examples – different kinds of regions

Values and philosophies change over time as well as differing between countries. Constitutional and administrative law and practice may move towards tighter central direction, or favour more devolved government, to relatively autonomous regions in the case of Spain. They may come to favour more or less civic participation and partnership across public, private and civil society sectors. A sustained critical event like the GFC may catalyse such a shift. We need to be alert to differences over time as well as within and between different countries and regions.

Constitutionally unitary and federal systems start from different positions. American and Australian States predate federation and the modern nation. They retain a distinct identity and harbour suspicion of federal transgressions of power. Modern Germany and Italy came into being only in the later nineteenth century; other nations within and beyond Europe are newer still. These histories affect the way that administrative–political sub-national regions operate. As for viable sub-regions within these States – States like Wisconsin and New South Wales – differences may result not just from diverse federal governments but from the States themselves. This diversity enriches the potential for within-country learning, if there are different policies for instance for managing 'tertiary' relations between college and university sectors as in Australia. The different attitudes and practices affecting devolution in unitary countries also change over time, making it harder to say confidently and in general how regions handle central and other government powers and controls. The interestingly named *United* Kingdom entered 2012 preoccupied by Scottish devolution and the prospect of a looming Scottish independence referendum.

Increasingly too in the global twenty-first century there are supra-national levels of governance and other forces powerfully affecting governance and policy with which to contend. These affect regions as well as nation states, notably but not only in Europe. The management of the affairs of Greece and now other European countries, down to fine details of social and economic policy that affect every community and village, is strongly influenced by the pronouncements of rating agencies and the 'troika' of international bodies charged by governments with resolving the GFC. International banks play a vital role. In other settings like North Africa, the Middle East and Burma (Myanmar), other kinds of international interest allow or prevent action by and even survival of governments. In Europe the EU recognises regions as an important aspect of governance and economic development. It funds many region-centred projects, and sustains and consults with its own Committee for Regions. A few EU regions cross the boundaries of member nation states.

Some PURE regions were in federal countries, Australia and the USA; others in unitary systems. Two in Africa were in young post-colonial societies. One was until recently part of the Soviet Union. The participating 'region' varied from recognised political and administrative entities within different systems to self-selected *de facto* regions as determined by a university catchment; one (short-lived) was a development zone straddling the regular second level divisions of government. One intending region was a more regular RDA covering several second level administrations. This also fell victim to the new policy of a new government dominated by the GFC and indebtedness. In another country the region taking part was the opposite: a new RDA straddling several local authority areas in a federal state. The experience of central government varied across these diverse kinds of regions.

What difficulties did they encounter? What strategies and tactics for confronting, managing or working around these difficulties does the project suggest?

One problem echoed time and again was the short-term behaviour, disruption and delay caused by frequent elections, sometimes at both national and regional level, coming at different times and in quick succession. It is wise to win support and commitment from continuing bureaucrats (in those systems where posts do not change as spoils of office) as well as political leaders. There is no easy solution in short-cycle democratic systems; acknowledging and managing these inevitable problems are part of the reality for regional administration. Embedding desirable practices culturally and doing what can be done by legislative means to protect the rights of regions to specific arenas of partial devolved policy-making as well as implementation in non-federal structures will help.

'Embedding desirable practices culturally' touches on a more subtle and less inaccessible aspect of central–regional relations outside tangible areas of law and policy. It has to do not with the formal division of responsibilities and duties but with the spirit and style of the behaviour of central government ministers, and especially their civil servants, in the exercise of their duties. They may attract and deserve unflattering names such as centralist control freak and micro-manager.

This includes the volume and style of intervention, monitoring and demands for time-absorbing reports. It includes low-trust supervision and interference, and the way these are handled in public and in more closed working settings. We found in the PURE work examples of central civil servants who were respected and highly regarded for their intelligence and their facilitative attitude of support for what regions were doing, despite representing rather unpopular central governments. In other instances the story was quite otherwise. It is within the gift of those working in central government to model and practise engagement across these power strata, based on trust and respect; or to make a region's work unproductive by behaving with disdain and undermining the stature and effort of the region.

Among PURE regions, national and regional elections and then sometimes a change of policy following a change of the party in power were at least disruptive and at times fatal to good ongoing work; fatal where a special-purpose regional authority was simply disbanded with the work devolved to more local levels and its capital fund ended. The whole national RDA system may be brought to an end, as happened in the UK. Similarly decisive in an OECD region in Korea was a change of national government; it abandoned both domestic and foreign policy initia- tives of the previous administration, including systematic decentralisation from Seoul. In Spain the interest of other OECD regions was snuffed out by changes of power in two autonomous regions. Melbourne in Australia gained somewhat from a national change before the project began; a change of party in power at State level complicated but did not destroy the work. Swedish regions worried about local authority mergers which would remove strong regional identity and loyalty to the administrative region. In Hungary change included central govern- ment abolishing the already weak region and loss of the central ministry which had provided resources.

Apart from sometimes decisively terminal events there are abiding tensions between a region with a deeply historic culture and traditions, and a central government that is felt to be out of sympathy, moving in tune with other values and in other directions. A good example is Scotland. Another is Puglia in the Italian south, far removed from the values, economy and lifestyle of the north where the separatist Northern League dramatises the national and regional division. Here an abiding cultural tension has to be managed. It may restrict, complicate and infect a region's exercise of responsibility and development aspirations, whether the unfavourable treatment is real or imagined. Where, as in Puglia and similarly the Malaysian State of Penang, the elected regional government is of a different persuasion from the central government, further problems may arise.

Central policies for higher and tertiary education

Governments tend to equate higher education with universities, making this the main focus of interest in engaging HEIs with the potential of a region. Not all show interest, although this appears to be changing in even the most laggard systems. The college sector, as it is generically called in this book, is of obvious importance to regions: for the initial preparation and updating of a skilled and semi-skilled workforce that underpins regional employment and growth; and in creating pathways into graduate and more advanced study as part of a wider HRD strategy.

The administrative separation of higher from further or 'non-higher tertiary' often means thinking in different compartments and through different ministries. State funds for the two sectors come through different channels and in different ways. Not surprisingly with divided minds and administrations, no strong tertiary cluster interest emerged in PURE despite its nomination by participants as of importance to regions. Central governments could better support coherent thinking and provision if they could stabilise integrated all-of-tertiary policy-making. This would materially enhance the capacity of HEIs and regions to work together.

More broadly, echoing a theme from Part I of this study, national governments might more purposefully nudge their own ministries and departments out of familiar silos and require them to connect, coordinate and communicate better. As it is, different parts of government with responsibilities for higher and tertiary education, for regional and local government, for development via industry, business, agriculture and trade, as well as health and welfare, each with an interest and some stake in HE and regional engagement, pursue unconnected policies. They may send mixed and incompatible messages to universities and other HEIs, generating irritation, confusion and perhaps cynicism about what government is doing.

At the highest level and prefiguring policy-making, governments need to clarify and make known their philosophies, assumptions and hence their aspirations and intentions for higher education. This is necessary as mass HE and other trends and changes in the global setting leave many in HE themselves uncertain; leadership is unsure what it should be doing. Older ideals of the autonomous public university 'telling truth to power' are challenged, perhaps abandoned, in the face of demands for the impact and utility of research and teaching. Higher education is seen as a powerhouse for international competitiveness. This may be translated into supporting a very few wealthy, elite research-led universities; or securing fitness for regional needs and purposes and balanced social and economic development.

Neo-liberal assumptions predominate in most of the countries where PURE regions took part, much less decisively in the several Scandinavian regions and less too in Puglia and the African regions. Ideas of a university and its work tend to become absorbed into this way of thinking. Not all governments understand well the value placed on academic freedom in choosing fields of study, research and teaching. If central governments are unaware of the importance of relations with other HEIs in a region, or of their contribution to a social inclusion and equity policy agenda and so of articulation with schools, colleges and even communities, they leave institutions confused. They are disabled from working well with diverse regional partners towards the required range of objectives and outcomes. More fundamentally, an instrumental approach to tangible outcomes devalues and ultimately excludes much of the civil and social, civilising and creatively inspiring work that HE can do. This enriches and sustains societies. Well managed it can strengthen inclusion. Central governments need a long and clear view on these matters. They should avoid inducing paranoia and schizophrenia in properly seeking utility and value for money.

National prestige is tempting and seductive. Governments and their ambitious political leaders are sadly vulnerable to the recent phenomenon of world ratings; some get fixated on the number of institutions appearing among the top 200 institutions in the multiplying world league tables. Pride and prestige then prevail over the greater importance, utility and value for money of a good national higher education system giving good regional service. Ratings and world tables are a serious threat to regional engagement. They pull institutions and their ambitious leaders away from balanced mission so as to concentrate on research as measured by a particular kind of published paper which may be of limited or no relevance nationally or regionally.

Central governments can take useful practical steps in the more tangible and obvious areas. In federal states there is usually a constitutional determination as to who controls and funds what. Exceptionally this may need to be changed by law. In some traditions, notably until recently the continental European, state systems are managed as part of state bureaucracy; the staff are civil servants. Increasingly these are being moved towards an 'Anglo-Saxon' more entrepreneurial model based on competition and selective state sponsorship, in a quasi-free-market contest system.

Where this prevails government needs to be mindful of the rules and criteria which exist, and of the unintended effects on universities' efforts to be useful regional partners. The work of PURE shows acute pressure on some universities, especially in the more entrepreneurial systems, to conform to research-driven global tables whereby some 3 per cent of universities drive the destinies and perhaps upset the good work of the other 97 per cent. This problem was less dominant in this project, because of the regions and universities which joined PURE, than in some other places. It is still a creeping threat as the priority of published research devalues and displaces other often more valuable work. Governments need to take a cold look at what investment gives the best returns: is it one or two 'world-class' universities, or a strong and balanced higher education *system* that meets the many different needs of complex societies?

How do central governments influence universities informally to nurture or weaken regional engagement? Universities may need to be more self-interested and less ideal-seeking as competition for resources gets more intense. The most prestigious enjoy high status and can be influential informally. Governments need to be alert to the flattering influence of dinner in a prestigious club. They should discourage excessive lobbying by the powerful and listen to all views. If they cannot prevent the formation of lobbying groups – what in the UK have been called 'gangs' – at least they should encourage the less prestigious but perhaps more workmanlike regionally oriented institutions and groups; and seek the views of partners in engagement of all HEIs that seek attention and financial support.

More formally, central government in some countries is cumbersomely bureaucratic. It is very slow, and funds on too short a timescale to enable good planning and management. This is unhelpful and not in principle hard to alter. Systems in many parts of the world suffer from this. They are unable to work freely in the businesslike and entrepreneurial ways demanded of them by competitive neo-liberalism. Redundant regulation limits proper operating freedom and the entrepreneurialism needed for effective diverse partnership. It should be removed as a priority. Similar scrutiny should be exercised, whatever the funding and quality assurance models being employed, especially when more nominal freedom comes hand in hand with new forms of scrutiny and audit. In general, national rewards, penalties and accounting systems for universities should be vetted systematically to encourage rather than hamper regional engagement.

Central governments may now find it timely to review universities' governance requirements, especially outside representation on university governing bodies. It is for universities so to manage their own affairs as to know the needs of other interests in their region: for example with representation on internal curriculum committees and by means of MOUs, contracts, agreements and advisory bodies. Central government may however need to require externality in governance, especially where older state control is being reduced or removed.

Looking more ambitiously wider, central goverments should consider the unintended consequences of competitive national funding and reward policies now exacerbated by competing global ratings. Faced with this they could adjust funding regimes so as to encourage rather than penalise local collaboration between HEIs in a region and across the spectrum of regional needs and partners. This could be done by adopting a system-wide policy for all tertiary higher education on a regional basis. It might include initial and ongoing low-cost funding to support regional HE consortia. This would help institutions in a region to work together and rationalise what each does, allowing greater specialisation and diversity of roles in ever more complex and demanding environments.

Probably all HEIs should do some work across the full spectrum of research and teaching. The mix would vary, and none should be expected to do everything. Ideally non-hierarchical differentiation would follow. Regional and national policies and requirements could be satisfied in this way. Meanwhile each institution could develop and take pride in its own chosen form of 'excellence'. The essential condition would be to bind institutions' interests and destinies together around those of the region by funding them collectively to meet the full range of requirements of that region. No region or university would wish to be without some outstanding research work, whether pure blue-skies big-science or more grounded Mode Two work in regional partnership. The requirements on the regional system would include the full range of social and economic as well as traditional academic targets and outcomes. The point is that all HEIs would collectively share the rewards of meeting targets, and together incur penalties if important areas were neglected. How the different kinds of work were shared out, and what else each institution also did by generating resources outside the contract, would then be local matters.

What can universities do?

How can universities mitigate problems caused by central government policies and practices? The answer varies between regions. Some of what has been said about regions and central government applies to universities also. European institutions now have the EU international level of government to contend with and gain from. Its influence goes beyond the well-known Bologna reforms. In terms of regional engagement the EU may be a source of regional project funds, some involving universities in R&D project partnership and in continuing networks. Targeted regional development funds also affect the work of HEIs. In the case of the PURE Hungarian region this was seen as a mixed blessing: welcome as a financial injection but flawed in being arranged between EU and the central government without adequate consultation or attention to the particular needs of that region.

Mainly in federal systems, there are two levels of government to consider within the country: national and federal – the State of New South Wales or Victoria in Australia, Illinois or California in the US. There are also strong semi-autonomous authorities as in Spain, and the systems of Scotland, Wales and Northern Ireland in the UK. These have now significantly distinct and different funding arrangements from the English, especially in the case of Scotland. Regions may have delegated powers in some systems, as do the US States, but none in others such as the English regions. When funding is split between the higher and the tertiary-college level, as in Australia, difficulties arise for internal management and parity of conditions in dual sector institutions, and for regional coordination and development when they are funded and managed through different levels and arrangements.

If they wish to alter government practices so as to make engagement easier, most HEIs must rely on a repertoire of arguments and persuasion, using whatever lobbying and supportive alliances they can muster. In today's information-rich era many comparative data are available. The OECD is a notably rich, reliable and authoritative source. It is used to argue for enhanced funding, generally and in areas of relative under-performance. This may include regional engagement and encompass all policy arenas and all partners where there is a political interest.

Indirect methods such as pressing for good national and regional data collection, analysis and comparison imply slow progress but may be essential for institutions in some regions. Also in the long-term, it is important to cultivate a wider public by making known the value of regional partnership locally and nationally in tangible ways. This means widening popular and media horizons beyond a handful of highly prestigious institutions and professors, balancing appreciation of top-level research with regard for wider contributions to give greater benefit overall.

A concurrent approach is to take examples and comparative data on the efficacy of approaches used elsewhere and suggest how resistance can be overcome and regional work improved. This applies to engagement enabled by carefully targeting funding that will benefit all. An example is paying a premium and otherwise favouring research undertaken in partnership and applied to regional benefit. Various kinds of impact assessment are being explored and adopted. Another example is the funding of regional HE–tertiary consortia suggested above. This might be done as a national programme, or case by case at local–regional level. Such development funds may also attract outside support, as from the EU.

Taking examples from approaches used in the systems of other countries and regions can help, for example through the PASCAL and PURE international network, via membership of Talloires, through national HE engagement networks and 'clubs', and by membership of the OECD's IMHE. Governments may be more persuaded by examples from other countries, especially if they are regarded as good and successful national models generally. On the other hand 'not invented here' remains an obstinate barrier for some individuals, places and cultures.

Using allies in the region who are themselves outside HE but seek and value partnership may be more effective than arguing one's own case; whether for direct funding or, with better prospects, for the removal of unnecessary bureaucratic or legal-technical obstacles to engagement. Where there are already established arrangements for engagement, joint approaches may be the most persuasive of all. In the majority of countries an industrial and commercial private sector presence may be more influential than an approach by regional government alone. Changes that facilitate technical–higher regional collaboration may have stronger appeal than single-institution lobbying.

National influence groups, clubs or 'gangs' of institutions with similar sector interests are influential in some countries, especially the very prestigious 'Ivy League' and now nascent 'Sorbonne league' institutions – Australia's 'Group of Eight' and Britain's 'Russell Group'. Ideally the whole sector would have a united and integrative approach; institutional gangs tend to be divisive and become ineffectual if played off one against the other by government. Ideally every interest from Harvard to the most locally oriented would share a commitment in practice as well as principle to regional engagement. The reality is commonly otherwise. It may be necessary for regionally oriented institutions committed to engagement as a high priority to make strong separate and joint representation for funding to their sub-sector and work. Sadly, where a competitive culture reigns and global league tables divert attention from regional realities, the contest for political attention and support becomes a zero-sum game. A more desirable situation would be for HEIs of all kinds to create consortia for regional collaboration, and for these to represent sector-wide interests on a locality basis.

Irrespective of the representational and lobbying tactics best calculated in each different and unique situation, leadership and courage, clarity and purpose are required in institutional heads. They need the confidence to make representations to government and to promote their cause via the media, alone as well as in association with others; and to hold fast to their chosen mission rather than be tempted by the glamour of a few research hot-spots into unproductive competition within a sector where there is pressure for all institutions short-sightedly to chase the same goals of research-based academic prestige.

Conclusions

Examples from the work of PURE that would illuminate the generalisations in this chapter can be found in the RVRs for each region on the PASCAL website. So far as their history and politics allow, central governments need to learn to trust regions, to delegate confidently and with integrity, and to support regions' efforts to translate national economic and other domestic policies and directions into successful development work in each different region. They need to consult across their own ministerial portfolios as well as with regional authorities direct, identifying optimal requirements to enable effective engagement between regions and higher education institutions. Usually, but with less restriction for some countries in recent times, this means working with official regional administrations and development authorities; it may however also include encouraging and at least pump-priming other partnerships, perhaps 'sub-regional' between a single university, or university and local colleges, with local SME industry, or with community enterprises.

Regional governments may need to promote their importance and expertise more forcefully, together as well as individually, establishing optimal as well as minimal requirements to enable effective collaboration and sustainable partnership between universities and colleges in their territory and the spectrum of stakeholders there. This includes specific attention to the behaviour of ministries and departments of higher and further education, special councils and quangos used to inform and execute HE policy nationally. Their representations will carry more authority than that of regional universities lobbying on their own behalf. It also implies looking out for ways that central government can help get better value out of regional higher education through the work of other central functional departments in health and welfare, industry, business and commerce.

13

Engaging horizontally
– leading, partnering, learning

How can regional administrations make engagement with others in their regions more productive and effective? Having discussed in Chapter 12 the impact of national governments on engagement between HEIs and their regions previously, this chapter focuses on regions before turning to individual universities and the HE sector locally. So far as regions are concerned, we discuss internal arrangements within the administration before turning to external relations: both with the university and tertiary sector and with other stakeholders in the private and third sectors.

Managing the local region

The internal dimension – managing the regional authority to engage better
The PURE project like earlier OECD studies of regional development and HEIs worked more with administrators than with elected politicians and their leaders in the region. Occasionally a local or national minister would take part in an event or meet the visiting consultative group; but the work was seen as a matter for planners and administrators rather than a major policy initiative.

This reflects the low salience of university regional engagement in the eyes of most national and regional governments. It is borne out by the limited interest and absence or low visibility of such partnership in regional strategic planning documents, perhaps because of regional governance issues or because of the rate and scale of economic and social change impacting regions. It also matches the low importance given to regional engagement by universities, as distinct from technically inclined college-level institutions, in most countries in modern times.

Given the short life expectancy of elected governments in countries where power tends to change hands between the main parties or coalitions thereof quite frequently, low visibility and political insignificance may be no bad thing. Engagement is better embedded into the natural way of thinking and doing things, the culture, of regional administrations throughout their departments and portfolios at all levels. It may still attract unwelcome political attention in terms of efficiency audit, or if it falls foul of a government of strong ideological persuasion that favours weak state authority and withdrawal from making and carrying out policy, or if some kind of partnership leads to embarrassing controversy. Administrators may on the other hand be cautious, too worried about such possibilities to build productive common purpose and collaboration with the different business and community interests in the region. They are required to serve their political masters, as is the region and the central government within the limits of constitutional powers. They do, however, tend to have longer periods of service and offer a more stable basis for developing a culture of engagement than will most elected politicians.

Long-term collaborative 'cross-sector' engagements are ultimately ways of being and behaving. They pervade or elude different whole countries, cultures and traditions. Ways of managing a regional authority also differ within their own structures. Working collaboratively across and between internal departments and divisions can be as important as managing regional and national political masters, fending off outside attacks, handling media and public relations, and working with business and community stakeholders.

Instincts to keep control, managing exclusively to the department's own specific ring-fenced targets, restricting information and minimising disclosure may produce a silo – indeed a laager – mentality within government. An authority that is unable to work across internal boundaries and share purposes, resources, processes and tactics between its component divisions is unlikely to be very good at engaging external partners where the uncertainty is much greater.

An administration, whether a national civil or public service or a local government authority, develops it own understandings and assumptions, language and codes of practice. These simplify and stabilise things. They can also cement hierarchies and hostilities in the course of facilitating day-to-day business in-house. Habits become entrenched. Conservatism finds expression in cumbersome bureaucratic delay. Chambers of commerce, entrepreneurs and community activists as well as HEIs then experience public administration as slow, unhelpful and self-serving. Without the trust and respect which this erodes, engagement and co-development become virtually impossible.

In the ever more complex and troubled world sketched in the first part of this book this is a recipe for bad regional governance. To engage effectively, connecting to the diverse energies and wisdom of different communities of interest, and fully tapping the resources of HE for development, administrations must first themselves learn to engage as open systems. Whatever devices are employed – internal staff mobility, matrix arrangements, project teams, short-lived task forces, shared cross-departmental targets and reward systems – until the administration learns to transgress or even remove internal boundaries, it will not be good at working with partners outside. Its capacity to lead and govern with any breadth and length of vision is compromised. Regional development and well-being suffer.

The external dimension – the region, its communities and interests
The price of closed-system management is paid in the inability to join forces and mobilise the resources of other stakeholders in the community and region across their different and changing sectors. The region needs the energy and resources of industry, commerce and its skilled workforce to achieve economic objectives.

Regional innovation systems (see Chapter 9) require entrepreneurialism inside government, higher education and training, as well as within industry from SMEs to multinationals. An administration working in non-collaborating silos cannot build partnerships and generate synergies outside.

The same applies to nurturing broader social, health and welfare, recreational and cultural well-being, including innovation and development, in and for the region; and to environmental management for health and sustainability. In most of these areas there are conflicting priorities, a choice and balance of goods and ills, which call for reconciliation and optimisation across conflicting priorities between different groups. This applies also to *active citizenship*, the interest and involvement of individuals, usually through their communities and interest groups, in what is being done about their present and future often local world. No government alone can know what is best in all matters, or arrange the dialogue, optimisation and reconciliation that are required. This needs both the expertise and active partnership of higher education and the willing involvement of diverse interest groups community-wide. Defensive inward-looking bureaucracy entrenched into different units, speaking its own language and protecting its own ramparts cannot tap these energies. Like the university it must learn to speak in many tongues, and systematically breach its own walls.

Economic and social–civic matters are themselves commonly and misguid-edly treated as silos. The multiple departments of local and regional, like central, government will fail in a world of chronic environmental, economic and fiscal crisis and changing demography unless they learn to work together in confronting interwoven needs and ends. This means working with diverse partners 'outside'. It may seem hard, complex and messy to achieve; the more so when regions find themselves constrained in personnel and other resources.

The alternatives are bleaker still. Regional leadership may have to remake its administration so as to be able to embed innovation into its own more collab-orative internal behaviour, processes and attitudes. Good internal collabora-tion enables external collaboration and resource mobilisation, including the knowledge, skills, passion and entrepreneurialism in the broadest sense that are latently available 'out there'. Embedded engagement may over time transcend what then become the hiccups of electoral cycles and changes of key personnel. It may survive political perturbation, compensating for reduced government resources by combined wider effort. The administration needs also to monitor and evaluate its performance and development; as a well-engaged partner as much as in terms of visible and measured outcomes. Here benchmarking can be an active tool for learning (see Chapter 10) and a measure of behaving as a learning region.

Engaging with the university and tertiary sector

Across the countries represented in PURE, regions have not in the main been good at engaging with universities, as was noted in Chapter 3. Universities on the other side have, one might argue with less justification, mostly been as bad or worse. The next part of this chapter reminds us why this is and what they might be doing better. Such a matter has simply not been there in the thinking and the doing of most regions or most universities, although the changing times have now made it of interest at least to some.

The onus for engagement rests mainly with the HEIs themselves. Regions can however be helpful and encouraging, or indifferent and even hostile, to universities and other tertiary institutions in their territory. To be constructive partners, regional administrations may themselves need to overcome barriers that they have erected or that are culturally widespread in the society. Are there inherited assumptions about what universities in particular are and do? Are they seen simply as teaching young people to their own privately chosen or nationally determined curricula, and pursuing the research of their choice within what are still sometimes called ivory towers? Are there stereotypes about arrogance, detachment or indifference; or about being self-seeking, interested in cooperating only with begging bowl in hand? If so they will be seen as largely irrelevant to regional needs, despite perhaps wishing to engage in useful and relevant ways.

At least authorities, and likewise other stakeholders in the region, may need to give the benefit of doubt to the institution, overcome any resistance and sense of insecurity masquerading as being in the 'real world', and try again. Such problems are made worse by the distancing and esoteric academic language and attitude practised by some rectors, vice-chancellors and other staff. But not by all: engagement leading to wider, systemic, change may occur through piecemeal linkages and project partnerships localised within different parts of a university. If circumstances are favourable these can yield small gains, connect up and ripple out, gradually shifting the conduct and culture of more of if not all the institution. Identifying where purposes can be shared and scarce resources combined to mutual benefit is one way that the regional government can help change the behaviour and outlook of locally based universities.

The higher education institution

(a) What kind of university? Pressures and trends
Convergence towards dominating common patterns of behaviour occurs in many fields of endeavour under twenty-first-century global free-market conditions. Mass higher education is no exception. The Bologna Agreement is a prominent example of European governments moving towards a common structure for degrees and for quality assurance. Internationalisation of the higher education market puts pressure on some non-European nations to approximate the same arrangements. EU policies and EC funding induce approximation if not harmonisation: in research collaboration and industry partnership; in free-market arrangements that support entrepreneurialism in HE; the adoption of a particular meaning of lifelong learning in education and training arrangements; and collaboration between HEIs and regions as part of regional innovation systems. The idea of the entrepreneurial university includes diversifying business and income streams.

Some of these global tendencies favour closer engagement and the more evident utility of universities nationally or by the more local region. Others pull in other directions, especially, as noted earlier, the new powerful siren call to excel in world ratings and league tables shaped by research excellence measured by traditional academic publishing criteria. So far (by early 2012) efforts to vary the bases for these ratings by privileging other criteria, notably teaching and even engagement, have confused rather than challenged the domination of internationally referenced research. This favours the most wealthy, usually older and more prestigious, institutions.

The common modern idea of a 'really useful university' is one that is relevant and valued, earns its prestige and is held in high regard. It is the ideal type for many nurtured in Western cultural, academic and civic conditions. It remains at the heart of most institutions' and rectors' ideal place to be and to lead. It is seen as under threat from commercialisation and from often private institutions, not-for-profit and increasingly now also for-profit. These can use new ICT with the freedom to pick easily marketed surplus-generating areas of work, without the obligation to offer the wide and balanced curriculum of the traditional public university. Of course many countries especially in the Americas and Asia have large and perhaps dominant private university sectors. Private status does not necessarily equate with narrow profit motive much less rapacity. Closer-scrutiny quality control, accounting and audit procedures and new measures for both quality and impact, the wider-than-academic utility of research, add pressure.

The old ideal of the autonomous public educative university creating, sharing and transmitting scholarly and research-based knowledge and able with impunity to 'speak truth to power' is under pressure from several sides. Policy analysts wrestle with different forms of system planning, and non-hierarchical diversity of mission. Pressure to excel in national and global tables blights this. Different categories of HEIs abound; competing 'mission groups' cluster or gang up around different 'types' and compete for relative standing and advantage. Arithmetically impossible numbers wish to be among the world's top twenty, fifty or two hundred. This passes by the great majority of universities but may still distort a natural and preferred mission based on what they can do best. It may even cost institutional heads their jobs if a governing body treats logically nonsensical aspirations as realistic.

To flourish in such an environment the institution requires steadfast institutional leadership that sets directions, encourages appropriate performance and ensures compliance. This means retaining the understanding and support of immediate governance, whether council, governing board or political masters. It means resisting group pressure to go with universities in pursuit of research excellence at the cost of all other priorities. For a majority, engaging with the region's other institutions and communities, for common purposes and mutual benefit, makes obvious sense. It may be the means of survival as well as success and reward. The chief executive – the president, director, rector or vice-chancellor – needs to affirm an appropriate mission, secure its active adoption throughout the institution, enlist the support of regional stakeholders and influence leaders to affirm and support it. It is important then to act with consistency in giving expression to this identity, whatever it is: world-class research-led, teaching mainly of young students, or the balanced profile as an engaged regional university.

External engagement with partners in different fields and sectors
If an institution determines to work with others across different sectors, especially in its home territory and travel-to-work travel-to-learn catchment area, possibly through branch campuses in different localities where these exist, what follows? There may be full and deep commitment led by the head of the institution in action as well as words, and made known regionally through diverse media. Similar attitudes and behaviour might then spread through the institution and echo in its behaviour in what it plans and does across virtually all curricula, teaching methods and research. This might be monitored by the different academic and business parts of the institution and the governing body, by explicit reference to partners and engagement.

A commoner reality shown in the PURE cases is an institutional affirmation of interest in the good of the region and in working with others there, but little or no recognition of this in the behaviour of senior leaders and in internal recognition and reward systems. It is then up to each faculty, school, department and often individual to consider external settings and local interests, identifying and meeting needs or not. Good work may be done in this way, applauded, approved or tolerated by the institution but not actively promoted and rewarded. In a few cases PURE CDGs wondered whether this was not the best that could be attempted and hoped for: keeping below the radar and avoiding unfavourable notice.

In these circumstances different regional community interests (using 'community' broadly and eclectically) give and gain benefit from different parts of the institution: industry in research and innovation from science and engineering in particular; SMEs from these disciplines and from management, business and law; public policy departments from the social sciences as well as those mentioned above; cultural and creative industries and activities from the arts and humanities as well as from design and IT; socio-educationally disadvantaged communities seeking wider access and opportunity from anywhere in the university, most probably the arts and social sciences.

At the least, a 'low-profile engagement university' will recognise and encourage these diverse efforts. An internal development fund may take bids to pump-prime such work; whether for wider participation or for sci-tech work that generates income rather than raises low socio-economic status student numbers. Such work can feature in defining academic and support roles, recruiting staff and rewarding success via promotion. Workloads may specifically include working with industry and communities: designing and teaching undergraduate and advanced curricula; undertaking workplace and community-based study; forging and managing external partnerships in research and R&D. An enterprise fund and administrative expertise may support science shop, science and business park, incubator and start-up activities.

A university's central administration may include an advisory service skilled in creating and managing partnerships with external partners: it needs *boundary-spanners* who can talk and work across language and related barriers. Institutions spend time and money coaching leaders and others in the public arena in public relations and public speaking. This kind of in-service training needs wider expression. A main barrier to successful engagement is the tendency to speak in the 'private language' of an academic field; or worse, to use esoteric language to adopt a pose of intellectual superiority which repels and distances.

At the worst, academic arrogance or simple social awkwardness may mean keeping such staff 'back office' and not doing university work out in the wider community. Being able to hear, talk and relate across different groups and communities is partly a matter of personality and instinct. It can also be improved with awareness and experience. Coaching and guidance may be drawn for this kind of staff development partly from within the institution; a medical school for example usually has a wealth of such experience across the full teaching–research spectrum, which is not always recognised as 'engagement': because that is just what medical schools do; often also because medical schools may be a world apart from the rest of the university.

When it comes to engaging with the wider world, internationally at fairs and overseas student graduation events, with central government, the 'big end of town', captains of industry, commerce and banking, vice-chancellors come into their own. The work of representation, public relations and profiling, winning resources and seeking philanthropic funds has gained in importance as universities have morphed into parts of big HE systems. The work may seem glamorous. It is certainly onerous; some institutions divide the work between two or more senior or chief executives, or with the chair of the governing body.

Where and with whom the chief executive dines sends a message. A vice-chancellor fully committed to regional engagement will be sure to spend time as an equal partner with regional leaders in different fields and sectors, private and community as well as governmental. Such an institutional head will expect an active place on regional strategic planning bodies, making clear the university's commitment to co-ownership of the short- and long-term future of the region's health, well-being and vibrant economy. For some of this work there is no adequate substitute for the boss: the modelling is the message. Workload may dictate some delegation to a senior deputy. The vice-chancellor should know and use relevant expertise within the institution that gives real value to what she or he has to say, thus showing why the HEI matters and belongs to its region.

Relating to other higher and tertiary education institutions

As seen in Part I, global complexity is an ever more 'wicked' problem. Its solution calls for sustained collaboration unknown and non-essential when universities were small, elite and somewhat detached from daily life. Meanwhile it is a sorry indictment and consequence of unshakeable faith in competition in neo-liberal market economies that HEIs, above all universities, find themselves almost unable to collaborate locally. Many associate more freely with more distant institutions not in local competition, which share similar characteristics and purposes.

These groups lobby and compete with others for recognition and resources. Examples of sustained city-based and regional collaboration are few and far between. In this study Melbourne made a bold start but pulled back to modest almost token partnership between just a few of the initial universities. The North-

East of England provides a rare example of sustained moderate success; Dublin has begun the attempt in financially difficult times. In other places inter-institutional doubts, rivalries or lack of confidence limit what can be done. The best places for regional collaboration are generally the more sparsely populated rural areas with only one institution. In large metropolitan areas less prestigious locally oriented institutions may develop strong many-stranded partnerships which truly engage, in a way that escapes the whole metropolis. In Greater Melbourne this applies to Deakin in the regional centre of Geelong, as to Victoria University in the City's Inner West.

In a number of the OECD and PURE study regions as elsewhere wasteful local competition caused confusion and duplication. This can put off potential regional partners, especially in cities with several universities. SMEs and community-based NGOs may find it impossible to know where to go for help. From the HEI side it may mean that some opportunities are neglected while institutions compete for obvious areas of activity and business. The same applies widely to collaboration between universities and the college-level tertiary-higher sector. It is not surprising that models of State-directed coordination and role separation found in parts of the US such as California, New York and Wisconsin attract international interest; or that new systems being created in some Central and East European countries are taking a stronger line over role segregation and national system planning.

As noted above a regionally engaged university with a more or less exclusive and natural catchment is in principle better placed to engage without the unavoidable competitive and boundary complications of a region like metropolitan London. This may make it easier to collaborate with the wider tertiary sector, such as a technical and further education institute in an Australian region, or with further education in the UK, where limited resources are stretched over a large and sparsely dispersed region.

Competition can still be intense. 'Catchment territories' and regional authority areas are not protected. In single-university regions branches and services of specialised universities located elsewhere may be present, for instance in agriculture, forestry or health. Collaboration with and by the 'in-residence' regional university is wise. Conversely, assuming the region offers rich enough pickings, private and other institutions may choose to create a competitive actual or virtual presence. There may be competition over college-level franchising arrangements and for direct provision: at pre-degree level and especially the first two years of undergraduate education which may carry a 'terminating' or associate degree qualification or lead to vocational awards. It benefits a region with lower participation especially of low socio-economic status families, as is common in rural areas, to have transparent cooperation, and clear pathways and links into higher education. While this concerns higher education it will be evident that similar questions also arise over pathways and cooperation, or conversely competition, for and with schools.

Internal dimensions – culture and processes, structures and roles

The case for open systems thinking and practices by regions applies no less to universities. Silos can be just as problematic, and guarded no less fiercely. Some universities are still stigmatised as ivory towers, or at least as remote, inaccessible and user-unfriendly. PURE also found examples where local universities were seen as right-minded and well meaning, but unable to talk comprehensibly and work effectively with other interests in the outside world.

Incomprehension through unseen barriers of language and assumption can also be common within the institution. The university is sometimes characterised as a holding company for diverse and competing scholarly interests. Its communities of practice are internationally referenced specialised academic sub-disciplines, talking and reading esoteric languages. Neither the employing institution nor the regional community have access or any place there. To alter this without destroying the value, authority and confidence of specialised (internal yet global) academic sub-communities calls for patience and a purposefully open management style.

The university's culture, structures and processes, as well as its leadership, values and capacity to learn and change, are all relevant. Heavily guarded internal territories and boundaries are an unpromising base for open and transparent external engagement leading to partnership based on trust that can be productive and sustainable. An open system means free transactions across divisions within the HEI as well as across the boundaries of the whole institution. It means removing or lowering barriers and requiring collaboration between the academic and the administrative, between levels in the internal hierarchy, and within and between academic divisions which dissect reality in ways often unfamiliar and unhelpful to a world and a local region needing integrative useful and useable knowledge.

Along with 'soft' issues of leadership style must go 'hard' policies and practices to support engagement internally as well as externally: from explicit and unequivocal mention in mission and strategy documents to organisational forms and structures that avoid the stereotyped tradition of faculty fiefdoms and baronial deans. Universities need strong central authority firmly directing engagement policy institution-wide, with rules, arrangements, reports and audit systems that inform the academic board or senate and the governing authority. Personnel and resource allocation policies and practices have to be aligned with the principles of open system engagement, inducing corresponding attitudes and behaviour. Traditions of university governance and academic autonomy vary; whatever they are, the governance level should play a vital leadership role.

Boundary-spanning skills are needed to work with outside partners across different 'languages' and assumptions. Chapter 4 discusses the problem of third stream–third mission discourse. It advises avoiding this way of thinking. Many institutions charge a senior member, perhaps a pro-vice-chancellor, a deputy rector or an assistant principal, with oversight and reporting duties in respect of engagement. It is difficult to say with confidence what arrangements best provide oversight and support for every system and institution. Much depends on national and local management practices, and the style of each unique institution. Some are instinctually collegial, others firmly managerial; others again may contain diverse local cultures from one area (college, faculty, school or department) to another.

A dedicated officer like a pro-vice-chancellor may lack the required stature, but senior monitoring, oversight and report responsibility is required. Busy pro-vice-chancellors and deputy vice-chancellors may have other duties that compete for time and attention. A typical error, for instance, would be to locate the oversight and monitoring of engagement with the oversight and recruitment of international students. Hard targets for enrolment numbers and fee income will win attention over the less tangible behaviours and dispersed outcomes of engagement. Because engagement is institution-wide and should embed into all research and teaching plans and programmes, it may in effect instead be overlooked and marginalised. Most universities do need specialised service units that support engagement and culturally embed habits, behaviours and skills such as what we have called boundary-spanning. Teaching and research should be treated as engagement, much as all research should be ethical, and accordingly accountable through an ethics committee. The trick is to avoid treating engagement and community service as a 'third mission', added on and separated from other academic endeavour.

In the end, learning to operate as an open system to which engagement with other parties in the environment of the region as partners comes naturally – giving to, taking from, learning with and from, doing business – is much the same as learning to be and behave like a learning organisation.

14

Wider reflections – engaging with the new imperative

Hyperbole or new reality?

Is it fanciful to write of a new imperative? Does it justify asserting that universities need therefore to engage more and better both generally and especially with their regions? In affirming that there is a critical new imperative this chapter summarises how it applies to the two main parties. Such terms imply being clear that the accelerating rate of change has indeed created survival-level urgency.

It is common to speak of a 'perfect storm' in respect of many different matters and of the fluttering butterfly-wing that can tumble distant empires. These expressions refer to the combination and interaction of formally separate and perhaps dispersed processes and events that can together prove toxic and catastrophic. Interconnectivity and interdependency have entered common awareness; changed practice takes longer to follow. For action to follow perception policy discourse needs to change from 'we can't possibly do that' to 'we cannot possibly not do this'.

For national and international governance the 'global problematique' embraces all ecological and environmental arenas: climate change and global warming; increasing scarcity of food and water relative to population rise and rising aspirations and demand; the exhaustion of non-renewable energy sources and the high costs, risks and damage of renewable alternatives; transport, waste disposal and the social and perhaps psychological costs of mega-city-region living. Costs and consequences are already evident in the scale and effects of human migration, social alienation and breakdown, massive environmental degradation and loss of species. The loss of bio-diversity accelerates apparently irreversibly. Extinctions multiply. The cost of what is lost in crude mercenary terms as well as in richness of life-forms and quality of living is incalculable. The management of mega-human systems threatens similar loss of diversity: standardisation for mass-management convenience has staggeringly severe consequences. The uniqueness of regions, of institutions of higher education, ultimately of individuals and their diverse qualities becomes an unaffordable luxury.

The alternative is rejected out of hand politically yet is already evidently unavoidable. It means massive cultural change: new economic models and the end of the automatic growth with accelerating consumption of finite resources that has fuelled growth and rising prosperity since the start of the industrial revolution. The 'knowledge economy' must become the 'knowledge society'. Applied wisdom succeeding clever knowledge must create the ethical wisdom society. This means feeling and valuing differently, as well as thinking smarter and more generously. It means creating and using essential survival and not merely consumption mentalities, tools and technologies. Most of the necessary resources are locally resident in inherited commonsense wisdom. They should be recognised, valued and used. Today in the main they are scorned.

The necessary creativity applied as innovation (see Chapters 1, 8 and 9) must be extended to include universally shared responsibility for seeing and being differently. Such fundamental cultural change grows up throughout society: slowly and hesitantly with surges and setbacks, protracted cost and pain; or possibly by transformation at the flutter of a butterfly wing. No clever government can achieve this alone: the buck stops everywhere with everyone. In this context – universal immersion in global crisis, an imperative for species-wide adaptation, inescapable interdependency – regions and higher education institutions must each engage if they are to flourish.

Interests and language

We need first to steer through language and interests, ideology, ethics and taboos.

Along with the perfect storm and fluttering wings another expression, capturing the narrative, refers to which interested party sets the public policy agenda. Managing the narrative is a potent public relations skill. It can give control of the agenda and of the outcomes of debate. For 'interested party' usually read 'political party in power'; for 'interested' read 'self-interested' at the expense of other interests and needs. Recent examples can be found in many countries over the causes of the global financial crisis and policy responses. The same is true of global warming and environmental policies. The eminent and scholarly critic of UK's New Labour, Stuart Hall, declared himself silenced: his critical tools of language and keywords had been appropriated and drained of meaning by government.

Other terms which feature prominently are a little different but no less confusing. Terms like community, lifelong learning, social capital, neo-liberal, free market, culture and globalisation, and less obviously bureaucratic, management/managerial, stakeholder, learning (versus education), even region, acquire colour and connotation that hamper understanding and may protect interests. Others stir old prejudices. They may wilfully divide and trigger hostility, closing minds and preventing open thinking: terms like capital(ism) with its added qualifiers and adjectives of abuse, likewise social(ism) and communitarianism; for both of these some hear 'communist'. The expression 'dog whistle' refers to terms that selectively and subliminally play to prejudices. On the other hand political correctness may inhibit and censor the kinds of open policy discourse essential to solving complex problems in ways that are intelligent, informed and ultimately consensual.

Other rhetorical devices avoid confronting unpleasant reality and making difficult and divisive choices. The charge of shroud-waving doomsayer is levelled against those who worry about climate change, degradation of the environment and the exhaustion of non-renewable resources. Climate-change denial is used as a riposte. There are many forms of obfuscation and self-delusion. Censorship may be subtle – social shaming and control – as well as overt. Interests resisting change that erodes privilege masquerade as practicality, inevitability and commonsense. 'The people's will' is laid claim, albeit as expressed by forceful, populist, seldom disinterested mass-circulation dailies and leading broadcast figures ('shock-jocks') who massively impact policy-making, especially in democracies.

Much policy-making is played out on a floodlit public stage heavily intruded by the surge and babble of instant social media – every citizen an active builder or wrecker. Many of the political–linguistic devices enumerated above are thus amplified. Meanwhile, in the wood behind the trees, simple but big and crucial questions demand answers for resolving the 'global problematique' effectively.

Ideology, ethics and taboos

The big debate and central choice has come to be couched in terms of the demise of global, financial or otherwise qualified capitalism as the best way of managing affairs: what Inglis calls 'the present splitting open of neoliberal capitalism' (in his review of Locke and Spender (2011) in *THE*, 26 January 2012, p. 57). Alongside this goes reconsideration of the role of government and the best conception of the state. The GFC continues to roll out, unpredicted and unpredictable. Policy choices compete over the best route to recovery and growth. In many countries in 2012 that means the best road and speed for debt reduction, at what cost, short and long term, to 'fairness', employment, social disruption and environmental damage. As economic success remains elusive and economies flat-line or contract, other voices advocate neo-Keynesian policies. Others again privilege a social agenda above the purely economic – meaning quality of life, health, well-being and even happiness.

These are cultural and ideological choices too big for politicians alone to tackle. They mean confronting difficult realities: not new in that the big ecological questions have long been evident but too hard to tackle; but new as joined and amplified by the GFC. The political economy of free-market liberalism or neo-liberal economics has prevailed since the 1980s. The political cost of debt reduction in southern Europe is becoming evident. This is predicated on making recovery through austerity and into growth as the only and apparently unassailable policy. The price of unrehearsed contraction under free-market rules is shown. Deep cultural change, the only alternative, means changing expectations of ever-increasing personal wealth. The vision of a communal, voluntarily fuelled Big Society lacks credibility so long as greater wealth and its quest remain dominant practice, competitive personal acquisition and enrichment the assumed sole driver.

Neo-liberal monologue haunts any formulation of alternative policies. Local regions and higher education institutions inhabit this ideological world. In Inglis's vigorous language, 'what happens when an economic system and its political order reach their terminus is that governments will try *anything*, at whatever human cost, to retain the old system ... to retrieve a familiar world'. US and much later UK universities were suborned by the all-American belief that there may be invented a metric technology for the enhancement of everybody's personal wealth – and if that is not a satisfactory meaning to give to life, what is?' (Inglis reviewing Locke and Spender 2011, p. 5).

How do these issues of interests and language, ideology, ethics and taboos apply to engagement? It takes courage, and some old and new kinds of resources, to choose another way. Such radical conclusions are none the less adopted in this study. Any taboo against addressing principles behind the 'real bottom-line issues' must be broken. An alternative political economy today branded naïve, scholarly and unrealistic may be tomorrow's self-evident commonsense.

The literature on engagement has grown exponentially in recent years, reflecting similar growth in associational networks and applied research projects. Much of it is steeped in wishful thinking. The evidence base for economically quantifiable value for money is (as of 2012) still tenuous. Some argue for good case studies of the benefits of engagement, avoiding reductionist efforts to quantify. Measuring (economic) benefit for proof within a marketising neo-liberal paradigm is doomed: the argument should be about the limits of these frameworks and the need to move beyond them. John Goddard, a world leader not just in the study of engagement but in its grounded practice and himself incurably optimistic and energetic in this cause, points out in forthcoming work that university engagement is an occasional and as yet perhaps still ephemeral phenomenon in the history of higher education (personal communication, January 2012). The criticism has with justice been made that the national and wider engagement networks tend to be strong in rhetoric but locked into short-sighted and superficial activity.

Any taboo on addressing ideology, using as well as acknowledging and challenging it, must be broken. Failing to do so locks the engagement movement into a delusional neutered comfort zone. It may be politically expedient but it is hazardous. Audit-ready target-based hard-number indicators built on economic values must also be challenged. Sinuous conformity that accepts underlying false value assumptions for quick gain ultimately sacrifices the grounds for a sustainable and balanced development agenda. The 'cultural dimension' should be asserted. Conceding it to be soft and irrelevant in hard times invites malign consequences in return for short-term gain.

Locke and Spender (2011) dissect the collusive and even corrupting lead role especially of US universities in their unquestioning adoption of neo-liberalism. There is, however, a new wave of ethical interest in business school curricula, through corporate social responsibility and in the 'triple bottom line'. Many universities seek to be 'ethical and green', although the expression of this can be limited to campus energy practices and a few optional courses in the curriculum. The currents are stirring. Any taboo on discussing morality, on the ethical dimension of governance, policy-making and institutional behaviour, must be broken.

The reality and the partiality of this study

PURE and PASCAL are INGO initiatives inhabiting the politica–economic and philosophical setting sketched above. They are committed to seeking new forms of governance for new times in a significantly altered world. The changing social structure and governance outlined in Chapter 2 includes a diminished state sector which is nevertheless often still growing in scale and reach of activity as well as into the international sphere. It includes a more empowered third sector: voluntary, civil society, NGO, community, not-for-profit, of which PASCAL is an example. While inter-sector collaboration becomes more necessary between these and with the private sector, sector boundaries themselves are breached and partly dissolve. Higher education adopts the language and practices of business and is prey to the same geopolitical GFC forces as afflict the public, private and third sectors. PASCAL shares the fuzzy image of the third sector, which explains in part its values, its *modus operandi* and also some limitations in the empirical base of this study.

It is timely to acknowledge what may long have been evident: this study, its empirical fieldwork and its reference and resource base are Eurocentric and Anglo-centric. This limitation occasionally influenced perception and behaviour in the PURE work, and occasionally hampered mutual intra-network under-standing when assumptions from one set of regions were applied without due care to others. The fieldwork lacks the breadth of casework comparison of a truly global study; only four out of six continents are directly represented. The direct knowledge and field experience of those involved is global, however.

It may yet be argued that a study drawn mainly from the Anglophone world and mainland Europe misrepresents global conditions. Of seventeen PURE regions, not forgetting literature and insights drawing from experience elsewhere across all world regions, twelve were European. Of these seven were continental, five in the UK. Three others made up a total of eight Anglophone regions. Of course English is also a first business and study language in most world regions, as increasingly in Europe. Although things are changing it remains true into the twenty-first century that the Euro-Atlantic cultures and economies dominate globally. They make rules and set directions from which other regions are diverging with increasing rapidity as what used to be called 'the South' asserts its different philosophies, traditions and ways forward in the face of the global crisis.

So the phenomena and issues in this study matter worldwide. The economically flourishing regions of Asia and South America are missing. As is observed in the text, the GFC was a North Atlantic and European affair. The aftermath of the initial GFC shock is, however, felt everywhere. Although GFC was a crisis of the greater Atlantic region the subsequent, protracted Euro crisis influences well-being and shapes economic calculations in many parts of the world. Findings suggested here have wider relevance than to the English-speaking world and Europe.

Announcing that 'stronger regions make for stronger nations' the 2011 OECD *Regions at a Glance* addressed the differential performance of regions within countries, where the gaps between rich and poor can be as wide as within countries themselves. Noting familiar concern about rising urbanisation it also observes that in some countries people are moving out of cities into 'intermediate zones'. The GFC hit rural areas harder than cities. The report emphasises the importance of improving education systems in these non-city regions and of creating stronger, fairer and cleaner regional economies to improve economic and lifestyle conditions (OECD 2011b and press release 7 July 2011). Garlick sees such regions as increasingly service centres and lifestyle places to the globally connected metropolises where growth has occurred with increasing disparities. He calls for targeted efforts to reverse the brain drain – the flight of human capital to mega-cities away from rural regions; and globally positioning such regions as local exemplars of the big issues of the day (Garlick, PASCAL correspondence, 22 July 2010).

Reality for regions

The future of the sub-national region remains clouded. Long sight and common sense suggest long life expectancy and rising importance in the lives of people in civil societies and in the governance of nations. Rising complexity can have it no other way. Not devolving responsibility proves incompetent and accident-prone. Government micro-managing the gamut of domestic social, economic and other policies is bound to fail. Local knowledge is essential: both to administer and enable well; and on the part of citizens (businessmen, employees, SME entrepreneurs, community leaders, voluntary workers, family members) to make intelligent input and to carry out policies and purposes emanating from national government but interpreted, energised and enacted locally.

Uncomfortable and dangerous roads lie ahead while the free-market paradigm prevails. Ironically, anxious central governments attempt to keep tight control. Devolution is likely to be nominally honoured but to go with reduced resources and little power and room to diverge and innovate effectively. Regional levels of government face being even less popular than national, so long as jobs, growth and prosperity are promised but austerities demanded by the global economy and eco-crisis prevail. Especially under post-GFC conditions regional administrations will find it difficult to take a long custodian's view of their duties, much less to be popular. Making time and freeing resources for anything non-urgent and developmental like building strong trust-based partnerships with universities takes a back seat, as some PURE regions quickly discovered. The essential minimal conditions for more than modest or token engagement may not exist.

A starting issue for the PURE project was to ask about the kinds of regions best fitted to engage with higher education, and to what effect. Is there any one best kind of 'engaging region'? Any finding would be conditioned by the higher education traditions and practices of the country, making generalisation unsafe. It also depends on the attitude and behaviour of central government, something this study has only alluded to in keeping its gaze more local. One huge question confronting humanity is the rise of the mega-city-region. These are already evident in China and other places including Japan, Brazil, West Africa and India. 'Mega-regions' growing out from existing mega-cities drive the world's distribution of wealth and lead to unprecedented inequality according to a UN HABITAT (2012) report noting that over half the world population now lives in cities. How universities engage with 'regions' in such mega-regions will be difficult and important.

The most obvious distinction is between officially recognised regional jurisdictions of the national state and *ad hoc* special-purpose-defined regions. These *ad hoc* regions have the advantage that they were self-identified or seen by an HEI as of interest, whether for commercial partnership, student intake and contribution to local human capital, or more broadly as communities of place and interest. On the other hand they are more loosely conceived and defined, lacking structures for formal publicly funded engagement.

Regions legally recognised in unitary and federal systems and by the OECD and the European Union as inter-governmental bodies owned by their Member States have the status and authority to receive, collect and disburse funds which may assist partnership-building and ongoing engagement. This authority comes at a price in political visibility and perhaps unpopularity, often with burdensome bureaucratic accountability. Many regions, especially the Provinces and States of federal systems, may be very large. They can perhaps create whole HE systems if the constitution so allows; for some purposes engagement may be more effective at a more local level where face-to-face contact, networking and tacit understandings provide foundations. California is the best example of a very large 'region', bigger and wealthier than most countries, with a single tertiary planned system; but perhaps less effective for local engagement than the smaller more communitarian regions in this study.

An inescapable conclusion is that for engagement purposes, 'region' has many meanings. In any but the simplest cases the larger territory of the whole participating region contains multiple largely discrete and overlapping sub-sets of engagement between region and higher education. Some are specific to particular interests and functions. Examples include industrial and commercial sector innovation, research and development; regional health including epidemiological and R&D studies as well as health care delivery; and culturally rich traditionally self-identifying historic sub-regions. Larger regions have one or more levels of sub-region where local universities and perhaps other tertiary colleges work closely across a wide spectrum of communities and businesses.

There is then no one sensible answer as to what constitutes the best or most effectively functioning region. What is certain is that diversity does and should prevail; the central requirement is that stakeholders are able to work across sectors and with academe in coming to grips with matters that simply cannot be handled in a one-size-fits-all top-down national way. The recognition by the EU and OECD of regions as important entities of social and economic development in Europe is one indication that they matter. Similar signs can be found in other world regions.

Reality for higher education institutions

In competitive free-market circumstances the prevailing reality will remain that each university competes for status, prestige and prosperity. The alternative option of regional tertiary systems that work together, collaborating with and for their regions, may remain unattainable – an ideal to some, anathema to competitive individualism.

Pressure is likely to mount, however, on the public university to change or be displaced by private for-profit institutions, and by other forms of private sector competition for teaching, training, research and think-tanks in place of the academy's public intellectuals 'speaking truth to power'. A good way to pose the key question about universities' engagement is to ask, in Garlick's elegantly simple formulation (Garlick 2011), whether they can move from 'what the university is good at' to 'what the university is good for'.

Chapters 4 and 13 sketch problems and possible ways forward for today's public university to engage in a difficult environment. Holmes (2012) provides a random example of ever-pressing issues. He looks at lessons learned from eight years of university rankings, arguing that to deal with a rapidly changing world, universities need above all to be independent. He continues by saying traditional universities 'should not be so quick to look down their noses at for-profit institutions', noting the blurring of boundaries between public and private higher education. He also reports on access to online journals and linking them with one another and the world and unpacks a recent report on think-tanks worldwide and finds them shifting away from academia. Adding to the pressure EU Research Commissioner Máire Geoghegan-Quinn (2012) warns that she will name and shame Member States that fail to speed up reform of research. 'With Europe crying out for growth, the European Research Area can't wait any longer,' she said.

A vigorous debate running for decades especially in the US and the UK about the perceived corruption of purpose and early demise of the public university had reached storm force by 2011. It grew with the rise and entrenchment of neo-liberalism from the 1980s, reaching a new pitch in step with the GFC 'crisis of capitalism'. The ethical basis of the university has come under question, perhaps as never before: more sharply even in the new context than with mid-twentieth century conflicts over the academic–military–industrial complex in the pre-mass HE era. The same issues recur over tainted donations and sponsorship, but alongside the new 'frugality' fashion and civic responsibility displayed by Bill Gates, Warren Buffet and some others of great wealth. A battle for the soul of the university is thus reinvigorated. Admittedly education tends to reflect rather than lead social values and social change, something to bear in mind while exhorting university leaders to show courage and defend academic freedom for worthy rather than venal reasons.

Questions about the future for and of higher and tertiary education systems and the public university mirror questions about the nature of civilisation, civil society and governance: does free-market competition continue to serve us best? Higher education will usually not be hugely and directly important for social amelioration much less transformation, although in some systems, students, faculty and campuses as symbols and places of conflict have played a crucial part in bringing about significant political and cultural change. More modestly, the study of engagement with regions in the second decade of the twenty-first century, especially in 'the North', suggests a balancing and civilising influence in places where universities reside. The effect extends from the most local neighbourhoods (student housing, transport and the very local economy) to areas of direct reach and draw of students, communities and businesses. The natural gravitational pull can in turn be extended further, purposefully and selectively, if will and leadership allow: to a wider region and beyond in some cases to the nation and globally. This book considers and exemplifies practical ways of exercising this influence to rising mutual benefit.

In reality, as we have seen, it is not easy. Universities must change inherited negative stereotypes of self-interested and perhaps arrogant intellectual superiority, detachment and ivory-tower conservatism. Some countries suffer a snobbish divide between universities and the vocationally oriented college sector. At best the influential middle classes may think of universities as they were thirty years earlier, unchanging stepping stones for aspiring children. Serving as local and global engines of the knowledge society is not part of this mindset; much less moving towards more interdependent and complementary tertiary systems that could serve the community and region better.

A big issue for higher education, perhaps the biggest for many vice-chancellors beyond their business viability, is the *identity* of the institution as the total number of institutions rises. A recent study by the Higher Education Policy Institute shows increasing convergence of mission among UK universities (one might add globally) in terms of recruiting overseas students, but only marginal change in diversity overall so far; this may change in the face of growing market pressures (HEPI 2012). There are competing forces: arguments about efficiency and national interest favour greater diversity of roles, which tend to be seen hierarchically; stigma often attaches to 'teaching-only' and 'regional' institutions. The idea of 'world class' with competitive global rankings drives ambition towards academically prestigious published research. On the other hand arguments are made in favour of an open, fluid HE system, ensuring that all universities do some research to expose students to 'research-based teaching'. The attitude and behaviour of national governments and local governing bodies can be fateful. Between these the voice of regional interest may go unheard.

Ultimately governments set the tone of debate, controlling the resources and conditions for the character, role and diversity at least of public universities. Most see higher education as a weapon in the political armoury of global competition, but how this is interpreted varies. If national pride and shame overrule calculated judgement then the urge to have at least one 'world-class' institution within the HE sector will win. Resources are concentrated in a few institutions. These gain prestige with wealth, success breeding success, while bleeding the national system. The big question is one mainly for national policy-makers. Sector lobbying can exploit vulnerability to national pride. Universities that are oriented more to the good health and wealth of their regions need their own moral strength and political cunning if they are to be heard and supported. Hard as this may be, for a majority it promises the only rewarding direction ahead. The question has yet to be answered officially and authoritatively: but the clear conclusion of this study and from evidence available in the global policy arena is that a good *system* matters far more to a country than having one or two top institutions. The pull of ambition makes this a hard argument to win.

It may be resolved through evidence accumulating of the rising contribution and success of the other 97 per cent' – the legions of non-globally ranked institutions. Discovering experientially and sharing understanding about the kinds of universities that can be effective partners for different purposes and outcomes in varied circumstances remains an important question to keep asking and answering. It includes recognising different kinds of engagement by different kinds and parts of different kinds of universities; but also exploring which open, interlocking and collaborating tertiary systems can be most useful for addressing the new imperatives.

For one heartening example of a highly prestigious 'world-class' university that appears to understand and seek to practise the deeper precepts of engagement, look at University College London (UCL). Engagement is central to its stated mission. In a recent interview Deputy Chief Executive Officer (Vice-Provost for Research) David Price explained the new UCL research strategy *Delivering a Culture of Wisdom*'.[1] Research-led universities must address major challenges and create wisdom as well as knowledge to justify their privileged funding and position. Aiming to be 'the engines of the knowledge economy' they had neglected wisdom, 'the judicious application of knowledge for the good of humanity'. This meant synthesising and contrasting 'the knowledge, perspectives and methodologies of different disciplines' – internal boundary-spanning. This did not 'just' happen; it had to be worked on through active leadership, as did speaking the language governments understand without doing only the research they want. Price posits a public and professional responsibility of academics, calls for collaboration with local less research-intensive institutions, and speaks of being a regional hub. Little wonder that the UCL Provost has publicly excoriated global rankings, despite UCL's success and top-twenty ambitions in that arena. The example shows that having a world-class university versus a good *system* is not an inevitable dichotomy: that even the best can in effect advocate a tertiary systems approach; and what it means to be *good for* and not only *good at* (see *THE*, 26 January 2012, pp. 22–23).

Is engagement 'natural' and feasible?

As we begin our conclusions let us ask a philosophical if not ideological question which might have a demonstrable and 'scientific' empirical answer. If engagement as almost instinctual collaborative behaviour (the capacity to work together on an essential basis of trust) is so obviously sensible, why is it occasional, unusual or exceptional rather than normal?

Instead, a competitive individualistic ideology has reigned at least from the Reagan–Thatcher years of the 1980s. It is now shaken; less by the serious global warming and global resources crisis than by the GFC, the fiscal-economic event that set a new tone for the second decade of the twenty-first century. The paraphrase that there is no such thing as society is being questioned in new ways as popular and student movements challenge the received orthodoxy of the free market with hesitation, defiance or violence in different places. There is new, widely shared 'mainstream' questioning of the efficacy of neo-liberal capitalism as a best way to manage our affairs.

Some people appear better able to trust and work together than others; it is apparently 'just the way we do things here'. If it were agreed – by public opinion, the media, government, in street behaviour – that a convivial society does matter, what might be done about it? This poses a parallel question about inter-regional learning and collaborative development across regions and nations: how do lessons transfer across cultures and traditions? Is it sensible to draw general lessons from multiple unique situations and contexts, as this and other studies attempt? Do people trust and collaborate less in some societies than others? If so, can this be changed? The answer to the first three questions is unequivocally yes, but to the final one, perhaps slowly and with difficulty.

Engagement is neither innately natural or unnatural – like instinctual good practice it comes from both nature and nurture. It may strengthen or wilt depending on the political and social environment, and ultimately the national and regional culture and the local community and institution. A series of American, British and other studies has explored these issues in recent years, following the triumph of neo-liberalism and the high tide of apolitical postmodernism. Robert Putnam's oft-cited *Bowling Alone* sought to document 'the collapse and revival of American community' (Putnam 2000).

More common are the critical studies of corporate greed and anti-social behaviour which fill many columns of contemporary journals and periodicals. Similarly themed monographs followed the 2008 financial crash (see for example Stiglitz 2010; Sachs 2011). A flow of articles asks similarly about the corporatisation of universities, as the pages of the UK's *The Times Higher Education* exemplify. A much-cited study of equality by Wilkinson and Pickett follows its series of correlations with 'Our social inheritance' in Chapter 14. It then resumes the central theme of equality and sustainability to explore building a future less ravaged by corporations and not 'letting the profit motive run amok' (p. 235) in considering social status and friendship, 'the social brain' and empathy (Wilkinson and Pickett 2010).

Richard Sennett's most recent book, *Together*, examines the rituals, pleasures and politics of cooperation, locating the capacity to cooperate with the deepening of informal links. Furedi's review summarises Sennett's magisterial outlook as suggesting that 'it is on the basis of learned expectations that people learn to trust and are prepared to make the leap of faith required for cooperation'. Waning capacity relates to loss of stability for informal networks with the changes of the 1980s – transactions displace relationships. The ethos of transaction devalues informality. With it comes managerial formalisation of process: in trying to enlist informal relations to its processes 'the managerial imperative empties informality of content and then retools it as a tool of management' (Sennett 2012; Furedi 2012, pp. 51–52).

Referring to Putnam, Sen and Nussbaum, Sennett examines the politics of cooperation, its relation to competition and the ways that cooperation can be weakened. He concludes with the outline of a 'new character emerging in modern society, an uncooperative self, ill-disposed for dealing with complexity and difference' (Sennett 2012, p. 30). Such a person is not well equipped to play the roles called for here: to span cultural and institutional boundaries or to lead an organisation engaging with the unlike. Recent research shows that many scholars feel they lack the skills to network with business leaders; 40 per cent of those questioned felt coerced into trying to sell, not a recipe for nurturing the successful boundary-spanners essential to effective engagement. Note too that the incoming Chair of the UK Political Studies Association, in calling on members to 're-engage people in democracy' and advocating local activism, also stressed the need to 'patrol the barriers between scholarship and government' – boundary-spanner or border patrol? (*THE*, 26 January 2012, pp. 17, 16).

The third part of Sennett's *Together* asks how cooperation might be strengthened. It is a far cry from checklists and toolkits for restructuring institutions, tweaking incentives, preparing MOUs and lobbying government; but it could be the place to start if we are to get better at making the collaborative response needed for the complexity and 'perfect storm' of crisis which the future promises. Chapter 8 applies 'everyday diplomacy', 'the craft of working with people we disagree with, perhaps don't like, or don't understand'. It refers to 'modernity's brutal simplifiers', and to us-against-them solidarity as compared with cooperation. Brutal simplifiers cannot erase the capacity to live together and to cooperate 'more deeply than the existing social order envisions' (Sennett 2012, p. 280).

The final chapter enlisting sixteenth century Montaigne's cat provides a fitting end-note. Was Montaigne playing with the cat, he wondered, or was it not playing with him? Does it matter, we might ask, of Montaigne or of a businessman, local community or of regional executive as they 'play with' a university, whether the university is also playing with them? Surely not, for this is the win–win of engagement. If we want to learn how to do a better job of regional engagement for development, we can examine case studies to see what worked elsewhere, enter agreements, set targets, reward performance and publicise success on which to build further. We might also with benefit reflect on the empathy and dialogics of Sennett and Montaigne; note Montaigne's capacity to take interest in others in an era when hierarchy and great inequalities separated them; and realise that it matters not who is playing with whom, so long as each and all are beneficiaries.

Practice and policy

The musing and explorations of Sennett are important in pointing to the increasing significance of civil action in the new global, social and political milieu. The evidence of the PURE project has been that local initiative blended with a good deal of altruistic intent can carry new forms of collaboration a long way.

The blunt reality, however, is that policy and legislative parameters also play a significant role in shaping both individual and institutional behaviour. The history of debate over very individual actions such as drink driving, on the one hand, and major social and environmental issues such as carbon pricing, on the other, shows that government intervention can bring about important social and cultural change. In the case of higher education purpose and functioning, many governments have been found wanting in their policy and allocative mechanisms. Contradictory messages about national priorities on the one hand, and the implementation of competitive markets on the other, have left little space for higher education institutions to position themselves as regional partners and to foster relationships which prompt the kind of mutual 'play' which generates new modes of knowing and acting.

The PURE project, and more generally PASCAL, has grappled with the twin challenges of understanding how policy affects institutional context and initiative as well as making sense of how effective collaborative partnerships do develop. Key insights are summarised in the Annex. While the cases of good and outstanding practice in various regions demonstrate the continuing importance of visionary individuals who act with great energy, sometimes courage and even heroically, there is no escaping that consistent, constructive and productive regional partnerships depend heavily on the determination and strategic nous of institutional and political leadership. While important examples can be found, there are at least as many instances where it is lacking.

Given the current economic, political and environmental challenges which all of us face, this is not good enough. As the OECD (2009) has noted, 'regions matter'. The PURE project, and the work of others such as Talloires, has demonstrated what is possible; we are entitled now to expect that higher education leaders and regional authorities will do what they can to ensure that regional systems of higher education become deeply embedded with regional purpose, even while they look also to global challenge.

Note

1 See www.ucl.ac.uk/research/UCL-Research-Strategy-2011.pdf (last accessed 15 December 2012).

Annex:
Twelve policy implications,
twenty-one questions and answers

The three sections in this Annex were derived from the final PURE workshop, conducted in Brussels in May 2011. The first is a summary of policy implications which emerged in the workshop, while the second is a set of questions about the key learning which was achieved through PURE. Each participant was asked to consider their own responses to these questions; one set of answers is included as the third section.

Twelve policy implications

1. It is important to win the support of top-level people in regions and in universities, to make engagement effective and sustain it. Engagement must be embedded in the culture and practice of institutions for continuity, as the leadership changes.
2. Partnership based in trust must be sustained between different stakeholders and made operational in practical ways.
3. This takes time but is the only way to get full returns on investment made in projects like PURE.
4. Regional Innovation Systems appear fundamental to the prosperity and well-being of regions.
5. Strong university governance requires good external representation. Regions may need to lobby national governments to enable this.
6. Regions and universities need to stimulate SMEs, involving the banks and exploring microfinance.
7. Green technology jobs and skills should be a central part of regions' regeneration policy, with strong university support.
8. The involvement of excluded and vulnerable groups in community activities and projects should be an active priority for all regions and university partners.
9. National administrations should work with supra-national jurisdictions such as the EU in supporting diverse and appropriate regional development.
10. All parties need to manage collaboration and partnership within competitive free-market conditions and in the face of global pressures and crises.
11. The implementation of lifelong learning at regional levels should be a principal policy objective.

12. All this implies permanent emphasis on learning by individuals and organisations, and more active involvement in inter-regional exchange.

Twenty-one Questions

The PURE processes

Q.1   Has a 'learning network' of regions been created? Do regions continue collaborating in difficult times?

Q.2   Can useful networking be built virtually, and when is direct exchange and working together essential?

Q.3   Does expectation of expert consultancy obstruct regions from self-reliance and learning from one another?

Q.4   Are ongoing partnerships established within regions with enough pay-offs to allow them to keep them with universities? (How is the momentum sustained, for example in Värmland?)

Q.5   Can a university take a project lead without taking over the regional agenda?

Regional initiative and leadership

Q.6   How do regions in different traditions and political systems make policy, and partner with universities?

Q.7   How should regions deal with central government instincts to direct and control? Can they avoid being drawn into national politics, political apathy and cynicism, and build on local resources and identity?

Q.8   How do regions win trust and get what is needed from central government to allow regional engagement – legislation, funding arrangements?

Q.9   How do regions create good 'joined-up' culture and arrangements?
(a) between the political and administrative arms of regional government;
(b) between departments in their own administration *horizontally*;
(c) with central government departments and policy-makers *vertically*;
(d) *externally* with the regional community, the private and third (NGO) sector, and HEIs, and equip themselves (human resources, structures and arrangements) for this work?

Q.10   How can regions turn a crisis into an opportunity, for example investing in green jobs and skills?

Leadership in higher education

Q.11A   Must the university CEO (rector, principal, vice-chancellor) give a clear lead in working with the region?

Q.11B   Or is action 'out and about in faculty-land' enough, with tolerant passive support from the centre?

Q.12   Are rewards and sanctions (sticks and carrots) the only reliable way to create an institutional culture of engagement?

Q.13   How can the commitment to engagement be sustained as leaders come and go?

Q.14   What formal governance and partnership measures are needed and work – *ex officio* seats on regional planning authorities, standing consultative bodies, MoUs and MoAs, strong lay presence on governing bodies?

The 'third mission' of universities

Q.15   Do regions see universities as a valuable resource?

Q.16A Should all universities be committed to regional development, with minimal requirements on all in terms of 'third mission engagement'?

Q.16B Or should the most prestigious be left to pursue 'world-class' objectives?

Q.17   Should we abandon the term 'third mission', and talk instead of community and regional service, engagement, interaction, co-production and use of knowledge?

Cooperation and collaboration between universities

Q.18   What formal arrangements and mechanisms work (examples from Melbourne, Manchester, Helsinki, Dublin, Puglia)?

Q.19   Do they need national or regional government authority, and a mandate with rewards and strong sanctions, to be sustainable?

How can regions get what they need?

Q.20   How can curricula be brought closer into line with the labour market development (skills training, HRD) needs of the region?

Q.21A Should regions require college and university higher education institutions to work together for regional development in a 'tertiary system'?

Q.21B Should it be planned and funded as a regional system rather than single institutions?

Q.21C Should regions lobby national funding authorities for rewards and penalties to all HEIs to provide between them the full range of necessary tertiary and higher education?

One Set of Answers

Q.1   Partly, and with difficulty.

Q.2   Still finding out.

Q.3   Yes, quite a lot.

Q.4   Too early to say, some probably, some probably not.

Q.5   Yes, in a few cases.

Q.6   This is varied and difficult.

Q.7   A crucial requirement; no easy answer in each case.

Q.8   Also often crucial; no one-size-fits-all solution.

Q.9   A key matter; it needs unceasing local effort to resist siloing.

Q.10   Little evidence of this happening so far.

Q.11   A challenge (B) to received wisdom (A) – sometimes the only way.

Q.12   Maybe in the short term, but it needs more long term.

Q.13   Embed a self-sustaining culture throughout the institution.

Q.14   Requires a many-stranded system of arrangements.

Q.15   Not usually, at least to begin with.

Q.16   (A) Deeply divisive and problematic.
           (B) I greatly dislike this aspect of globalisation but incline towards pragmatism on this.

Q.17   Yes.

Q.18   There are several examples; but the urge to compete is always strong.

Q.19   A formal requirement with rewards and sanctions will usually be necessary for some time.

Q.20   Requires a sense of university self-interest followed by a lot of effort with the detail, and sustained collaboration with regional partners.

Q.21   Yes (A), yes (B) and yes (C), if at all feasible.

Bibliography

Amin, A. and Thrift, N. (eds) (1994) *Globalisation, Institutions and Regional Development in Europe*. Oxford: Oxford University Press.

Beere, C., Votruba, J. and Well, G. (2011) *Becoming an Engaged Campus: A Practical Guide for Institutionalizing Public Engagement*. San Francisco: Jossey-Bass.

Bekessy, S., Samson, K. and Clarkson, R. (2007) The Failure of Non-binding Declarations to Achieve University Sustainability – a Need for Accountability. *International Journal of Sustainability in Higher Education*, 8(3), pp. 301–316.

Benner, C. (2003) Learning Communities in a Learning Region: The Soft Infrastructure of Cross-Firm Learning Networks in Silicon Valley. *Environment and Planning A*, 35, pp. 1809–1830.

Benneworth, P. and Dassen, A. (2011) Strengthening Global–Local Connectivity in Regional Innovation Strategies: Implications for Regional Innovation Policy. *OECD Regional Development Working Papers*, 2011/01.

Berry, M. (2003) *Innovation by Design: The Economic Drives of Dynamic Regions*. Melbourne: Lab.3000.

Bjarnason, S. and Coldstream, P. (eds) (2003) *The Idea of Engagement: Universities in Society*. London: ACU.

Borish, S. M. (1991) The Land of the Living: The Danish Folk High Schools and Denmark's Non-violent Path to Modernization, Nevada City, CA: Blue Dolphin.

Boyer, E. L. (1996) The Scholarship of Engagement. *Journal of Public Service and Outreach*, 1(1), pp. 11–20.

Bradley, D. (2008) *Review of Australian Higher Education: Final Report*. Canberra: Commonwealth of Australia.

Brennan, J., Little, B. and Locke, W. with Allen, L., Osborne, M., Storan, J., Doyle, L., McKay, G., Bogdanovic, D., Lebeau, Y., Longhurst, B., Cochrane, A., Hudson, A. and Hick, R. (2006) Higher Education's effects on disadvantaged groups and communities: report of an ESRC network on cross-regional perspectives on the transformative impact of higher education on disadvantaged groups and communities. London: CHERI. www.open.ac.uk/cheri/documents/esrc-crossregional-final-report.pdf (last accessed 15 December 2012).

Brown, A. and Massey, J. (2001) *Literature Review: The Impact of Major Sporting Events*. Manchester: UK Sport, Manchester Institute for Popular Culture, Manchester Metropolitan University.

Brown, L. R. (2011) *World on the Edge: How to Prevent Environmental and Economic Collapse*. New York: W. W. Norton.

Buffett, W. (2011) Stop Coddling the Super-rich. *Bangkok Post*, 17 August 2011, p. 9 from New York Times News Service.

Burton Clark, R. (1998) *Creating Entrepreneurial Universities*. Oxford: Pergamon.

Camilleri, J. and Falk, J. (2009) *Worlds in Transition: Emerging Governance Across a Stressed Planet*. Cheltenham and Northampton, MA: Edward Elgar.

Camp, R. (1989) *The Search for Industry Best Practices that Lead to Superior Performance*. Portland, OR: Productivity Press.

Campbell, D. (1984) *The New Majority: Adult Learners in the University*. Edmonton: University of Alberta Press.

Campbell, D. (2011) Personal Communication, 9September.

Castells, M. (1996) *The Rise of the Network Society*. Cambridge, MA: Blackwell.

CEDEFOP and ICO (2010) *Skills for Green Jobs – European Synthesis Report*. Luxembourg: European Commission.

Chambers, W. (2011) Liverpool Culture Campus: Linking Higher Education and the Arts. In L. Komlosi (ed.) *Inclusion through Culture*. Proceedings of the 4th Annual Conference of the University Network of European Capitals of Culture, Pécs, 14/15 October 2010

Charles, D. (2003) Universities and Territorial Development: Reshaping the Regional Role of UK Universities. *Local Economy*, 18(1). pp. 7–20.

Charles D. and Benneworth, P. (2001) *The Regional Mission: The Regional Contribution of Higher Education: National Report*. London: UUK.

Charles, D. and Benneworth, p. (2002) *Evaluating the Regional Contribution of an HEI: A Benchmarking Approach*. Higher Education Funding Council for England, April 02/23 www.hefce.ac.uk/pubs/hefce/2002/02_23.htm (accessed January 2012).

Charles, D. R, Benneworth, P. Sanderson, A., Taylor, J. and Goddard, J. (2001) *The Regional Mission: The Regional Contribution of Higher Education: The North East*. London: Universities UK.

Clover, D. and Sanford, K. (2011) Editorial – Special Issue. *Journal of Continuing Education* 17(2), pp. 1–4.

Clugston, R. and Calder, W. (1999) Critical Dimensions of Sustainability in Higher Education. In W. L. Filho (ed.) *Sustainability and University Life*. Berne: Peter Lang.

Cooke, P. (2001), Regional Innovation Systems, Clusters, and the Knowledge Economy. *Industrial and Corporate Change*, 10(4), pp. 945–974.

Crouch, C. (2011) *The Strange Non-Death of Neoliberalism*. Cambridge: Polity Press.

CURDS (1998) The Dialogue of Universities With Their Partners: Comparisons between Different Regions of Europe (project for CRE and the EC examining the North-East Region of England). Newcastle: University of Newcastle CURDS.

Dahlof, U. and Selander, S. (1994) *New Universities and Regional Context*. Uppsala: University of Uppsala Press.

Darmon, I. (2012) Personal Communication, 10 January.

Davies, J. (1997) The Regional University: Issues in the Development of an Organisational Framework. *Higher Education Management*, 9(3), pp. 29–42.

Defourny, J. and Nyssens, M. (2006) Defining Social Enterprise'. In M. Nyssens(ed.) *Social Enterprise*. Oxford: Routledge.

Delanty, G. (2001), *Challenging Knowledge: The University in the Knowledge Society*. Buckingham: Open University Press.

Deloitte (2011) *Making the Grade 2011*, available at www.deloitte.com/assets/Dcom-Canada/Local%20Assets/Documents/ca_en_ps_making-the-grade-2011_041811.pdf (last accessed 28 December 2012).

Department for Education and Employment (DfEE) (1998) *Universities and Economic Development*. Sheffield: DfEE.

Department for Victorian Communities (DVC) (2004) *Changing the Way Government Works* . Melbourne: IPAA Victoria.

Doyle, L. (2007) Cultural Presence and Disadvantage: What Difference Do HEIs Make? In M. Osborne, K. Sankey and B. Wilson (eds), *Researching Social Capital, Lifelong Learning Regions and the Management of Place: An International Perspective*. London: Routledge.

Doyle, L. (2010) The Role of Universities in the 'Cultural Health' of their Regions: Universities' and Regions' Understandings of Cultural Engagement. *European Journal of Education*, 45(3), pp. 466–480.

Duke, C. (2008) University Engagement: Avoidable Confusion and Inescapable Contradiction. *Higher Education Policy and Management*, 20(2), pp. 87–97.

Duke, C. (2009) Trapped in a Local History: Why did Extramural Fail to Engage in the Era of Engagement? In P. Cunningham with S. Oosthuizen and R. Taylor (eds) *Beyond the Lecture Hall – Universities and Community Engagement from the Middle Ages to the Present Day*. Cambridge: University of Cambridge. At www.educ.cam.ac.uk/events/conferences/past/beyondthelecturehall/BeyondtheLectureHall_VirtualBook.pdf (last accessed 15 December 2012).

Duke, C. (2010) Learning Cities and Regions. In *International Encyclopedia of Education*, 3rd Edition, vol. 1, pp. 144–149. Oxford: Elsevier.

Duke, C. (2011a) Winning the University Engagement Narrative (review article). *International Journal of Lifelong Education*, 30(5), pp. 699–707.

Duke, C. (2011b) *Regional Development and Higher Education – the Next Decade*. Glasgow: Glasgow University PASCAL Office http://pobs.cc/92 (last accessed 15 December 2012).

Duke, C. (2012a) Lifelong Learning and the Autumn of Europeanisation in Asia. *International Journal of Continuing Education and Lifelong Learning*, 4(2).[[. 17–34.

Duke, C. (2012b) The Impact Debate: Hazards of Discourse in the UK. *Journal of Adult and Continuing Education*, 17(1), pp. 115–129.

Duke, C., Osborne, M. and Wilson, B. (eds) (2005) *Rebalancing the Social and Economic: Learning Partnership and Place*. Leicester: NIACE.

Duke, C., Hassink, R., Powell, J. and Puukka, J. (2006) *Supporting the Contribution of Higher Education Institutions to Regional Development: Peer Review Report: North East of England*. Organisation for Economic Co-operation and Development: Paris, http://www.oecd.org/document/35/0,3343,en_2649_35961291_35602979_1_1_1_1,00.html (accessed January 2012)

European Commission, Enterprise and Industry Directorate General (2009) *Think Small First – Considering SME Interests in Policy-Making*. Report of the Expert Working Group, Brussels.

Ewu, J. (2007) Crossing the 'Zaure': Theatre for Development and Women's Empowerment in Northern Nigeria. *African Performance Review* 1(2/3), pp. 75–97.

Faure, E., Herrera, F., Kaddoura, A.-R., Lopes, H., Petrovsky, A. V., Rehnema, M. and Ward, F. C. (1972) *Learning to Be*. Paris: UNESCO.

Fine, B. (2010) *Theories of Social Capital: Researchers Behaving Badly*. London: Pluto Press.

Florida, R. (1995) Towards the Learning Region. *Futures* 27(5), pp. 527–536.

Florida, R. L. (2002) *The Rise of the Creative Class: and How it's Transforming work, Leisure, Community and Everyday Life*. New York: Basic Books.

Florida, R. L. (2004) *Cities and the Creative Class*. London: Routledge.

Florida, R. L. (2005) *The Flight of the Creative Class: The New Global Competition for Talent*. New York: Collins.

Furedi, F. (2012) Keep It Light, Keep Them Close (review of Sennett 2012). *The Times Higher Education Supplement*, 2 February, pp. 50–51.

Gardiner, S. (2006) *A Perfect Moral Storm: The Ethical Tragedy of Climate Change*. Oxford: Oxford University Press.

Garlick, S. (1998) *Creative Associations in Special Places: Enhancing the Partnership Role of Universities in Building Competitive Regional Economies*. Canberra: DEETYA, EIPHED.

Garlick, S. (2011) Personal Communication, 4 August.

Garlick, S. and Matthews, J. (2009) Engaged Learning and Enterprise through the 'Ecoversity': Implementing and Engagement Theory to Meet Sustainability Concerns. Paper presented to the National Conference of Australian Universities' Community Engagement Alliance, Whyalla, South Australia.

Geoghegan-Quinn, M. (2012) Consultation on ERA Finds Opportunities and Challenges for EU Research Landscape. European Commission press release, 30 January, ref. IP/12/84. http://europa.eu/rapid/press-release_IP-12-84_en.htm (last accessed 15 December 2012).

Gibbons, M. (2001) *Engagement as a Core Value of a University: A Consultation Document*. London: ACU.

Gibbons, M., Limoges, C., Nowotny, H., Schwartzman, S., Scott, P. and Trow, M. (1994) *The New Production of Knowledge: The Dynamics of Science and Research in Contemporary Societies*. London: Sage.

Ginsberg, B. (2011) *The Fall of the Faculty: The Rise of the All-Administrative University and Why it Matters*. Oxford: Oxford University Press.

Goddard, J. (1997) *Universities and Regional Development: An Overview*. Background paper to OECD Project on the Responses of Higher Education to Regional Needs. Paris: OECD.

Goddard, J., Charles, D., Pike, A., Potts, G. and Bradley, D. (1994) *Universities and Communities*. London: CVCP.

Goddard, J., Charles, D., Pike, A., Potts, G., Bradley, D. (1997) Managing the University/Regional Interface. *Higher Education Management* 9(3), pp. 7–28.

Grinsted, T. H. (2011) Sustainable Universities – from Declarations on Sustainability in Higher Education to National Law. *Environmental Economics*, 2(2), pp. 29–36.

Guile, D. (2009) *Questioning the Simplistic Link between Qualifications and Labour Market Entry: New Forms of Expertise and Learning in the Creative and Cultural Sector*. London: Centre for Learning and Life Chances in Knowledge Economies and Societies. www.llakes.org.uk (last accessed 15 December 2012).

Hall, C. (1992) *Hallmark Tourist Events: Impacts, Management and Planning*. London: Bellhaven Press.

Halsey, A. (1992) *Decline of Donnish Dominion*. Oxford: Clarendon Press.

Hamilton, C. and Sneddon, N. (2004) *Scoping Study on Cultural Engagement and Knowledge Transfer in Scottish Universities*. Glasgow: Centre for Cultural Policy Research.

Harvey, D. (1989) *The Condition of Post-Modernity*. Oxford: Basil Blackwell.

Hazelkorn, E. (2009) Rankings and the Battle for World-Class Excellence: Institutional Strategies and Policy Choices. *Higher Education Management and Policy*, 21(1), pp. 55–74.

Hazelkorn, E. (2011) *Rankings and the Reshaping of Higher Education: The Battle for World-class Excellence*. London: Palgrave Macmillan.

HEFCE (2000) *Regional Profiles of Higher Education*. Bristol: HEFCE.

HEFCE (2010) *The Higher Education Knowledge Exchange System in the United States*. Bristol: HEFCE.

HEPI (2012) *Institutional Diversity in UK Higher Education*. Oxford: HEPI.

Holden, M. and Connelly, S. (2004) *The Learning City*. The World Urban Forum 2006, Vancouver Group Working Paper. Vancouver: Simon Fraser University.

Holmes, R. (2012) World Blogs. *University World News Newsletter*, 207, 5 February.

Howkins, J. (2001) *The Creative Economy*. London: Allan and Lane.

Inman, P. and Davidson, K. (2012) *Assessing the Suburban Cook County Food System: Setting the Table for Collaboration*. Report for the Suburban Cook County Food System Steering Committee. De Kalb: Northern Illinois University.

International Regions Benchmarking Consortium (2010) *Research Universities and the Knowledge Region*. Preliminary draft. IRBC: Seattle.

Jones, C. (2001) Mega-events and Host-Region Impacts: Determining the True Worth of the 1999 Rugby World Cup. *International Journal of Tourism Research*, 3(3), pp. 241–251.

Judt, T. (2010a) What Is To Be Done? (Manifesto for a Brighter Future). *The Guardian Review*, 20 March 2011, pp. 2–4.

Judt, T. (2010b) *Ill Fares the Land: A Treatise on our Present Discontents*. London: Allen Lane.

Kane, L. (2001) *Popular Education and Social Change in Latin America*. London: Latin American Bureau.

Kanter, R. (1995) *World Class: Thriving Locally in the Global Economy*. New York: Simon and Schuster.

KEA European Affairs (2006) *The Economy of Culture in Europe*. A Report to the DG Education of the European Union (accessed February 2012 at http://www.keanet.eu/ecoculture/studynew.pdf)

Kim, H. J., Gursoy, D. and Lee, S.-B. (2006). The Impact of the 2002 World Cup on South Korea: Comparisons of Pre- and Post-Games. *Tourism Management*, 27(1), pp. 86–96.

Knox, A. (2011) Creativity and Learning. *Journal of Continuing Education*, 17(2), pp. 96–111

Langworthy, A. (2009) Benchmarking Community Engagement: The AUCEA Pilot Project. Lismore: Australian Universities Community Engagement Alliance.

Locke, R. and Spender, J.-C. (2011) *Confronting Managerialism: How the Business Elite and Their Schools Threw Our Lives Out of Balance*. London: Zed Books.

Longworth, N. and Osborne, M. (2010) Six Ages Towards a Learning Region – A Retrospective. *European Journal of Education*, 45(3), pp. 368–401

Macneil, J., Testi, J., Cupples, J. and Rimmer, M. (1994) *Benchmarking Australia: Linking Enterprises to World Best Practice*. Melbourne; Longman Business and Professional.

Malfas, M., Theodoraki, E. and Houlihan, B. (2004). Impacts of the Olympic Games as Mega-events. *Municipal Engineer*, 157, pp. 209–220.

Matthews, J., Garlick, S. and Smith, J. T. F. (2009) Ecoversity: Towards a Sustainable Future. *Journal of the World Universities Forum* 2(3), pp. 114–124.

Mobiot, G. (2011) The True Value of Nature is Not a Number with a Pound Sign in Front. *The Guardian*, 7 June 2011, p. 27.

Morris, P. (2001) Learning Communities: A Review of Literature. Working Paper 01–32, Research Centre for Vocational Education and Training, University of Technology Sydney.

Mullen, A. (2011) *Degrees of Inequality: Culture, Class and Gender in American Higher Education*. Baltimore: Johns Hopkins University Press.

National Committee of Inquiry into Higher Education (1997) The Local and Regional Role of Higher Education. Chapter 12 in *Higher Education in the Learning Society* (The Dearing Report). London: HMSO DfEE.

Newman, H. K. (1999) Neighborood Impacts of Atlanta's Olympic Games. *Community Development Journal*, 34(2), pp. 151–159.

Novotny, H., Scott, P. and Gibbons, M. (2001) *Rethinking Science: Knowledge in an Age of Uncertainty*. Cambridge: Polity Press.

Nyssens M. (ed.) (2006) *Social Enterprise*. London: Routledge.

OECD (1974) *Recurrent Education: Towards a Strategy for Lifelong Learning*. Paris: OECD.

OECD (1997a) *The Response of Higher Education Institutions to Regional Needs*. Paris: OECD, CERI.

OECD (1997b) *Higher Education and Regions: Globally Competitive, Locally Engaged*. Paris: OECD, CERI.

OECD (1999) *The Response of Higher Education Institutions to Regional Needs*. Paris: OECD.

OECD (2007) *Higher Education and Regions: Globally Competitive, Locally Engaged*. Paris: OECD.

OECD (2008) Higher Education Management and Policy, Special Issue, Higher Education and Regional Development. *HEMP*, 20(2).

OECD (2009) *Regions Matter: Economic Recovery, Innovation and Sustainable Growth*. Paris: OECD.

OECD (2011a) *Cities and Green Growth: A Conceptual Framework*. Paris: OECD

OECD (2011b) *Regions at a Glance*. Paris: OECD.

OECD (2012) *Equity and Quality in Education – Supporting Disadvantaged Students and Schools* Paris: OECD.

Ohmann, S., Jones, I. and Wilkes, K. (2006) The Perceived Social Impacts of the 2006 Football World Cup on Munich residents. *Journal of Sport and Tourism*, 11(2), pp. 129–152.

Orr, D. W. (1992) *Ecological Literacy: Education and the Transition to a Postmodern World*. Albany, NY: SUNY Press.

Osborne, M. (2003) United Kingdom. In M. Osborne and E. Thomas (eds) *Lifelong Learning in a Changing Continent: Continuing Education in the Universities of Europe*. Leicester: NIACE.

Osborne, M. and Houston, M. (2012) United Kingdom: Universities and Lifelong Learning in the UK – Adults as Losers, but Who are the Winners?' In M. Slowey and H. Schuetze, *Global Perspectives on Higher Education and Lifelong Learning*. London: Routledge.

Pinderhughes, R. (2006) Green Collar Jobs: Work Force Opportunities in the Growing Green Economy. *Race, Poverty & the Environment*, 13(1), pp. 62–63.

Porter, M. (1990 (1998)) *The Competitive Advantage of Nations*. New York: Free Press.

Pratt, A. C. (2008) Creative Cities: The Cultural Industries and the Creative Class. *Geografiska Annaler: Series B – Human Geography*, 90(2). pp. 107–117.

Princen, T. (2010) *Treading Softly: Paths to Ecological Order*. Boston, MA: MIT Press.

PURE (2010) *Green Jobs Study Report*. http://pure.pascalobservatory.org/pascalnow/forums/cluster-4-green-skills-and-jobs-gs/melbourne-green-jobs-study-report (last accessed 14 December 2012).

Putnam, R. (2000) *Bowling Alone: The Collapse and Revival of American Community*. New York: Simon and Schuster.

Readings, B. (1996) *The University in Ruins*. Cambridge, MA and London: Harvard University Press.

Roberts, C. and Roberts, J. (2007) *Greener by Degrees: Exploring Sustainability through Higher Education Curricula*. Cheltenham: Centre for Active Learning.

Rockström, J. *et al.* (2009) A Safe Operating Space for Humanity. *Nature*, 461(7263), pp. 472-475.

Ruiz, J. (2004). *A Literature Review of the Evidence Base for Culture, the Arts and Sport Policy*. Edinburgh: Social Research Unit, Scottish Executive Education Department.

Sachs, J. (2011) *The Price of Civilization: Economics and Ethics after the Fall*. London: Bodley Head.

Salmi, J. and Saroyan, A. (2009) International University Ranking Systems and the Idea of

University Excellence. *Journal of Higher Education Policy and Management*, 29(3), pp. 245–260.

Scott, P. (1984) *The Crisis of the University*. Beckenham: Croom Helm.

Sennett, R. (2012) *Together: The Rituals and Pleasures and Politics of Cooperation*. Londn: Allen Lane.

Small, K., Edwards, D. and Sheridan, L. (2005). A Flexible Framework for Evaluating the Socio-cultural Impacts of a (Small) Festival. *International Journal of Event Management Research*, 1(1), pp. 66–77.

Spendolini, M. J. (1992) *The Benchmarking Book*. New York: AMACOM Press.

Srietska-Ilina, O., Hofmann, C., Durán Haro, M. and Jeon, S. (2011) *Skills for Green Jobs – A Global View*. Geneva: International Labour Organisation.

Steiner, M. (ed.) (1998) *Clusters and Regional Specialisation*. Norwich: Pion.

Stiglitz, J. (2010) *Freefall: Free Markets and the Sinking of the Global Economy*. London: Allen Lane.

Tapper, T. and Palfreyman, D. (2000) Oxford and the Decline of the Collegiate Tradition. London: Woburn Press.

Taylor, M. (2010) Keynot Presenation at Equity Challenge Unit Conference, Accelerating Equality in Higher Education, November.

Thomas, I., Sandrip, O. and Hegarty, K. (2010) Green Jobs in Australia: A Status Report. *Sustainability*, 2, pp. 3792–3811.

Thompson, J. and Bekhradnia, B (2011) *Higher Education: Students at the Heart of the System – an Analysis of the Higher Education White Paper*. Oxford: HEPI.

Tilbury, D. (2012) Higher Education for Sustainability: A Global Overview of Commitment and Progress. In Global (ed.), University Network for Innovation. *Higher Education in the World 4. Higher Education's Commitment to Sustainability: from Understanding to Action*. London: Palgrave Macmillan.

UN HABITAT (2012) *State of the World's Cities 2012/13: Prosperity of Cities*. Nairobi: UN HABITAT.

UNEP/ILO/IOE/ITUC (2008) *Green Jobs: Towards Decent Work in a Sustainable, Low-Carbon World*. Nairobi: UNEP/ILO/IOE/ITUC.

UNCSD (2011) *Green Jobs and Social Inclusion, Rio 2012 Issues Brief 7*, available at www.uncsd2012.org (last accessed 29 December 2012).

University of Glasgow (2012) HLF Gives Green Light for Kelvin Hall Development. www.gla.ac.uk/hunterian/about/news/headline_221635_en.html (last accessed 14 December 2012).

University of Newcastle (1997) *Universities and Economic Development* (Report for the DfEE). Sheffield: DfEE.

Vinson, T. (2007) *Dropping off the Edge: The Distribution of Disadvantage in Australia*. Richmond, Victoria: Catholic Social Services Australia and Jesuit Social Services.

Watson, D. (2007) *Managing Civic and Community Engagement*. Maidenhead: McGraw-Hill, Open University Press.

Watson, D. (2010) Universities' Engagement with Society. In *International Encyclopaedia of Education*, Vol. 4, pp. 398–403. Oxford: Elsevier.

Watson D., Stroud, S. E., Hollister, R. and Babcock, E. (2011) *The Engaged University: International Perspectives on Civic Engagement*. London: Routledge.

Wenger, E. (1998) *Communities of Practice: Learning, Meaning and Identity*. Cambridge: Cambridge University Press.

Wilkinson, R. and Pickett, K. (2010) *The Spirit Level: Why Equality is Better for Everyone*. London: Penguin.

Wintour, P. (2011) PM tells Britain 'To Show Some Fight' as Economy Flatlines. *The Guardian*, 6 October 2011.

Wissema, J. G. (2009) *Towards the Third Generation University: Managing the Universities in Transition*. Cheltenham and Northampton MA: Edward Elgar.

Yanming, H. (2011) Reflections on the Value of Higher Education in Lifelong Learning. In J. Yang and R. Valdés-Cotera (eds) *Conceptual Evolution and Policy Developments in Lifelong Learning*. Hamburg: UNESCO Institute for Lifelong Learning.

Yarnit, M. 2011) *The Learning City : Dead as a Dodo?* Posted on PASCAL Website, http://pobs.cc/mpby (last accessed 15 December 2012).

Zipsane, H. (2011) *The Changing Roles of Museums*. http://pobs.cc/mq8a (last accessed March 2012).

Index